# EXPERIENCING SPORT

# EXPERIENCING SPORT

## Reversal Theory

*Edited by*

JOHN H. KERR

JOHN WILEY & SONS

Chichester · New York · Weinheim · Brisbane · Singapore · Toronto

*Other Wiley Editorial Offices*

John Wiley & Sons, Inc., 605 Third Avenue,
New York, NY 10158-0012, USA

WILEY-VCH Verlag GmbH, Pappelallee 3,
D-69469 Weinheim, Germany

Jacaranda Wiley Ltd, 33 Park Road, Milton,
Queensland 4064, Australia

John Wiley & Sons (Asia) Pte Ltd, 2 Clementi Loop #02-01,
Jin Xing Distripark, Singapore 129809

John Wiley & Sons (Canada) Ltd, 22 Worcester Road,
Rexdale, Ontario M9W 1L1, Canada

**British Library Cataloguing in Publication Data**

A catalogue record for this book is available from the British Library

ISBN 0–471–97531–1

Typeset in 10/12pt Times by Dorwyn Ltd, Rowlands Castle, Hants
Printed and bound in Great Britain by Bookcraft (Bath) Ltd,
Midsomer Norton, Somerset
This book is printed on acid-free paper responsibly manufactured from sustainable forestry,
in which at least two trees are planted for each one used for paper production.

To

**OSCAR RANDALL BRAMAN,**
**Emeritus Professor, University of Guam**

For his sense of humour and enthusiasm for life, astute understanding of human behaviour, knowledge of the history of psychology and critical support in the development of reversal theory and the study of sport.

No matter what 'kind' of psychologist a person is, he is a student of human behaviour. To my mind the history of psychology shows that if he shuts himself up narrowly in any particular small sphere of conduct inside or outside the laboratory (but specially inside), he will tend to get over-immersed in a terrific lot of detail about behaviour problems which he cleverly imagines for himself, and will approximate to a sort of puzzle solving which is often extremely interesting and, in a debating sense, intellectually attractive, but which leaves him revolving round and round his limited area. This works both ways, and if it is true that the general, or the laboratory, psychologist must be prepared to keep his problems alive by going outside the study or beyond his immediate experimental settings, it is equally true that the field psychologist must seek his executive solution with loyalty to that rigour of scientific method and that honest sense of evidence which only the study and the laboratory appear to instil.

Bartlett, F. C. (1949). What is industrial psychology? *Occupational Psychology*, **23**, 212–218.

# CONTENTS

## SECTION III   RECREATIONAL PARTICIPANTS

## APPENDICES

# ABOUT THE EDITOR

Since 1994, John Kerr has been a professor at the Institute of Health and Sport Sciences at the University of Tsukuba in Japan. Prior to this, he worked at Nijenrode University in the Netherlands. His first degree was in physical education and physical sciences at Loughborough University, after which he completed his Masters degree in educational psychology at the University of Ulster. He later completed his doctoral studies in psychology at Nottingham University in England. He has held visiting positions at the Universities of British Columbia, Sydney, and Oregon, and at Curtin University of Technology in Perth. He has co-edited or written five books on reversal theory and had numerous papers published in academic journals on sport psychology. John played rugby for Loughborough and Ballymena and has taught physical education to children in primary and secondary schools and to students at university. He has coached high-level rugby players in England, Ireland, Canada, Australia and Holland and continues to coach at the University of Tsukuba in Japan.

# ABOUT THE CONTRIBUTORS

**Michael J. Apter**   Michael and his father, Ken Smith, were the originators of reversal theory. Michael is currently Visiting Professor of Psychology at Georgetown University in Washington, DC. After achieving his PhD in 1965 at Bristol University, he spent three years in industry, followed by twenty years at University College Cardiff, where he attained the rank of Reader in Psychology. In recent years he has held a series of visiting university appointments, including positions at Purdue, Northwestern, Loyola, Chicago and Yale. He is the author or co-editor of thirteen books. He is also a Fellow of the British Psychological Society and the Netherlands Institute of Advanced Studies.

**R. Iain F. Brown**   Iain is a member of staff in the Department of Psychology at the University of Glasgow in Scotland. He has been a regular presenter at reversal theory conferences and has made several important contributions to reversal theory books. Iain specializes in the study of addictions and has linked reversal theory to his Hedonic Tone Management Model of Addictions which shows how addictions, including substance abuse, follow the same basic stages in their development. Iain has been dubbed the 'Flying Scotsman' by his reversal theory colleagues, this in connection to his nick-of-time arrivals and subsequent flying departures from reversal theory conferences, rather than his experience with train-spotters or his expertise as an occasional jogger.

**Nicola A. Cogan**   Recently graduated from the University of Glasgow with first-class honours in psychology, Nicola was awarded the Henry J. Watt prize in experimental psychology for highest academic performance in final-year examinations. She has worked for Mental Health Services in Grampian Healthcare, which provides services for the mentally handicapped, the mentally ill, and the elderly, as well as other community health and general hospital services. She is currently involved, through Royal Cornhill, in collaborative research involving the assessment of patients with Alzheimer's disease, schizophrenia, frontal lobe dementia and Huntington's chorea. Nicola also enjoys risk sports. She is an avid snowboarder at home in Scotland and abroad and has completed several parachute jumps for charity. In addition, she is keen on kung-fu and is training for her blue sash.

**Kurt P. Frey**   Kurt was born in Albany, New York, and grew up in Texas, England, North Dakota, Puerto Rico and Pennsylvania. He attended the University of Pittsburgh, Franklin and Marshall College, and eventually graduated from Millersville University (all in Pennsylvania) with a BA in Psychology in 1986. He obtained an MSc and PhD in Social Psychology from Purdue University in 1990 and 1993, respectively. In 1993, Kurt joined the faculty at Yale University as an Assistant Professor of Psychology. He has published a number of articles on topics in social and personality psychology and has given presentations at numerous universities and professional conferences. His research has focused on various areas, including why people spend money, how people cognitively represent relationships, the important dimensions of intimacy, how, why and with what consequences people evaluate their own or someone else's moral character, in what ways the content or structure of dreams are distinctive, often fantastic, and what various forms ecstasy and agony take. He has received several academic and early career awards, including the Purdue University Fellowship and the Yale Junior Faculty Fellowship. His avocations include a passion for long-distance running and the game of chess.

**Koenraad J. Lindner**   Koenraad graduated from the Academy of Physical Education in The Hague, the Netherlands, with a primary/secondary Teaching Certificate, and earned MEd and PhD degrees from the University of Toledo, USA. He was previously with the Faculty of Physical Education and Recreation Studies at the University of Manitoba, Canada, and joined the Physical Education and Sports Science Unit of the Faculty of Education, University of Hong Kong, in 1992, with responsibility for teaching and research in psychological aspects of physical activity and sport. His research is in the areas of youth sport participation and sport injury epidemiology. Koenraad's competitive sporting career was in elite volleyball in the Netherlands and the United States, but since coming to Hong Kong he has returned to soccer, the favourite activity of his youth, and taken up the sport of cricket. In the summer vacation he likes to be in a quiet spot on a Manitoba lake fishing for the big ones that usually get away, with his cooperation. He has played as a violinist with various orchestras over the last 25 years, and is an avid reader of just about any type of book under the sun.

**Jonathan R. Males** After representing Australia at four world slalom canoeing championships, Jonathan coached his national team at the Barcelona Olympics, and was sport psychologist with the Great Britain Olympic canoeing team at the 1996 Atlanta Olympics. He completed a psychology degree at the University of Tasmania in 1991, where he used reversal theory to test the efficacy of different goal-setting strategies. His PhD studies at Nottingham University, in Britain, have led him to explore emotion and motivation during elite performance in individual and team sports. He is currently a director of Sporting Bodymind Ltd., a London-based management consultancy, where he works with individuals and teams in both sporting and business environments.

**Ian P. Purcell** Ian is a lecturer in psychology in the School of Social Sciences at the Northern Territory University in Australia and a member of the Australian Psychological Society. His research interests include the impact of stress and emotion on human performance and the role of motivational factors in the acquisition of cognitive-motor skills. He is currently completing his PhD on the relationship of metamotivation and emotion in the decision making and performance of golfers. His main sporting interest is in soccer, both as a player and a Level 2 Coach. To maintain his fitness, Ian regularly works out at the gym and is also a Level 2 Strength and Conditioning Coach. He has acted as a consultant to individual athletes and sport teams on performance enhancement issues.

**Sven Svebak** Sven recently took up a position as Professor of Medicine at the Norwegian University of Science and Technology in Trondheim, Norway. Prior to this, he worked in the Department of Biological and Medical Psychology at the University of Bergen for over 25 years. Sven has been involved in reversal theory since the first international meeting organized by the reversal society in Wales in 1983. He has published widely on the psychobiology of motivation, emotion and health, including pioneering research on several reversal theory constructs, particularly in the medical and sport contexts. His leisure and sport interests generally involve spending time in the Norwegian mountains where he enjoys hiking, rock climbing, fishing and shooting.

**Paul Tacon** Paul is Professor Emeritus of Psychology at York University, Ontario, Canada. He has been at York University since 1969, where he has held a variety of academic and administrative positions. His interest in reversal theory spans many years, during which he has presented his research at a number of reversal theory conferences. He has published in various journals and texts. Now retired, he enjoys farming and fishing, both of which he has been able to indulge in more frequently than when professing psychology in his pre-retirement years. Apart from psychology,

Paul is a talented artist and his other interests include collecting antiques and vintage French wine, and traditional Canadian winter sports.

**George V. Wilson**    George is a Senior Lecturer in the Department of Psychology at the University of Tasmania, where he started in 1974. He completed his PhD in the area of biofeedback at the University of Queensland and has teaching and research interests in the psychophysiology of arousal and stress reactivity. He is an enthusiastic user of reversal theory, both to complement and extend traditional psychophysiological methodology, and as a coherent system for the measurement and understanding of the emotions generated in different situations. He has served as Deputy Head and Acting Head of the Department of Psychology and has a long involvement with the profession of psychology, serving as Secretary and Chairperson, and currently as Treasurer of the Tasmanian branch of the Australian Psychological Society. His recreational interests incline towards low-impact activities such as gardening and walking, and he is an 'optimistic angler', fly fishing for trout in Tasmania's clear rivers and lakes, on the rare occasions when weather and work permit.

# PREFACE

The origins of this book are to be found at the 1st International Workshop on Motivation and Emotion in Sport held at the University of Tsukuba in 1996, supported by a grant-in-aid from the Tsukuba Expo '85 Memorial Foundation. There could hardly have been a more appropriate place for hosting the first reversal theory meeting dedicated solely to sport. As I write this preface, it is Wednesday afternoon and I can hear the shouts and calls of people practising in the nearby basketball and volleyball halls. Out of my window to my left I can see that the tennis courts and the soccer, American football and rugby pitches are also occupied by practising players. Beyond this, in the martial arts central, others will be concentrating on traditional Japanese sports judo, sumo, and kendo (Japanese sword fighting) with their tremendous bodily and mental control combined with fast, aggressive and potentially violent moves. In the archery area, students will be engaging in kyudo, the traditional Japanese form of archery. They will be trying to meld body and mind quietly together, combining poise, fine motor control, complete concentration, and a sense of mastery that I have rarely encountered anywhere else. Their efforts will be observed and quiet feedback given by their sensei. It is like this on most afternoons and evenings at Tsukuba University; young people putting enormous effort into sport.

Tsukuba University, and its forerunner Tokyo University of Education, has a long and distinguished history of producing sport champions. I well remember, on my first visit, being proudly shown a large plaque in the foyer of the university's central hall by Vice President Masa Eda. On that plaque were listed the names of students, their events and the year in which they had won Olympic medals. I also remember attending the annual department barbecue for the first time and, towards the end of the evening, seeing a quiet unassuming man squatting down, poking the embers of the fire. Another colleague noticed this and I was introduced to Sawao Kato.

Later, that same colleague told me that Katosan had won eight gold medals in gymnastics over three Olympic Games. Had there been a mistake in translation, was the number eight correct? I was assured that it was correct: three at the Mexico games in 1968, three at the Munich games in 1972 and two at the Montreal games in 1976. For days afterwards I was left pondering the motivation and other attributes needed to achieve the almost inconceivable feat of winning eight gold medals, not to mention the three silver and a bronze that he also won.

The plaque in the central hall takes no account of the countless others, like Yuki Mimura, who have won medals at World, Asian and other Championships. A couple of years ago Yuki, one of the Masters students in my sport psychology class, politely asked for time off to attend the World Karate Championships. Interested, I asked a few questions about where the championships were being held and how she thought she would perform. Modestly and unaffectedly she told me that she had already been World Champion three times. As it turned out, she became World Champion, for the fourth time, in South Africa. Yuki is just one example. Every year I encounter numerous world-class athletes from a whole variety of sports, as well as many others who never reach the real elite level, but whose dedication and resolve to strive to reach the limits of their ability is admirable. I consider myself particularly fortunate to be able to work in such an environment.

Few non-Japanese will know much about Tsukuba University or Tsukuba Science City where it is located, 60 kilometres north-east of Tokyo. Tsukuba University is one of the most, if not the most, prestigious universities for Physical Education and Sport Sciences in Japan. There are well over 100 teaching staff in Physical Education and over 30 in the Institute of Health and Sport Sciences which deals with the scientific aspects of sport, like biomechanics, physiology, biochemistry and, of course, psychology.

Towards the end of September 1996, each one of an invited group of psychology researchers from as far apart as Trondheim and Perth, Washington and Hong Kong and London and Guam, began their separate journeys from their local airports to Japan. As they arrived in Tsukuba, my excitement grew as I welcomed old friends and anticipated the start of the workshop I had been planning for some time. All the researchers had found their way into sport psychology in their own unique way. Some were talented and high-level sportsmen, others were respected psychologists who found sport an intriguing context in which to examine human behaviour. In other circumstances, such a mix might have led to problems, but in Tsukuba they engaged in the most concentrated series of reversal theory presentations and discussions on any individual subject to date.

I would like to record my thanks to those people without whose help the reversal theory sport workshop would not have taken place. I am grateful to Tsukuba University for hosting the Reversal Theory Workshop and both the University and the Tsukuba Expo '85 Memorial Foundation for providing generous financial support. Thanks are especially due to Shigeru Katsuta and Shinji Tochibori in this regard. I would also like to thank my sport psychology colleagues at Tsukuba—Soichi Ichimura, Shigeru Yoshida, Shiro Nakagomi, Hiromi Miki and Hironobu Tsuchiya, as well as Takehisa Hagiwara, Mitsuhiko Takei, Misao Miyashita, Toshio Mori, Nariaki Sato and Takeo Nomura—for their help and cooperation. I am also deeply indebted to Yasuo Iyoda (Yas), my good friend and colleague, whose tremendous organizational and social skills ensured that the events of the workshop ran smoothly and all those in attendance had an experience in Japan that they would never forget.

As I have mentioned, the material covered in the Tsukuba Workshop forms the core of this book. As such, the contents focus on a batch of new reversal theory sport research which has recently been completed. Reversal theory explanations of human behaviour in sport are making a valuable contribution to sport psychology knowledge and literature and it is important for the results of these new research studies to be reviewed and discussed in one specialized research-oriented volume. This book is designed to both add to the sport psychology knowledge and literature and to extend the empirical evidence in support of reversal theory. Of interest is that these research studies have adopted a range of different research methodologies to obtain information about feelings and motives in actual sport situations. Further, the studies are nicely balanced between recreational and elite level sport.

An attempt has been made to gear the contents of the book to the same high level as previous Wiley sport and exercise psychology publications. To this end, in addition to the research-based chapters, others have been included which (a) explain the basic concepts of the theory for those readers unfamiliar with reversal theory, (b) outline the challenges and difficulties facing reversal theory researchers in sport, (c) draw together a summary of general conclusions in the wider context and (d) provide an overview of some of the critical issues facing reversal theory sport research in the future. It is the third reversal theory book focusing on sport, and follows *Understanding Soccer Hooliganism* (1994) and the student textbook *Motivation and Emotion in Sport: Reversal Theory* (1997).

For researchers interested in carrying out reversal theory sport research, this book will prove invaluable. Not only will it provide a review of the latest research findings, but it will also provide details of a range of different research strategies and measurement techniques used in these studies. It should also be a rich source of ideas for future research. In addition, practising sport psychologists who want to keep up with the latest research developments as a way of improving the advice they offer to sport performers should find this book of value.

# ACKNOWLEDGEMENTS

I wish to thank Mieke Mitchell for her contribution to this book. She understands reversal theory better than most of us and has strengthened all the contributions to this book by her constructive criticism. What we have said and how we have said it has been vastly improved by her efforts. I am also grateful to Comfort Jegede for her support and patience and the rest of the publishing team at Wiley, without whom this book project would never have come to fruition. Thanks are also due to Mary Cook, Mary Gerkovich, Miriam Potocky and Kathy O'Connell, and to Judith Calhoun and Kathy O'Connell for granting permission to reproduce the Somatic State Questionnaire and the Telic/Paratelic State Instrument, respectively, as Appendices.

# SECTION I

# BASIC CONCEPTS AND MEASUREMENT ISSUES

# 1

# Reversal Theory: Basic Concepts

**Kurt P. Frey**

*Yale University, USA*

## INTRODUCTION

Before taking to the court, field, ring, track, or water, the sport enthusiast often takes some time to warm up. In like manner, you, the reader, may need to 'warm up' before embarking on the discussions that follow. This chapter is designed to help you do so, by providing an outline of the basic concepts in reversal theory. If you are already familiar with reversal theory and are already in a sense warmed up, feel free to skip this chapter and move on to the rest of the book.

Reversal theory (Apter, 1982, 1989) is concerned primarily with *motivation*: the needs or desires that guide a person's behaviour, and how these needs and desires change from one state of mind to another. Reversal theory is also concerned with *experience*: how one interprets, and responds emotionally to, a given situation. As such, the theory is relevant to a wide range of human activities and phenomena – addictions, religious devotion, sexual behaviour, humour, family relations, and so on. It is also, as the present book will show, applicable to sport. Indeed, the examples

---

*Experiencing Sport: Reversal Theory.* Edited by J. H. Kerr.
© 1999 John Wiley & Sons Ltd.

used in this chapter to illustrate the theory will all be taken from the world of sport.

# METAMOTIVATION

One of the central arguments of reversal theory is that individuals, throughout their daily lives, alternate between opposite psychological states. These opposite states are operative in everyone and entail distinctive motives, perceptions, and emotions. For example, in a particular state one wants to feel very aroused (stimulated or excited), while in another state one wants to feel quite unaroused (calm or relaxed). However, if one desires to experience high arousal, but in fact does not, one will feel bored, and if one desires to experience low arousal, but does not, one will feel anxious. Thus, different states represent opposite ways of experiencing the same level of a particular psychological variable, such as arousal.

What is being described is summed up in the term *metamotivation*. Metamotivation refers to the way in which a person's motives can change and fluctuate during the course of activities and daily life, because these motives are state determined. Each state is *meta*-motivational in the sense that it 'sets' what the person wants, at least for the time being. Consider, for example, someone participating in a pick-up basketball game at a local gym. What, essentially, does this person want to experience? This question has several possible answers. For example, it may be that he or she simply wants to have fun, to enjoy the action on the court – the energetic dribbling and lightning passes, show-off shots, and 'trash talk'. In contrast, he or she might be in a very different frame of mind: determined to win, cognizant of team strategies, anxious about personal performance, alert to the changing score, and so on. In other words, there are various 'ways of being' while 'playing' pick-up basketball. One can also enter a game in one metamotivational state, and 'switch' from one state to another, any number of times, during the course of a game.

Reversal theory claims that metamotivational states occur in pairs of opposites. When one state is active, its opposite is inactive (the theory derives its name from the fact that one can *reverse* back and forth between opposite states). States are opposite in the sense that they involve opposite desires and opposite subjective responses to the same objective experiences. Another way of putting this is to say that individuals are *bistable* with respect to certain psychological dimensions. There are two specific points (towards the extreme ends of a dimension) that are stable or 'optimal'. However, only one of these points is optimal at any one time – determined by prevailing metamotivational states and changing as these states change. In this respect, the theory departs from simpler homeostatic accounts of motivation, which generally claim that motives revolve around some single optimal point.

Metamotivational states also have emotional consequences. More specifically, for each state there is both a *preferred* level and an *actual* level of a particular experiential variable, such as how aroused one feels. While the preferred level is determined by the state itself, the actual level is determined by one's situation and perception of that situation. If the preferred and actual levels of a variable match, one will experience a specific positive emotion, such as feeling relaxed. If the preferred and actual levels of a variable do not match, one will experience a specific negative emotion, such as feeling anxious.

Reversal theory contends that there are four pairs of opposite metamotivational states. This means that, at any given moment, an individual is experiencing a total of four states, one from each pair. Normally, however, one or more of the states will be salient – that is, they will have the greatest influence on one's behaviour and experience. These four active states, then, and especially the one or two that are salient, determine the person's temporary 'personality' – what the person wants, how he or she thinks and behaves, and the kinds of emotion that he or she is likely to experience.

All of this may seem a bit abstract at this point, but as each pair of states and the other elements of the theory are described, detailed examples will be given that will make the aforementioned concepts more vivid and compelling.

# SOMATIC STATES

The first two pairs of metamotivational states are referred to as *somatic* states because they pertain primarily to how one generally experiences one's own bodily arousal. This subjective experience of arousal is important and is the reason why, in reversal theory, arousal is referred to as *felt arousal*. Felt arousal is defined as 'the degree to which an individual feels himself to be 'worked up' at a given time'.

## Telic and Paratelic

The first pair of states to be conceptualized (and the one that has received the most research attention) comprises the *telic* and *paratelic* states. A person in the telic state is primarily goal oriented: a particular objective is seen as being more important than whatever means are used to achieve it.

The goal is also seen as having important repercussions beyond the present situation (achieving the goal will help one achieve a larger goal, which will help one attain an even larger goal, and so on). Although the telic person wants to be energized enough to pursue his or her objective, he or she does not want to be unnecessarily 'worked up'. In fact, any source of arousal, especially if it seems frivolous or represents an obstacle to goal attainment, will produce such negative emotions as fear and anxiety. A common (though less precise) word to describe being telic is 'serious'.

In contrast, a person in the paratelic state might be described as 'playful' (though, again, this word lacks precision). The paratelic person is primarily activity oriented, enjoying the very process of whatever he or she is doing. Although the paratelic person may adopt some goal, the goal is somewhat arbitrary, serving only as an excuse to engage in the activity. Another key feature of being paratelic is wanting to attach little, if any, importance to what one is doing. In fact, the paratelic state involves feeling (realistically or not) 'protected' and 'encapsulated' – unaware of, or unconcerned with, any significant negative outcomes (Apter, 1993). The person who is paratelic also delights in arousing surprises and intense physical sensations. Without these, he or she would quickly succumb to boredom.

The example given earlier of playing basketball either for 'fun' or for more 'serious' purposes illustrates some of the differences between being paratelic and being telic. The same distinction could be made regarding the way one participates in any sport – one might be focused on simply enjoying the various sensations the sport produces or on performing well, winning, or achieving some related goal. Consider, for example, a 'fun' game of beach volleyball: music is blaring from a radio, players are slicked down with sun tan lotion, bottles of beer are close at hand (if not in hand), no one is fussing about infractions or out-of-bounds plays and no one is keeping a close check on the score. In contrast, think of a 'serious' game of beach volleyball: plays are well coordinated, each spike and dig has grave consequences, onlookers have taken sides, a referee is at hand, and winning is 'crucial'. Most of the players in the 'fun' game would likely be in the paratelic state, while most of the players in the 'serious' game would probably be in the telic state. (Although there is not necessarily a relationship between a given activity or situation and one's metamotivational state, and as reversals can and do occur between pairs of metamotivational states, there is always the possibility that players may reverse from the telic to the paratelic state, or vice versa.)

In terms of the experience of arousal, if the action is stimulating enough in the 'fun' game of volleyball, players (in the paratelic state) may be pleasantly excited, but if the action slows, they may become bored. In contrast, if the 'serious' game becomes too arousing or threatening, players (in the telic state) may become anxious, but if they are making undeterred progress towards their goal of winning, they may remain pleasantly calm. Thus, it is possible to see how one can experience a given level of a particular psychological variable, such as high arousal, in opposite ways in different states.

## Conformist and Negativistic

The second pair of somatic states comprises the *conformist* and *negativistic* states. While the telic and paratelic states have to do with emphasizing *ends* versus *means*, the conformist and negativistic states have to do with how one temporarily regards any restrictions (rules, norms, traditions, or others' expectations) on one's behaviour. The person in the conformist state wants to abide by rules, comply with others' wishes, and respect the status quo. In contrast, the person in the negativistic state seeks to be free of such constraints: he or she wants to break rules, mock norms, overthrow traditions, and defy others' expectations (Dennis Rodman, the 'bad boy' of US professional basketball, quickly comes to mind here). The negativistic person tends to behave as if he or she is 'exempt' from particular restrictions (Apter, 1993). Thus, in moments when a person is aware of some specific constraint, he or she will be inclined to either accept it or defy it, build it up in some way or tear it down in some way. In fact, there are two opposite ways of experiencing *felt negativism* (the perception that one is to some degree violating rules and expectations): the person in the negativistic state will relish it while the person in the conformist state will cringe from it. Indeed, being negativistic can also enhance felt arousal, the key variable for the somatic emotions.

Having described both pairs of somatic states, it is now possible to describe how, when combined, they produce interesting blends of meta-motivation. For example, one could simultaneously be telic and conformist, perhaps nervously demonstrating certain karate kata before a panel of black-belt judges, or one could be telic and negativistic, perhaps experiencing sudden anger at being thrown a threatening baseball pitch. One could be paratelic and conformist, perhaps indulging in a leisurely game of tennis while being respectful of the various rules and proper etiquette of the game, or one could be paratelic and negativistic, perhaps mischievously poking fun at a friend during a round of golf. Figure 1.1 shows the telic and paratelic experiences of felt arousal in combination with (a) the conformist state (resulting in the four emotions relaxation, anxiety, excitement and boredom), and (b) the negativistic state (resulting in the emotions placidity, anger, provocativeness and sullenness).

In connection with the somatic states, it is worth mentioning that in the paratelic state, emotions that are otherwise experienced as negative and unpleasant in the telic state can paradoxically become positive and pleasant

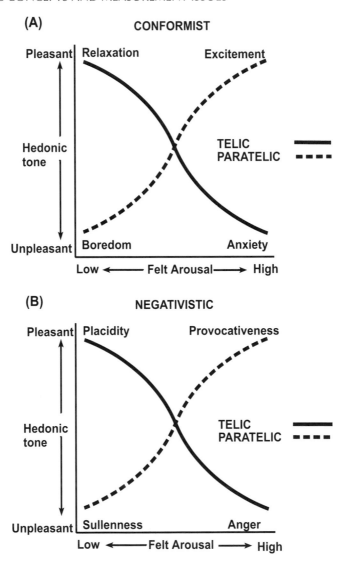

**Figure 1.1**   Relationship between felt arousal and hedonic tone for the somatic states (from Frey, 1997).

if experienced in the paratelic state. These form a special case in reversal theory and are known as *parapathic emotions*. In fact, any unpleasant emotion (e.g., anxiety or anger) that involves high arousal can be enjoyed in the paratelic state as a parapathic emotion, as when one delights in seeing or reading something 'disgusting' or 'terrible'.

# TRANSACTIONAL STATES

The third and fourth pairs of metamotivational states, referred to as *transactional* states, pertain to one's interactions with other people or objects. In other words, these states concern *felt transactional outcome* – what one perceives oneself to be 'gaining' or 'losing' as a result of a particular 'transaction'.

## Mastery and Sympathy

The first pair of transactional states (and third pair overall) consists of the *mastery* and *sympathy* states. The person who is in the mastery state views an interaction as a kind of power struggle and evaluates relationship outcomes in terms of who is winning and who is losing, who is strong and who is weak, who is dominating and who is submitting. Obviously, much of sport reflects the mastery state – ask any offensive lineman in American football, world-class competitor in the 100 metre dash, or jai alai professional about his or her sporting objectives! The mastery state often involves 'objectifying' others – viewing them as objects (rather than as people) to be manipulated, used, and controlled to one's own advantage (Apter, 1993).

In contrast, the person who is in the sympathy state views an interaction as an opportunity for being attentive, considerate or generous, or for showing affection, intimacy, or nurturing behaviour. Although sport mostly reflects mastery motives, it also provides opportunities to satisfy desires in the sympathy state: consider the camaraderie typically felt among the members of any sports team (bobsledders or synchronized swimmers, for example) or the intimacy shared among fellow golfers at the 19th Hole pub or among fellow marathoners at a post-race pasta dinner. Indeed, sport probably provides fellowship and friendship as much as it does competition and fitness.

## Autic and Alloic

The second pair of transactional states (and fourth and final pair overall) consists of the *autic* and *alloic* states. The person in the autic state is concerned primarily with his or her own outcomes in an interaction, while the person in the alloic state is more concerned with the other's outcomes.

As with the somatic states, it is thought that one is always experiencing one state from each pair of transactional states, with reversals between these pairs occurring more or less frequently. For example, a boxer in the mastery state dominating his opponent might reverse to the sympathy state if his opponent starts bleeding profusely following a right hook after the bell. Of course, two of the four somatic states would also be active simultaneously in a four-way metamotivational state combination, and might become salient.

Just as the somatic states combine to produce distinct blends of metamotivation, so too do the transactional states. For example, one could be autic and mastery oriented and feeling proud after placing a penalty kick past a goalie in soccer, or autic and sympathy oriented and feeling grateful when being comforted after a dismal gymnastics performance. One might be alloic and mastery oriented and feeling modest and perhaps actually glad to be trounced by a tennis protegé, or alloic and sympathy oriented and feeling virtuous, perhaps, as a basketball coach, reassuring a bench-warming player that he is a valuable member of the team. Figure 1.2 shows the autic and alloic experiences of felt transactional outcome in combination with (a) the mastery state (resulting in the four emotions modesty, shame, pride and humiliation) and (b) the sympathy state (resulting in the emotions virtue, guilt, gratitude and resentment).

There are some additional points that should be mentioned in respect to interactions in the transactional states which have relevance for sport.

The transactional states also pertain to one's interactions with *things*. Most of the time, it is the autic and mastery states that are involved in interactions with things during sport, as when a bowler attempts to put a curve on a ball, a rodeo rider manages to remain atop a feisty barebacked bronc, or a sprinter races against the clock. But sometimes the alloic state is involved, as when a baseball player safeguards a lucky bat or an auto-racer extols the power (in this case horsepower) of his Formula 1 car. Although it probably occurs more rarely, the sympathy state can also be active in various ways in one's interactions with things during sport, as when one lovingly cleans and tinkers with one's racing bike.

The autic and alloic states also possess some special nuances which are consequential for understanding the experience of sport. Specifically, the 'other' with whom one is relating can, at times, be oneself, as in the interaction between *I* and *me* – and this is referred to as the *intra-autic* state (Apter, 1988). When the person is simultaneously mastery oriented, *I* wants to dominate, control, or subjugate *me*: a gymnast attempts her first back flip on the balance beam, a wrestler does a daily regimen of 200 push-ups and 200 sit-ups, a middle distance runner endures a gruelling interval track workout. When the person is simultaneously sympathy oriented, *I* sympathizes with, appreciates, or nurtures *me*: a roller-blader attends to blistered feet, a golfer treats herself to a new set of clubs, a cross-country skier stops at an inn for its warm fire and cold beer.

Also important (especially for understanding the experience of watching sport) is the fact that a person will often vicariously identify with another

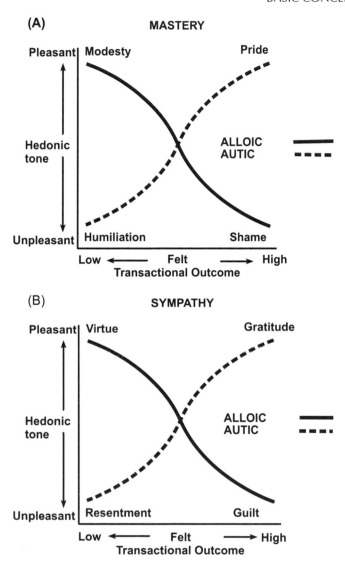

**Figure 1.2** Relationship between felt transactional outcome and hedonic tone for the transactional states (from Frey, 1997).

person who is interacting directly with someone or something else, wanting the person he or she is identifying with to be powerful in some way (a mastery orientation) or appreciated and loved in some way (a sympathy orientation). For example, one might devotedly watch a particular sports team (the Philadelphia Flyers ice-hockey team, for example) throughout an entire season, feeling 'up' or 'down' depending on that team's performance. Or one might identify closely with a particular person, such as the odds-on favourite in the Olympic track and field decathlon. Such experiences, which involve vicariously experiencing another person's interactions, represent a special case of the alloic state, referred to in reversal theory as the *pro-autic* state (Apter, 1988).

## REVERSALS

As mentioned earlier, a reversal is a switch from one state to the opposite state in any one pair, resulting in a drastic transformation in one's outlook and emotional experience. In Figures 1.1 and 1.2, a reversal involves moving vertically from one curve to the other (or, in some cases, horizontally from one graph to the same position on another graph – for example, from anxiety in Figure 1.1(a) to anger in Figure 1.1(b) when a conformist-to-negativistic reversal occurs). Reversals are especially dramatic when they occur at the ends of a particular dimension, as when one goes from extreme anxiety to extreme excitement or from intense pride to intense shame.

A common cause of reversal from one state to another is *contingency*: something occurs in the environment to instigate the reversal. For example, one NBA game found Michael Jordan playfully attempting to hold the hand of the player who happened to be guarding him – although the other (probably telic) player at first rebuffed Jordan's playfulness on the court, he suddenly broke into a smile and began to laugh, likely indicating a reversal to the paratelic state (though no doubt this was soon followed by a reversal back to the telic state as the guard once again became aware of the drubbing his team was suffering).

A second mechanism of metamotivational reversal is *frustration*: when a person in a particular state goes for too long without achieving the satisfactions of that state, he or she may reverse to the opposite state. Something like this may have happened to Mike Tyson in his recent boxing bout with world champion Evander Holyfield, when Tyson bit a sizeable chunk out of Holyfield's ear (frustration is likely to have induced a reversal from the conformist to the negativistic state).

A final mechanism of reversal is *satiation*: even in the absence of any contingencies or frustrations, a person will eventually undergo a reversal. One can only remain in a state for so long, before spontaneously reversing to the opposite state. For example, on an 18-mile training run, a marathoner might feel calm and 'relaxed' (if that is the right word!) for the first few miles, as she concentrates on regulating pace and conserving energy, then, following a spontaneous reversal from the telic to the paratelic state, suddenly feel bored with the bland landscape and lack of stimulation as she lopes along at her monotonous pace. At another point in the run, she might feel pleasantly aroused, perhaps relishing the intensity of the heat reflecting off the macadam, the sweat dripping from her body, and the euphoria of a 'runner's high', then, following a spontaneous reversal from the paratelic to the telic state, suddenly feel anxious, perhaps wondering if she will dehydrate before finishing or worrying about a future race.

It is important to note that reversal theory asserts that individuals do not have direct control over reversals. An individual cannot wilfully activate a certain combination of states. The best that one can do is to choose activities and settings that are likely to bring about certain reversals and maintain certain states. For example, one might forgo a heavy meal, put on a pair of racing flats, and head for a local track, all in order to generate the right mood before embarking on an intense speed workout. There is no guarantee, however, that on arrival at the track one will be, for example, telic–conformist and intra-autic–mastery oriented, the state combination likely to contribute to a successful workout.

# DOMINANCE

A concept in reversal theory that relates to reversals (although not a mechanism of reversal *per se*) is that of *dominance*. Although reversal theory is mostly concerned with *intra*-individual differences (differences within a person over time), the concept of dominance reveals that the theory also allows for important *inter*-individual differences (differences between people). Dominance implies that each person possesses a 'bias' for one or the other state in a given pair of states. For example, a person might be telic dominant, spending more time in the telic state than most people; conversely, one might be paratelic dominant, spending more time in the paratelic state than the average person (see, e.g., Svebak & Murgatroyd, 1985). In the same way, one is either conformist or negativistic dominant, mastery or sympathy dominant, and autic or alloic dominant. It is thought that an individual will contingently reverse more easily into his or her dominant state, and will satiate more slowly and become frustrated less easily in that state.

The concept of dominance differs from that of *trait*, which has received widespread acceptance in psychology. Possessing a particular trait – being an introvert or an extrovert, for example – suggests that the characteristic is a stable aspect of one's personality. Dominance, however, while suggesting that one spends more time in a particular state, recognizes that one is often in the non-dominant state and experiences that non-dominant state as fully as someone for whom it is dominant. The concept of dominance (more so than the concept of trait) allows for the self-contradictions individuals often display.

Specific dominances may influence one's preferences for certain sports and manner of entering into those sports (Kerr, 1997). For example, paratelic dominance has been shown to be related to a preference for physically dangerous sports (such as rock climbing or stock-car racing) (Kerr, 1991; Kerr & Svebak, 1989), while telic dominance has been shown to be related to how seriously or professionally one undertakes a sport (Kerr, 1987). Autic dominance might be related to a preference for individual sports (such as fencing, arm wrestling, or bicycle racing) over team sports (such as lacrosse, soccer, or volleyball), and sympathy dominance might lead one to gravitate towards non-competitive sports (like roller-blading or scuba diving). A particular combination of dominances might cause one to prefer sports which involve direct competition and physical contact (e.g. rugby or water polo), sports which generally avoid physical contact (e.g., baseball or tennis), sports which involve competition without participants directly confronting each other (e.g., harness racing or swimming), or sports in which participants take turns demonstrating some skill (e.g., bowling or pole vaulting).

# EIGHT SELVES RUN A RACE

Having described each of the eight metamotivational states and the three inducing agents for reversal, it is now possible to provide a fuller example of how one's motivation and experience can be 'structured' during sport performance. The following account is of an individual's experiences shortly before, during, and after a 5-mile running road race. References to particular metamotivational states are italicized to emphasize the person's various operative states, the salience of those states, and reversals during this relatively brief period of time. As the subtitle above indicates, these metamotivational states may also be referred to as 'selves', since each represents a unique aspect of the person, a distinct way of his 'being-in-the-world'.

> I arrived for the race an hour early in a *telic* frame of mind; I was worried about having enough time to pre-register and adequately warm up. Jogging from my car to the race site, I went over mile-splits in my mind and engaged in a kind of *intra-autic* 'pep talk' – 'I' reminded 'me' of the previous months of diligent training. Noticing other runners jogging about (some too enthusiastically, wasting their energy, I thought), I made quick comparisons of such things as running shoes, attire, and general physique. These momentary *autic mastery* evaluations fuelled my self-confidence: in most cases, I looked more

like a 'true runner'. For a few moments, I *paratelicly* fantasized that I was an out-of-town 'ringer', about to win the race in record time.

It was during this reverie that I ran into an old friend whom I hadn't seen since the previous year's race. I immediately reversed to a *sympathy* frame of mind – but as the conversation got on and we started talking about our recent training and goals for the race, I reversed back into the *mastery* state (we had been running rivals since junior high school). *Autic* oriented, I proudly described the intense training I'd been doing – only to learn that he had done little to prepare for this race; he was just running 'for the hell of it' and planned to run considerably slower than me. I promptly reversed to the *alloic* state, feeling suddenly ashamed of my having gone off bragging as I did. I reminded him of a previous race (in which he had 'dusted' me) to bolster his ego.

Seeing others flock to the pre-registration table, I was immediately reminded of the short time to the race, and reversed to the *telic* state. I abruptly ended the conversation I was having with my friend (even briefly feeling *negativistic* towards him for wasting my time). I generally remained *telic, intra-autic*, and *mastery* oriented up to the start of the race. However, as the 1,500 or so runners began to congregate at the starting line, I reversed momentarily into the *paratelic* state, delighting in the animated horde of runners and jocose announcements made by a city official. Recognizing a few 'local legends', I reversed fleetingly into the *alloic* state (with a *pro-autic* focus), imagining the fierce duels soon to occur at the front of the pack.

The sound of the starter's gun immediately reversed me back into the *telic* state: I started my stopwatch and concentrated on setting a steady pace. Someone in the stampede of runners stepped on my heel, almost pulling my shoe off, prompting me to mutter a *negativistic* comment. His snide retort (something about me slowing faster runners down) left me in this state for most of the first mile.

I ran most of the remainder of the race in a *telic mastery* frame of mind. Once the field of runners thinned out, I encountered a series of one-on-one 'battles' – which always found me in the *autic* and *mastery* states. But I was also often *intra-autic* oriented: for the most part, I was running against myself. Several times a runner near me dropped off to the side, apparently quitting the race. While I clearly felt *mastery* oriented pride in passing one such runner, I reversed briefly into the *alloic* state in response to another such runner.

The first three miles were all clearly marked – allowing me to *telicly* monitor my progress during the race. However, I did not see (or perhaps missed) the fourth mile marker. The gradual realization of this as the fourth mile seemed to drag endlessly on reversed me to the *negativistic* state ('incompetent race organizers', I thought).

Although I remained *telic* throughout most of the final mile, I experienced an obvious reversal to the *paratelic* state as I neared the finish line and felt buoyed by the boisterous crowd (which had cheered the first-place finisher nearly five minutes earlier).

Making my way on wobbly legs through the final 'shoot' and over to family members, I was definitely in the *autic* and *sympathy* states. It was only after about ten minutes that I began to focus on runners who were still finishing – I cheered them on in an *alloic (pro-autic)* frame of mind.

I stuck around for the awards ceremony and remained in the area after most of the other runners had left, mainly in the *paratelic* and *autic* states.

Although the account just given may seem a bit contrived (it is actually the author's own retrospective analysis of a recent race experience, with a few embellishments), it serves to convey the textured fabric of human experience. Moreover, although this account describes one kind of sporting experience, there is no reason why similar analyses could not be given of other sporting experiences: working out with weights at a gym, riding horseback, driving in a stock-car race, playing in a doubles tennis tournament, speed skating, or tossing horseshoes at a barbecue. Such an analysis reveals how the intensity and complexity of sport complements the intensity and complexity of human motivation.

## CONCLUSION

This chapter offers a 'crash course' in reversal theory. Fuller discussions of the theory (including various types of experimental, psychometric, psychophysiological, and experiential evidence for the theory) can be found elsewhere (e.g., Apter, 1982, 1989; Kerr, 1997). Brief as this chapter is, however, it should serve as an adequate warm-up for those that follow.

As you embark on subsequent chapters and delve further into the psychology of sport, keep two things in mind. First, reversal theory claims that behaviour of any kind – sporting behaviour no less – cannot be fully understood without inquiring into the motivation that underlies it. There is never an absolute one-to-one correspondence between motivation and behaviour. Nor, for that matter, is there a simple link between behaviour and experience. Two individuals can engage in the same behaviour but be in different metamotivational states, resulting in different, even opposite, experiences, or the same individual can engage in the same behaviour at different times in different states, again resulting in disparate experiences.

A second point to keep in mind is that reversal theory views individuals as being inconsistent and self-contradictory, conspicuously capable of undergoing radical changes in their 'personalities' during relatively short periods of time. Indeed, it is impossible to comprehend the psychology of sport without recognizing such frequent, rapid, and drastic transformations. Human personality is dynamic and fluid, not lethargic and inflexible, an assertion that becomes exceedingly obvious when one probes the rich and vibrant world of sport.

## REFERENCES

Apter, M. J. (1982). *The experience of motivation: The theory of psychological reversals*. London: Academic Press.

Apter, M. J. (1988). Beyond the autocentric and the allocentric. In M. J. Apter, J. H. Kerr & M. P. Cowles (Eds.), *Progress in reversal theory* (pp. 339–348). Amsterdam: Elsevier.

Apter, M. J. (1989). *Reversal theory: Motivation, emotion, and personality.* London: Routledge.

Apter, M. J. (1993). Phenomenological frames and the paradoxes of experience. J. H. Kerr, M. J. Apter & S. Murgatroyd (Eds.), *Advances in reversal theory* (pp. 27–39). Amsterdam: Swets & Zeitlinger.

Frey, K. P. (1997). About reversal theory. In S. Svebak & M. J. Apter (Eds.), *Stress & health: A reversal theory perspective* (pp. 3–19). Washington: Taylor & Francis.

Kerr, J. H. (1987). Differences in the motivational characteristics of 'professional', 'serious amateur' and 'recreational' sports performers. *Perceptual and Motor Skills*, **64**, 379–382.

Kerr, J. H. (1991). Arousal-seeking in risk sport participants. *Personality and Individual Differences*, **12** (6), 613–616.

Kerr, J. H. (1997). *Motivation and emotion in sport: Reversal theory.* Hove, UK: Psychological Press.

Kerr, J. H. & Svebak, S. (1989). Motivational aspects of preference for and participation in risk sports. *Personality and Individual Differences*, **10**, 797–800.

Svebak, S. & Murgatroyd, S. (1985). Metamotivational dominance: A multimethod validation of reversal theory constructs. *Journal of Personality and Social Psychology*, **48**, 107–116.

# 2

# Measurement Challenges in Reversal Theory Sport Research

## Michael J. Apter

*Georgetown University, USA*

## INTRODUCTION

As will be clear from the first chapter of this book, reversal theory provides a systematic framework for understanding many aspects of human behaviour, including motivation, emotion, personality, and stress. It also emphasizes many kinds of behaviour which do not figure prominently in mainstream psychological research, but which appear to play an important part in most people's lives. These include behaviour associated with art, with humour, with religion – and with sport.

Generally speaking, the psychological study of sport has been objective and behavioural, with much emphasis on motor skills and associated physiological processes. Nor is this surprising, since sport itself represents an attempt to objectify human competition, so that success and failure can be quantified, and winning and losing can be determined by objective decision procedures. In a sense, both modern psychology and sport stem

*Experiencing Sport: Reversal Theory.* Edited by J. H. Kerr.
© 1999 John Wiley & Sons Ltd.

from the same desire to put human nature to the test: a sporting event is a kind of experiment, and a laboratory experiment in human psychology is a kind of game.

The problem with all this, from the reversal theory perspective, is that if we are fully to understand what is happening in sport – as in any human activity – we have to know something about the way that it is experienced by its participants. To understand any activity, we have to be able to follow the changing meanings that are attributed to it, the various values that it serves, and the subjective significance which it has at different times. In other words, we have to understand something of its phenomenology. The reversal theory framework provides a systematic way of dealing with this phenomenology, and especially with the motivational and emotional meanings that are experienced as an integral part of the meaning of every human action. In the case of sport, the fundamental claim of reversal theory would be that objective measures of performance outcome (and also of physiology) will be related in some way to such subjective meanings, and especially to the meanings associated with different metamotivational states. For example, what is it to be 'in the zone'? What happens when someone 'chokes'? What are runners experiencing when they experience 'runner's high'?

Psychologists have of course, over the years, called on a set of increasingly sophisticated psychometric techniques and developed a wide variety of instruments for measuring subjective judgements, self-evaluations, and the like. It is this tradition which reversal theory calls upon when it attempts to 'get a handle' on subjectivity. But reversal theory raises two kinds of difficulties for this approach, and underlines them both for sport research in particular and psychology in general. The first derives from the observation that subjective meanings can be subtle and full of nuances, and therefore difficult to capture, and yet still be of profound importance. The second is that these meanings are continually shifting and changing, so that single static 'snapshots' may be misleading.

The aim of the present chapter is to outline the various measures that have been generated from within reversal theory, to look at their various strengths and weaknesses, and to see how they might be usable in the context of sport research. The main kinds of measures, of course, are dominance measures and state measures and we shall look at each of these in turn. (It should also be recognized that in the future some other kinds of tests will need to be developed, especially tests of lability – the frequency with which an individual reverses between states – and of the strategies which people tend to use within each state.)

More time will be spent in what follows on state than on dominance measures, since the state concept is both more central to the whole thrust of reversal theory and is arguably more central to the interests of sport psychology – and this focus on the state level of analysis is reflected in the chapters which follow in this book. (By 'state', of course, is meant the metamotivational state, from a pair of states, which is active in the individual at a given time, and by 'dominance' the individual's bias towards one or the other metamotivational state in any one pair of states over time.)

# A SURVEY OF REVERSAL THEORY DOMINANCE MEASURES

Although the idea of 'state' is at the heart of reversal theory, measures of dominance emerged earlier, largely because they could be treated in a trait-like way and conventional statistical techniques (such as those involved in item analysis) could be brought to bear on their development.

The first psychometric instrument to be developed in this way was the Telic Dominance Scale (Murgatroyd, Rushton, Apter, & Ray, 1978), related to the telic and paratelic concept in reversal theory, and this has subsequently been the mainstay of much reversal theory research on personality (e.g., Martin, Kuiper, Olinger, & Dobbin, 1987; Murgatroyd, 1985; Svebak & Murgatroyd, 1985). The scale and item key will be found in Apter (1982), Apter, Kerr, and Cowles (1988) and Kerr (1997). Norms will be found in Tacon and Abner (1993). Although this scale has given rise to interesting and useful data, a number of psychometric problems have arisen with it over the years (Hyland, Sherry, & Thacker, 1988), and this has led to alternatives being developed, such as the Paratelic Dominance Scale (Cook & Gerkovich, 1993). A telic dominance scale for children, the Nijmegen Telic Dominance Scale, has also been constructed (Boekaerts, Hendriksen, & Michels, 1988).

The negativism dominance dimension was explored by McDermott, who developed the Negativism Dominance Scale (McDermott, 1988a, 1988b). Norms for this scale will be found in Tacon and Abner (1993), and the scale itself in Apter, Kerr, and Cowles (1988) and Kerr (1997).

All dimensions – that is, every type of dominance recognized in the theory – are measured in the Motivational Style Profile (originally called the Personal Orientation Profile) which measures the salience of each dimension in comparison with other dimensions, as well as dominance on the dimension itself (Apter, Mallows, & Williams, 1998). A more detailed review of psychometric dominance measures will be found in Apter and Apter-Desselles (1993).

Most of these scales have been used in sport research as well as in other contexts. For example, the Telic Dominance Scale has been used in studies by Kerr (e.g., Kerr, 1987, 1988) on the personalities of players of different sports, and by Chirivella and Martinez (1994) on the participants in risk and non-risk sports. The Negativism Dominance Scale has been used by

Vlaswinkel and Kerr (1990) in their comparison of high-level performers in risk and team sports. The Motivational Style Profile was used by Evans in his study of soccer referees (Evans, 1994). A comprehensive review of all the research on metamotivational dominance which has been carried out in relation to sport is provided by Kerr (1997) in his book *Motivation and emotion in sport: Reversal theory*, especially in chapter 3.

# A SURVEY OF REVERSAL THEORY STATE MEASURES

The technique of state measurement is far less well developed in psychology than that of trait measurement. There are basically three different ways of measuring state – self-report scales, verbal accounts, and objective indices – and reversal theory research has made use of all of them. It should be noted here that the prime interest in this reversal theory research is in identifying which metamotivational state is operative at a given time, rather than in other aspects of the ongoing experience.

## Self-report Scales

Self-report scales are simple questionnaires or rating scales which ask the participant to state or rate something about how he or she feels in certain respects at the moment in question (or at a definable moment in the recent past; for example, by asking after a game about feelings before going on to the field of play).

The most widely used of these so far has been the Telic State Measure (TSM) (e.g., Svebak & Murgatroyd, 1985), which has been used successfully in sport by, for example, Cox and Kerr (1989), Kerr and van Schaik (1995), and Kerr and van den Wollenberg (1997). It has a set of five rating scales: three are used to determine whether the telic or paratelic state was or is operative, including a preferred level of arousal scale; one is a measure of experienced level of arousal; and one measures the degree of 'effortfulness'. A further derived scale, the discrepancy between the actual level of arousal and the preferred level of arousal, gives rise to a measure of arousal discrepancy or 'tension.' The items for this measure will be found in Kerr (1997), together with the rating scale descriptions which are provided to respondents to help them to understand exactly what they are being asked to rate.

Other reversal theory self-report state measures are now available, although these have not yet been used to a significant extent in sport research. In particular, the Somatic State Questionnaire (SSQ) has been developed by Cook, Gerkovich, Potocky, and O'Connell (1993; see Appendix A). This consists of 12 items, making up three 4-item subscales (serious/playful, arousal-avoidance/arousal-seeking, and negativistic/conformist). A derivative of this instrument is the Telic/Paratelic State Instrument (T/PSI) developed by Calhoun (1995; Calhoun & O'Connell, 1995; see Appendix B) and consisting of 12 items comprising a 7-item serious/playful subscale and a 5-item arousal-avoidance/arousal-seeking subscale. While the TSM has single items measuring each dimension, the SSQ and T/PSI have multiple-item subscales with good psychometric properties.

A number of other self-report instruments are currently in development, including an instrument devised specifically for use in the sport context and covering all of the metamotivational states as well as aspects of arousal, the State of Mind Indicator for Athletes (SOMIFA), by Kerr and Apter (see Appendix C).

Another measure, the Tension and Effort Stress Inventory (TESI), has also been used to measure state. It has been used to good effect in this way in the sport context by Kerr and Svebak (1994), Males and Kerr (1996), and Purcell (1999) (see also Chapter 3 by Wilson in this volume). Devised by Svebak (1993), this self-report scale was originally designed to measure experienced stress, and changes in the 16 primary emotions hypothesized in reversal theory (Apter, 1988), over some specified time interval, measuring separately what Apter and Svebak (1989) defined as *tension-stress* and *effort-stress*. It has been used in a variety of investigations (e.g., Svebak, 1997; Svebak, Mykletun, & Bru, 1997). The time interval can be made sufficiently small for the TESI effectively to become a state measure, and inferences can be drawn about which metamotivational states are operating (over the complete set of states) from the pleasant and unpleasant emotions which the respondent has to identify. The scale items can be found in Svebak (1993) and Kerr (1997).

## Verbal Accounts

The use of verbal accounts allows the researcher to uncover the states of mind that were operative by reference to what the participant says. This has been done in three ways in reversal theory research: interview, interview and later coding, and think-aloud verbal protocols.

### Interview

In the first of these ways, an interviewer conducts a conversation with the participant about the state of mind that he or she was in at the time of interest, and does so in such a way that the state can be identified during the interview itself. For example, in one study, respondents were interviewed in a laboratory experiment on muscle tension (electromyographic gradients) about what their metamotivational state had been during the experimental task (Apter & Svebak, 1986). The interviewer followed a basic structured set of questions, but was allowed follow-up questions to elucidate unclear responses. He was blind to the respondent's psychophysiological record. Harré and Secord (1972) have aptly described this kind of interview as involving a process of negotiation between the interviewer and interviewee.

### Interview and later coding

In the second method, the participant is interviewed on audio-tape. This tape is listened to by independent judges, or is transcribed and the transcriptions are read by the judges. The experiences described in the interview may then be coded by the judges into reversal theory categories. For this purpose, a coding schedule, known as the Metamotivational State Coding Schedule (MSCS) was developed by Potocky, Cook, and O'Connell (1993) and a detailed manual for its use has been drawn up (O'Connell, Potocky, Cook, & Gerkovich, 1991).

The MSCS is used in the following way: The verbal protocol is divided into coding units, each unit representing a single state in each pair, a single goal and a single environment or situation. If a change of goal, a change of environment or situation, or a reversal in any of the metamotivational pairs occurs, then a new coding unit is formed. For each unit, the judges make a series of decisions about the way in which the situation is being viewed, and which emotions and feelings are being experienced by the interviewee, to determine the prevailing metamotivational states. To date, this painstaking method has been used in a series of studies on smoking cessation (e.g., O'Connell, Cook, Gerkovich, Potocky, & Swan, 1990) and in sport research by Males, Kerr, and Gerkovich (1998), Purcell, Kerr, and Pollock (1996), and Purcell (1999), using a modified version of the MSCS.

### Think-aloud verbal protocols

In the third approach, the participant thinks aloud and his recorded utterances are later analysed and coded in terms of metamotivational state. Purcell uses this technique effectively in the research on golf, which is described in Chapter 4 in this book.

## Objective Indices

The third general way of measuring state is by means of some relatively simple response which can be measured objectively and which can be taken (on the basis of previous research) to represent one or another state. This can then be used to indicate the presence or absence of that state during some activity of interest to the researcher, such as activity in the classroom, the workplace, or the playing field. For example, Walters, Apter, and Svebak (1982) used colour preference as an indicator of the telic and paratelic states, basing this technique on previous research showing that 'hot' colours are preferred when an individual wants to increase arousal and 'cool' colours when he or she wants to lower arousal. In an extension of this work, Kerr and Vlaswinkel (1993) estimated the states of mind of the runners in their study by using colour preferences as a sign of the telic and paratelic states, with a preference for red being taken as a sign of the paratelic state and for blue as a sign of the telic state. Runners simply had to indicate either a red or a blue board as they passed it at a fixed point on the trail to represent their preference at that moment.

In another example, Lafreniere, Cowles, and Apter (1988) used the participant's choice of materials to work with (computer video games or a computer statistics teaching program) as an index of telic or paratelic state, this relationship being established independently of the main experiment. As more is known of the psychophysiological concomitants of the telic and paratelic and perhaps other states, psychophysiological measures may also be used to make inferences about state. (A summary of such concomitants, as explored by Svebak and his colleagues, will be found in Apter and Svebak, 1992.) Combined with telemetric monitoring, this could be a powerful procedure.

More detail on reversal theory state measures can be found in Cook *et al.* (1993), and their use in sport has been reviewed in detail by Kerr (1997).

# WHAT TYPE OF STATE MEASURE SHALL WE USE IN SPORT RESEARCH?

If one is going to engage in state-oriented research in the area of sport and performance which requires, among other things, identifying metamotivational states, then one will need to decide between the different approaches outlined in the previous section of this chapter. Whether one wants to use one (or two in combination) of the already developed approaches/measures or to develop new materials, this initial choice will still need to be made. Let us, therefore, look at some of the advantages and disadvantages of each.

## Self-report Scales

The overriding advantage of paper-and-pencil self-assessment devices, like rating scales, is that they are relatively easy to administer and score, and can also be given out to groups rather than individuals. This means that they can provide an inexpensive way of gathering extensive data. This advantage lessens with scales that measure state rather than trait, since they often have to be administered individually at appropriate times *in situ* (e.g., at a sport venue). But this is still likely to be a more convenient and less labour-intensive method than individual interview. The other advantage is that such tests are often regarded by some psychologists as somehow more objective (and therefore 'legitimate') than interviews, even though they still depend on subjective judgements – albeit judgements of the respondent rather than the observer.

A major disadvantage, which it is possible to overcome to some degree with interviews, is that the respondent may misinterpret the meaning of items. That is, there is no way of checking what the words in each item actually mean to each person taking the test, and this may be critical when such words refer to the subtleties of emotional life. In contrast, puzzlement can be noted during an interview, clarification asked for by the interviewer when responses seem off the point, and so on. This language problem is something which will be returned to later in this chapter.

A second problem is that a choice must typically be made by the investigator between an instrument which has satisfactory psychometric properties, but which may be a little lengthier than one would like, or a shorter scale which does not have these desirable properties, but which interferes less with ongoing activities. That is, on the one hand there are instruments with multiple items representing each characteristic to be measured, in which subscales produce acceptable alpha coefficients, and reflect the factor structure disclosed through factor analysis, and on the other there are instruments with only single items representing each characteristic to be measured, but which take little time to complete, and therefore cause less of an interruption to an activity which is in progress. This problem becomes more acute the greater the number of characteristics to be assessed, so while it is not necessarily too great a problem to have multiple items when dealing with a single pair of metamotivational states, it becomes much more difficult when there is an attempt (as in the SOMIFA) to measure all pairs of metamotivational states in the same global state measure. In this case, the respondent must stop whatever he or she is doing and attend to the test for a significant time, even when the test comprises single items, and even where these single items involve no more than dichotomous choices.

# Verbal Accounts

The advantage of using freely-given narrative verbal information from respondents is, firstly, that their responses are not confined or prompted or pre-packaged, or at least not in such obvious ways as occurs with self-report questionnaires or scales. The second is that the information is likely to be fuller and richer.

The specific benefits of the interview method for assessing state are many. As noted in the discussion of 'objective' self-report tests, one great advantage is that it is possible to ask follow-up questions which remove ambiguity from answers, and which clarify what respondents actually mean by the words they use – something which is not necessarily obvious with emotion and emotion-related words. A good interviewer will also avoid prompting the interviewee, and in this way receive detailed and sometimes unexpected accounts which can give rise to new insights and hypotheses. A further advantage of the interview is that it is possible to obtain accounts retrospectively, the 'talking through' prompting memory in a way that is less likely to occur with questionnaires. Since such a retrospective interview does not interfere with the actions that it is asking about, it is possible to take considerably more time and to ask, if one wants to, about all the pairs of meta-motivational states (see, e.g., Males, Kerr, & Gerkovich, 1998).

But if the advantages are considerable, so are the disadvantages. For one thing, interviews are not as standardized as questionnaires, even if they can be structured in terms of a basic set of questions, and so it may be difficult to compare the results of different respondents. And, of course, there is always the danger that interviewers will prompt the respondent to give expected or desirable answers. In any case, interviewers need to be well-versed in reversal theory to be able to spot potential problems and to ask the right kinds of follow-up questions. Furthermore, if the interview takes place long after the event, there may be memory problems – not only loss of memory but memory fabrication to please the interviewer. This problem may be at least partially overcome by using cues and prompts from the activity itself. For instance, McLennan and Omodei (1995) used the ingenious method of having orienteers wear helmets with mini-video recorders which recorded their field of action during a run. The resulting recordings were later used when discussing the participants' feelings at each point in their runs.

An alternative interview strategy, as we have seen, is for the interviewer to ask questions rather than engage in too much interpretative dialogue, and for the transcripts (recorded or transposed into written form) to be coded by independent judges. One problem here is what to do when judges cannot agree, although Cook et al. (1993) report that agreement is high when their coding schedule is used. And if interviewing in general is labour intensive, interviewing in conjunction with later work on coding can be prohibitive.

The use of think-aloud, or internal monologue techniques removes even further the possibility of the researcher prompting particular responses by the questions that are asked, although there is still the possibility of encouraging certain kinds of responses through a subtle reinforcement of certain kinds of statements if the researcher is present. The downside of this technique is that, without prompting, the respondent may verbalize in ways that do not reflect the actual aspects of experience that are of interest to the researcher, and a great deal of material may be 'off the point' with respect to the particular research question that is being asked. The power of this technique, however, will be evident from Purcell's chapter in the present volume (see Chapter 4).

## Objective Indices

The overriding advantage of using indices is twofold. Firstly, they can be completely objective and easily quantifiable. Secondly, they either do not interfere with the activity at all, or interfere only minimally. The basic disadvantage is that of validity. Indices need to be validated in some way so that one may be confident that they really are associated with states in the way that is being assumed. This means that they need to be validated against other more subjective methods (e.g., interview and self-report). This leads us back into some of the problems which we have now noted to be associated with self-report, and so these problems are not completely avoided in this approach. A lesser but very real practical problem may be that of actually identifying indices which can be used for specific states in specific situations. This will need a great deal of inventiveness and imagination in the future.

While thinking critically about state measures, there is a further methodological point which should perhaps be mentioned, even though it is not about measurement as such: one needs to analyse, very carefully, the inferences that are drawn from state measures about cause-and-effect relationships. Suppose, for example, that a relationship is found between the paratelic state and excellence of performance for some sportsperson in some sport. How does one know which caused which? Did the paratelic state constitute a prerequisite for the high performance, or did the success of the performance induce the paratelic state? To have a hope of sorting out this kind of question, very precise ways of determining sequence are needed, and this is why some previous studies in sport have measured states, pre-, post- and, where possible, during performance. This problem is, of course, not restricted to reversal theory sport research.

# ISSUES IN ASSESSING METAMOTIVATIONAL STATE

The attempt to identify metamotivational states is one that gives rise to many issues. Some of these have already been mentioned in the previous section of this chapter, in relation to choosing between the different possible approaches, but there are two more general problems that we shall need to look at more extensively. In doing so, we should bear in mind that these kinds of difficulties are not peculiar to reversal theory, but will inevitably arise with any approach that attempts to get a handle on subjective meaning, especially as it relates to the life of the emotions. Indeed, it is perhaps a sign of the sensitivity, maturity, and seriousness of an approach that it comes up against, and recognizes, such problems rather than ignoring them.

## Language Considerations

Whatever technique is used, one is confronted by the problem of language – even, as noted, where indices are used. Although several of the reversal theory measures discussed above include detailed explanations of the terminology used, it may be useful to look at some of the specific problems.

The difficulty with asking people about their emotions is that most emotion words have a variety of meanings: they are what linguists call polysemic. Of course, context can influence the way that individuals interpret the meaning of words, but let us look at this in terms of the emotion words used in reversal theory to depict the somatic emotions excitement and anxiety. Firstly, 'excitement' can mean any kind of feeling of being worked up, as in the phrase 'It excited my attention'. But it can also mean something much more specific, namely sexual excitement. Neither of these captures the reversal theory sense of any kind of pleasant high arousal. Secondly, 'anxiety' can mean 'determination' as in 'I was anxious to do well', rather than unpleasant high arousal.

The existence of parapathic emotions also complicates matters here, because a respondent may choose a telic emotion word but actually be experiencing the emotion concerned in the paratelic state. For example, someone may experience parapathic anxiety.

One possible way to overcome some of these problems would be to train respondents in reversal theory, at least to the extent that they can use words consistently in certain ways that are well established within the theory and so that they can understand, for example, the difference between a parapathic emotion and its 'normal' form. This would mean flying in the face of one of the tenets of twentieth-century psychology – namely that participants should be naive. But it has a great deal to recommend it, and it is already being used in some so-far unpublished but promising lines of reversal theory research. The present writer believes that this could represent a major way forward.

## Considerations in Test Assessment

The accuracy of state measures is particularly difficult to assess, since one is not making predictions in the way that occurs with measures of more enduring characteristics. In this context, it should be realized that reliability in its traditional psychometric sense is an inappropriate criterion for a state measure, since the whole point of a state measure is that it tracks the way in which people *change* over time. Such a measure would be suspect, and indeed of little use, if it always showed high test-retest reliability.

As far as validity is concerned, a number of techniques have been used:

1. *Face validity:* It is a good idea to get a consensus of opinion on items to be used in a state questionnaire or rating scale, and most of those who have developed reversal theory scales have checked items at an initial stage with a panel of judges familiar with the theory.
2. *Manipulation by experimental procedure:* This means manipulating the situation in which respondents find themselves in such a strong way that it is reasonable to assume that most respondents will find themselves in a particular metamotivational state. This technique has been used with success by Sven Svebak and his colleagues with the TSM, using such manipulations as the threat of electric shock or watching a comedy film (e.g., Svebak & Apter, 1987).
3. *Ecological validity:* This means testing people in strong real-life situations in which it is reasonable to assume that particular metamotivational states will be induced – for example, before an examination, at the theatre, and so on. Thus Cook *et al.* (1993), in developing the SSQ, compared respondents who were leaving on a ski vacation with respondents waiting to see the dentist.
4. *Testing against ideal vignettes:* Here the respondent is asked to rate how he or she would feel in certain described situations which are highly likely in the normal way of things to induce or maintain a particular state. For instance, Calhoun (1995; Calhoun & O'Connell, 1995) used this method in developing the T/PSI.

There is another validation criterion which, in a sense, is the most important of all, but which is difficult to determine in more than an impressionistic way. One might call it pragmatic utility. Does the measure give rise to patterns rather than noise? Do these patterns 'tell a story'? Does the measure generate interesting results? Can one make progress with it?

# THE PROBLEM OF PSYCHOLOGICAL MEASUREMENT IN SPORT

A number of the problems indicated earlier in this chapter, especially in relation to the identification of experiential states, may become even more problematic and exacerbated in the context of research on sport. This is true of all attempts to understand the motivation and emotional life of the sportsperson, but here we shall discuss these problems with particular reference to reversal theory. In any case, it is a reasonable assumption that any approach that does not seriously face up to such problems of measurement as these will produce at best no more than a superficial account of the psychology of the athlete.

One of these is the problem of measuring ongoing state without interfering with the activity concerned. In some situations, this is not a major difficulty. For example, in the research by Walters, Apter, and Svebak (1982) cited earlier, the office workers, whose metamotivational states were being tracked during the working day, showed no signs of annoyance at the regular request (every 15 or 30 minutes) for information, and the response requirements were so minor that little if any disruption was caused. One could imagine that in certain sports, and with certain athletes, it would also not be an issue. For example, many golfers seem to like to chat to spectators and others between shots, and being asked to reply to some questions may not seem too onerous for these sportsmen and sportswomen, as Purcell found (see Chapter 4).

More typically, however, it might be considered unfair and inappropriate to ask questions very close to critical moments of performance, and athletes are unlikely to acquiesce. To ask questions during the activity itself, unless there are natural breaks, could be very difficult. However, with the cooperation of the performers, some successful attempts have been made in reversal theory sport research (e.g., Cox & Kerr, 1989; Males & Kerr, 1996).

But the problem is not just that of fairness to the athlete and the possible negative impact on performance, it is also methodological. That is, the asking of questions, especially at critical moments, may in itself change the metamotivational state (and other aspects of the ongoing experience) of the athlete so that what is to be measured is changed by the measuring instrument. For example, the questions may induce a negativistic state in the athlete who may then become angry, or they may help to induce an alloic state (with the athlete wanting to help the questioner) rather than the autic state that would have prevailed without the intervention. (This whole topic of the way in which measurement can change that which is being measured is, of course, one that is well known in the modern physical sciences, and is epitomized by the impossibility of simultaneously measuring both the momentum and position of a particle in quantum mechanics.)

Post-performance testing remains a possibility for overcoming these potential barriers to good data collection, and many athletes have shown themselves ready, for example, to talk to researchers immediately after performing (Males, Kerr, & Gerkovich, 1998; Purcell, 1999). Even with athletes who are willing to respond, the testing should be rapid. Overly long questionnaires or interviews should perhaps be avoided, unless these are administered outside the performance context altogether – for example, at home when the athlete is at leisure. But now the problem of memory arises. This always presents a difficulty when asking questions about states of mind on some previous occasion, but it becomes a particular source of difficulty in the sport context since knowledge of victory or defeat will have been gained by the time of questioning. And this may well colour the whole recollection.

On the positive side, athletes may be much more willing than others to take part in studies, because they believe that what is discovered will help them to improve their personal performance. This optimism has not always proved to be well-founded in the past, but it is a legitimate motivation which can be used in a non-cynical way by the researcher to recruit participants to studies. Seen from the perspective of the experimental psychology of motivation, sport is a wonderful area for research because participants are genuinely motivated to succeed, and also outcome variables are already objective and quantified.

## CONCLUDING COMMENTS

We have now looked at the challenge of measurement in sport from the perspective of reversal theory, and much of the remainder of this book will provide detailed examples of the successful use of a variety of measurement techniques derived from this theory. All the techniques are concerned with understanding, in a systematic manner, the way in which the athlete experiences his or her world of competition. While the measurement tools being used at present are not necessarily ideal, by continually refining these tools, and by using a variety of tools, it will be possible to get closer to the essential nature of the athlete's experience than would otherwise be the case. Certainly this chapter has emphasized the problems involved, but it is only by recognizing the difficulties that arise when one attempts to describe and measure subjective meaning and emotion that real progress can be made. Unlike some other approaches to sport, reversal theory confronts these problems and deals with them in an imaginative and insightful way. In particular, instead of looking only at anxiety, and using only self-report scales – as so many sport researchers have done in the past – reversal theory insists on dealing with the full range of emotional experience and has developed a number of contrasting techniques for doing this.

Meanwhile it is encouraging to see, as will be apparent from the chapters in the rest of this book, that (a) reversal theory researchers in sport are now concentrating increasingly on dynamic issues to do with state, and the changes of state known as reversals, rather than the more conventional and static problems of enduring dispositions; (b) they are increasingly examining all the different pairs of metamotivational states in their work, rather than just the telic and paratelic pairs of states that attracted most of the reversal theory research initially (both in sport and more generally); and (c) some standard techniques and instruments are emerging that will allow research from different sports, different settings, and different cultures to become comparable. The future looks particularly bright for reversal theory sport research.

# REFERENCES

Apter, M. J. (1982). *The experience of motivation: The theory of psychological reversals.* London: Academic Press.

Apter, M. J. (1988). Reversal theory as a theory of the emotions. In M. J. Apter, J. H. Kerr & M. P. Cowles (Eds.), *Progress in reversal theory* (pp. 43–62). Amsterdam: North-Holland/Elsevier.

Apter, M. J. & Apter-Desselles, M. L. (1993). The personality of the patient: Going beyond the trait concept. *Patient Education and Counseling,* **22**, 107–114.

Apter, M. J., Kerr, J. H. & Cowles, M. P. (Eds.) (1988). *Progress in reversal theory.* Amsterdam: North-Holland/Elsevier.

Apter, M. J., Mallows, R. & Williams, S. (1998). The development of the Motivational Style Profile. *Personality and Individual Differences,* **24**, 7–18.

Apter, M. J. & Svebak, S. (1986). The EMG gradient as a reflection of metamotivational state. *Scandinavian Journal of Psychology,* **27**, 209–219.

Apter, M. J. & Svebak, S. (1989). Stress from the reversal theory perspective. In C. D. Spielberger, I. G. Sarason & J. Strelau (Eds.), *Stress and emotion,* Vol. 12 (pp. 38–52). Washington, DC: Hemisphere–McGraw-Hill.

Apter, M. J. & Svebak, S. (1992). Reversal theory as a biological approach to individual differences. In A. Gale & M. W. Eysenck (Eds.), *Handbook of individual differences, biological perspectives* (pp. 323–353). Chichester, UK: Wiley.

Boekaerts, M., Hendriksen, J. & Michels, C. (1988). The assessment of telic dominance in primary school children. In M. J. Apter, J. H. Kerr & M. P. Cowles (Eds.), *Progress in reversal theory* (pp. 265–274). Amsterdam: North-Holland/Elsevier.

Calhoun, J. E. (1995). *Construct validity of the Telic/Paratelic State Instrument: A measure of reversal theory constructs.* Unpublished doctoral dissertation, University of Kansas School of Nursing.

Calhoun, J. E. & O'Connell, K. A. (1995, July). *Construct validity of the Telic/Paratelic State Instrument: A measure of reversal theory constructs.* Paper presented at the 7th International Conference on Reversal Theory, Melbourne, Australia.

Chirivella, E. C. & Martinez, L. M. (1994). The sensation of risk and motivational tendencies in sports: An empirical study. *Personality and Individual Differences*, **16**, 777–786.

Cook, M. R. & Gerkovich, M. M. (1993). The development of a Paratelic Dominance Scale. In J. H. Kerr, S. Murgatroyd & M. J. Apter (Eds.), *Advances in reversal theory* (pp. 177–188). Amsterdam: Swets & Zeitlinger.

Cook, M. R., Gerkovich, M. M., Potocky, M. & O'Connell, K. A. (1993). Instruments for the assessment of reversal theory states. *Patient Education and Counseling*, **22**, 99–106.

Cox, T. & Kerr, J. H. (1989). Arousal effects during tournament play in squash. *Perceptual and Motor Skills*, **69**, 1275–1280.

Evans, R. (1994). A psychological profile of top Australian soccer referees. *Sports Coach*, April–June, 17–18.

Harré, R. & Secord, P. F. (1972). *The explanation of social behavior.* Oxford: Basil Blackwell.

Hyland, M. E., Sherry, R. & Thacker, C. (1988). Prospectus for an improved measure of telic dominance. In M. J. Apter, J. H. Kerr & M. P. Cowles (Eds.), *Progress in reversal theory* (pp. 287–295). Amsterdam: North-Holland/Elsevier.

Kerr, J. H. (1987). Differences in the motivational characteristics of 'professional', 'serious amateur' and 'recreational' sports performers. *Perceptual and Motor Skills*, **64**, 379–382.

Kerr, J. H. (1988). A study of motivation in rugby. *Journal of Social Psychology*, **128** (2), 269–270.

Kerr, J. H. (1997). *Motivation and emotion in sport: Reversal theory.* Hove, UK: Psychology Press.

Kerr, J. H. & Svebak, S. (1994). The acute effects of participation in sport on mood. *Personality and Individual Differences*, **16** (1), 159–166.

Kerr, J. H. & van den Wollenberg, A. E. (1997). High and low intensity exercise and psychological mood states. *Psychology and Health*, **12**, 603–618.

Kerr, J. H. & van Schaik, P. (1995). Effects of game venue and outcome on psychological mood states in rugby. *Personality and Individual Differences*, **19** (3), 407–409.

Kerr, J. H. & Vlaswinkel, E. H. (1993). Self-reported mood and running under natural conditions. *Work and Stress*, **7**, 161–177.

Lafreniere, K. D., Cowles, M. P. & Apter, M. J. (1988). The reversal phenomenon: Reflections on a laboratory study. In M. J. Apter, J. H. Kerr & M. P. Cowles (Eds.), *Progress in reversal theory* (pp. 247–254). Amsterdam: North-Holland/Elsevier.

Males, J. R. & Kerr, J. H. (1996). Stress, emotion and performance in elite slalom canoeists. *The Sport Psychologist*, **10**, 17–36.

Males, J. R., Kerr, J. H. & Gerkovich, M. M. (1998). Metamotivational states during canoe slalom competition: A qualitative analysis using reversal theory. *Journal of Applied Sport Psychology*, **10**, 185–200.

Martin, R. A., Kuiper, N. A., Olinger, L. J. & Dobbin, J. (1987). Is stress always bad? Telic versus paratelic dominance as a stress moderating variable. *Journal of Personality and Social Psychology*, **53**, 970–982.

McDermott, M. R. (1988a). Measuring rebelliousness: The development of the Negativism Dominance Scale. In M. J. Apter, J. H. Kerr & M. P. Cowles (Eds.), *Progress in reversal theory* (pp. 297–312). Amsterdam: North-Holland/Elsevier.

McDermott, M. R. (1988b). Recognising rebelliousness: The ecological validity of the Negativism Dominance Scale. In M. J. Apter, J. H. Kerr & M. P. Cowles (Eds.), *Progress in reversal theory* (pp. 313–325). Amsterdam: North-Holland/Elsevier.

McLennan, J. & Omodei, M. M. (1995, July). *Studying dynamic psychological phenomena in real-world settings*. Paper presented at the 7th International Conference on Reversal Theory, Melbourne, Australia.

Murgatroyd, S. (1985). The nature of telic dominance. In M. J. Apter, D. Fontana & S. Murgatroyd (Eds.), *Reversal theory: Applications and developments* (pp. 20–41), Cardiff: University College Cardiff Press.

Murgatroyd, S., Rushton, C., Apter, M. J. & Ray, C. (1978). The development of the Telic Dominance Scale. *Journal of Personality Assessment*, **42**, 519–528.

O'Connell, K. A., Cook, M. R., Gerkovich, M. M., Potocky, M. & Swan, G. E. (1990). Reversal theory and smoking: A state-based approach to ex-smoker's highly tempting situations. *Journal of Consulting and Clinical Psychology*, **58**, 489–494.

O'Connell, K. A., Potocky, M., Cook, M. R. & Gerkovich, M. M. (1991). *Metamotivational State Interview and Coding Schedule: Instruction manual.* Kansas City: Midwest Research Institute.

Potocky, M., Cook, M. R. & O'Connell, K. A. (1993). The use of an interview and structured coding system to assess metamotivational state. In J. H. Kerr, S. Murgatroyd & M. J. Apter (Eds.), *Advances in reversal theory* (pp. 135–150). Amsterdam: Swets & Zeitlinger.

Purcell, I. P. (1999). *Expertise, decisions and emotions in the performance of male golfers.* Unpublished doctoral dissertation, Curtin University of Technology, Perth, Australia.

Purcell, I. P., Kerr, J. H. & Pollock, C. M. (1996). *Plans, decisions and emotions in golf. Coaches Report of the Applied Sports Research Program.* Canberra: Australian Sports Commission.

Svebak, S. (1993). The development of the Tension and Effort Stress Inventory (TESI). In J. H. Kerr, S. Murgatroyd & M. J. Apter (Eds.), *Advances in reversal theory* (pp. 189–204). Amsterdam: Swets & Zeitlinger.

Svebak, S. (1997). Tension- and effort-stress as predictors of academic performance. In S. Svebak & M. J. Apter (Eds.), *Stress and health: A reversal theory perspective* (pp. 45–56). Washington, DC: Taylor & Francis.

Svebak, S. & Apter, M. J. (1987). Laughter: An empirical test of some reversal theory hypotheses. *Scandinavian Journal of Psychology*, **28**, 189–198.

Svebak, S. & Murgatroyd, S. (1985). Metamotivational dominance: A multimethod validation of reversal theory constructs. *Journal of Personality and Social Psychology*, **48**, 107–116.

Svebak, S., Mykletun, R. & Bru, E. (1997). Back pain and work stress. In S. Svebak & M. J. Apter (Eds.), *Stress and health: A reversal theory perspective* (pp. 57–67). Washington, DC: Taylor & Francis.

Tacon, P. & Abner, B. (1993). Normative and other data for the Telic Dominance and Negativism Dominance Scales. In J. H. Kerr, S. Murgatroyd & M. J. Apter (Eds.), *Advances in reversal theory* (pp. 165–176). Amsterdam: Swets & Zeitlinger.

Vlaswinkel, E. H. & Kerr, J. H. (1990). Negativism dominance in risk and team sports. *Perceptual and Motor Skills*, **70**, 289–290.

Walters, J., Apter, M. J. & Svebak, S. (1982). Colour preference, arousal and the theory of psychological reversals. *Motivation and Emotion*, **6**, 193–215.

# SECTION II

# HIGH-LEVEL AND ELITE PERFORMERS

# 3

# Success and Failure and Emotional Experience in Sport

**George V. Wilson**

*University of Tasmania, Australia*


## INTRODUCTION

One of the most obvious features of sporting competition is the pervasiveness of the full spectrum of emotional responses: happiness, joy, pride, and gratitude may be evidenced in response to winning; anger, dismay, frustration, or shame may be shown in losing (McAuley & Duncan, 1990). Research to assess emotions experienced in sport indicates that emotional reaction to success and failure affect a range of factors such as self-confidence and self-esteem that may ultimately influence an individual's performance level, expectation of success, and motivation to compete in future competition (e.g., Kerr & Cox, 1990; Reeve, 1992).

Emotion is a complex psychological phenomenon which has been the basis for a large number of attempts at theoretical explanation. Few theoretical approaches have attempted to describe the effects of success

*Experiencing Sport: Reversal Theory.* Edited by J. H. Kerr.
© 1999 John Wiley & Sons Ltd.

or failure (winning or losing) in competitive situations, including those encountered in the outcome of sporting competition.

# ATTRIBUTION THEORY APPROACHES TO EMOTIONAL EXPERIENCES IN SPORT

One theoretical approach which has been applied to emotional experiences in sport and sporting competition is Weiner's (1985) attribution theory of achievement and motivation. The theory proposes that in achievement-related situations there are three sources of emotion: the first and strongest is tied to outcome; the second to luck, task difficulty, and the influence of others on success or failure; the third is the result of self-ascriptions of either ability or effort. A key postulate of the Weiner theory is that emotions produced by outcome are very general (namely, success produces happiness and failure produces sadness), whereas emotions which are the product of luck, task difficulty, influence of others, ability, or effort are more specific. The theory argues, for example, that failure attributed to effort produces feelings of guilt and shame, whereas failure attributed to lack of ability produces feelings of incompetence. The rigid structure of the attribution theory of achievement and motivation restricts and limits the ability of the theory to account for emotions engendered in achievement-related situations, especially when inappropriate emotional responses and emotional variations are involved (e.g., McAuley & Duncan, 1989, 1990; McAuley, Russell, & Gross, 1983; Russell & McAuley, 1986). For example, McAuley and Duncan (1990) argue that it is possible to lose a squash match against a superior opponent and still experience positive emotions because one feels that one has played well: this emotional reaction is not catered for by Weiner's theory. In addition, there are a variety of factors not incorporated into the theory which have been shown to contribute to emotional reactions: expectations of success (McAuley & Duncan, 1989), closeness of match outcome (Martin & Gill, 1991), and choice of performance or outcome goal (Martin & Gill, 1991). While Weiner's theory has received partial support from research, its inability to describe the full range of emotion and to cover important determinants of emotional experience, reveal major limitations.

Vallerand (1983, 1987) developed the intuitive–reflective appraisal model of emotion in sport from the theoretical approaches of Weiner (1985) and others. The model proposes that emotions in sport are the result of intuitive and reflective cognitive appraisals. Intuitive appraisal represents the immediate perception of how well one has performed in a game and is always involved in the formation of emotion. Reflective appraisal involves a cognitive process that assimilates and accommodates performance information in new or existing cognitive structures: it is used only in situations when control of arousal is required. Reflective appraisal is proposed to take many forms, including intellectualization, comparison processes (self, outcome, and social), information-processing functions, mastery-related cognitions, and causal attributions – all of which may be used in a variety of sporting situations. The structure of the intuitive–reflective model has been tested with basketball players (Vallerand, 1987) and gymnasts (McAuley & Duncan, 1990): intuitive appraisal was implicated in both studies but reflective appraisal processes were used in only some situations. McAuley and Duncan could not find a relationship between some of the emotions experienced and either appraisal process. While there was support for the intuitive–reflective model, Vallerand only measured six emotions, which represents a restricted emotional palate, and McAuley and Duncan found that not all emotions were accounted for by the appraisal processes, which suggests that the model is not comprehensive.

## ATTRIBUTION THEORY RESEARCH ON WINNING AND LOSING IN COMPETITIVE SPORT

While there are a number of attribution theory studies on performance in sport and other situations, there are few studies of the effects of winning or losing in real competitive sporting situations. Spink and Roberts (1980) performed an attributional analysis on winners and losers, using a single game of racquetball with randomly paired players who had played against each other previously. Following each game, players were assessed about causal attributions to outcome concerning levels of skill, effort, task difficulty, and luck. Wins and losses were classified as 'clear' when game outcome and subjective performance satisfaction were consonant, and 'ambiguous' when outcome and performance satisfaction were not consonant (e.g., when a player lost the game but was satisfied with the level of performance, this outcome would be classified as an 'ambiguous loss'). Spink and Roberts found that clearly perceived outcomes (either clear wins or clear losses) were attributed internally (e.g., one's own competence) while ambiguous losses were attributed externally (e.g., a more competent opponent, luck, etc.). They also concluded that success and failure were not necessarily synonymous with win and lose. Actual emotions were not measured in this study.

McAuley, Russell, and Gross (1983) studied the emotional consequences and causal attributions of winning and losing, using the outcome of a competitive table tennis game involving players of matched ability. They used a single post-game assessment to measure nine 'attribution depend-ent' emotions and to assess causal attributions. Emotional responses were very clearly differentiated by outcome. Winners felt significantly more sat-isfied, proud, confident, and grateful than losers; losers felt more angry, depressed, incompetent, and surprised than winners. Losers were more ashamed than winners, but this difference was not statistically significant. For winners, satisfaction was the only significant causal attribution (along the causal dimensions of locus of causality, stability, and controllability); for losers there were no significant effects. McAuley *et al.* (1983) inter-preted their results as clearly not supporting Weiner's attributional model of emotions. They suggested that differences between studies probably reflect the type of competitive performance (e.g., academic vs. sport) and level of ego involvement, with sport outcomes making perceptions of con-trol more salient to participants.

Both the Weiner and Vallerand models share common faults. They can-not explain why individuals have different emotional experiences of the same event on different occasions and they do not provide an explanation of the important role of physiological arousal on emotional reactions. Re-versal theory (Apter, 1982, 1989) does not share these common faults and is a comprehensive theoretical model from which it is possible to explore emotional experience in competitive sport.

# REVERSAL THEORY IN SPORT

Emotional responses are determined by both the person and the situation: any theory which is capable of determining how an individual will react must be interactive and link the situation experienced and the person's motivations or reasons for his or her behaviour in this situation. Reversal theory incorporates this property into its structure to explain individuals' emotional responses to various situations and different motivational states. The theory proposes that human emotion is produced via bistable pairs of opposite and mutually exclusive metamotivational states. Each state moti-vates an individual to process information and to behave in a distinctive fashion.

The somatic states consist of the telic–paratelic pair and the conformist–negativistic pair. In competitive sporting situations, an individual in the telic state feels the need to be oriented towards some essential future goal (e.g., to win) and any obstruction to this goal will be experienced as un-pleasant as it interferes with the attainment of the goal. By contrast, in the paratelic state an individual will be playful and activity oriented: any asso-ciated goal will simply provide a justification for the activity. Experiences of high felt arousal are interpreted as pleasurable as they add to the quality and enjoyment of the activity in which one is participating. In the negativistic–conformist states, an individual's experience will depend on whether his or her behaviour is seen as conforming to or resisting rules, social pressures, or social expectations. Individuals in the conformist state will comply with rules and social pressures and are uncomfortable when they perceive that social expectations have been violated. In the negativistic state, individuals experience most pleasure when they perceive their behaviour as rebellious or defiant (e.g., 'beating the odds', swearing, being abusive, or even cheating). This framework of somatic states, in conjunction with level of arousal, provides for eight somatic emotions.

- An individual in the conformist and paratelic states will experience low arousal as boredom and high arousal as excitement.
- An individual in the conformist and telic states will experience low arousal as relaxation and high arousal as anxiety.
- An individual in the negativistic and paratelic states will experience low arousal as sullenness and high arousal as provocativeness.
- An individual in the negativistic and telic states will experience low arousal as placidity and high arousal as unpleasant anger.

The transactional states consist of autic–alloic and mastery–sympathy pairs of states. Reversal theory proposes that at any one time an individual will be self-focused (autic state) or 'other focused' (alloic state). In the autic state, an individual will experience most pleasure if he or she is on the gain side of felt transactional outcome (FTO) (e.g., a win against a sporting rival); in the alloic state most pleasure will be experienced if one is on the loss side of FTO (e.g., giving good advice to a weaker player). The mastery–sympathy states are differentiated on the basis that, in the mastery state, one will seek to control, dominate, or win, while the sympathy state is concerned with liking or being liked by self or others. Reversal theory predicts that participants engaged in competitive sport will be predominantly in the autic–mastery state combination – the concern is to win or dominate over others. Reversal theory also proposes that the two pairs of transactional states, moderated by FTO, provide for a set of eight transactional emotions.

- An individual in the mastery and autic states will experience low FTO (e.g., losing to a weaker opponent) as humiliation, and will experience high FTO (e.g., winning against a stronger opponent) as pride.
- An individual in the mastery and alloic states will experience low FTO (e.g., giving advice to a weaker opponent) as modesty, and will experience high FTO (e.g., mercilessly trouncing a much weaker and inexperienced opponent) as shame.

- An individual in the sympathy and alloic states will experience low FTO (e.g., comforting a fellow player in a time of need) as virtue, and will experience high FTO (e.g., behaving in an unsporting manner to an opponent) as guilt.
- An individual in the sympathy and autic states will experience low FTO (e.g., not receiving expected support from fellow players) as resentment, and will experience high FTO (e.g., being praised by the coach) as gratitude.

Reversal theory proposes that somatic and transactional emotions can be elicited concurrently: the relative strength of each emotion and its salience will determine which is experienced as the strongest.

A reversal between state pairs is an unconscious or automatic process which is not under voluntary control and is precipitated by a number of factors. These include *frustration*, caused when an individual's needs are not being met; *satiation*, the effect of being in one state for too long a time; *contingent situations*, such as a funeral or hospital ward, or alternatively a lively party or football grand final; and *contingent events*, which are environmental and psychological events that act as triggers for reversals. In sport there are many contingent events that can trigger reversals; for example, pain caused by injury, making a mistake, success and failure, umpire decisions, heckling from the crowd, and unpleasant inputs from opponents. Reversal theory also proposes that individuals have an innate consistent tendency to prefer one state, the dominant state, over its opposite. Most of an individual's time will be spent in the dominant state: the concept of state dominance thus reflects the probability or likelihood that an individual will be in the dominant state at a particular point in time. When the non-dominant state is engaged, it is enjoyed as much as the dominant state and is experienced as just as real and not inferior in any way.

## REVERSAL THEORY PREDICTIONS ABOUT WINNING AND LOSING

Reversal theory facilitates some general predictions about the specific states and emotions which are appropriate to (1) the playing of competitive sport and (2) winning or losing as an outcome of sport competition:

1. The playing of competitive sport (e.g., team games, racquet sports) should involve the high arousal somatic emotions (excitement, provocativeness, anxiety, anger). The somatic states are all involved, and individuals may occupy some or all of the paratelic–conformist, paratelic–negativistic, telic–conformist, and telic–negativistic state

combinations, depending on each individual's dominance, game progression, and incidents which could trigger reversals. The low arousal somatic emotions would not seem to be likely or appropriate during most highly active competitive sport competition.

The pleasant mastery transactional emotions (modesty, pride) would be the most appropriate in both individual and team sports which demand high standards of individual personal performance. It is unlikely that much time would be spent in the sympathy state during the playing of competitive sport, but the pleasant sympathy emotions (virtue, gratitude) may be evoked, especially in team sports, if concern becomes focused on feelings of others, or for others, rather than on actual competitive performance.

2. The effects of winning or losing should produce very different emotions in both the transactional and somatic emotions. Winning should produce the pleasant transactional emotions, particularly the mastery emotions (modesty, pride) but also the sympathy emotions (virtue, gratitude) as the fact of winning is enjoyed and is shared with others. The somatic emotions should reflect the pleasant conformist emotions (excitement, relaxation) as winners enjoy their victory, or feel satisfaction in the attainment of their goals.

   Losing should produce the unpleasant transactional emotions, especially the mastery emotions (humiliation, shame) but the unpleasant sympathy emotions (resentment, guilt) may become salient if concern is focused on the feelings of other people or for other people. The somatic emotions should show unpleasant negativistic emotions (sullenness, anger) as losers are denied or frustrated in the attainment of their goal.

These are general predictions about the emotional effects of competitive sport and the differential effects of winning and losing. It is to be expected that individual factors and concerns, such as injury, exceptional performances, luck, and the reactions of others, will produce some deviations from the general pattern of predicted outcomes.

# RESEARCH DESIGNS USED IN REVERSAL THEORY INVESTIGATIONS OF SPORT

Kerr (1997) has produced a useful review and summary of six studies which have used a reversal theory approach to investigate winning and losing in sport. These studies, plus a recent study of emotional responses to winning and losing of rugby players by Wilson and Kerr (1999), form the basis for the methodological considerations in this section. It is important to understand the various types of research method used, the different sporting situations (the participants, type of sport, type of competition and outcome), the methods used to measure the dependent variables, and the measurement of related or control variables.

## Different Sporting Situations

The sports described by Kerr (1997) comprised gymnastics and canoeing, two individual performance sports; squash, a competitive 'one-on-one' sport; and rugby, a contact team sport. The nature of the competition involved in different types of sport involve different behavioural and somatic requirements during play. It is highly likely that the salience of the emotions elicited during play and the emotional response to winning or losing will also differ from sport to sport.

In the individual sports there is a single winner, two place-getters, and the rest of the field (losers): in order to win, the aim is not so much to beat an opponent or a specific other competitor, but rather the competition involves optimizing one's own performance, score, luck, preparation, one's 'state' on the day, and so on. The competition is impersonal and is almost entirely focused internally on self and the performance of self: win or lose may or may not translate directly onto the gain or loss FTO dimension of the transactional emotions.

On the other hand, 'one-on-one' sports like squash are more personal and involve a decisive competition (combat) between oneself and a single other person. There is a winner and there is a loser and the outcome is determined by the superiority of relative performances of the two players on the day: one can play one's best ever game and still lose, and one can play abominably and yet win. The dyadic situation, as epitomized by squash, produces a very simple and unambiguous win or lose outcome in terms of the transactional outcome which simplifies methodological considerations.

In competitive contact team sports, one plays as a member of a team and one's opponent is a team of players rather than any individual person or persons. The experience of winning or losing is not conferred personally, but via one's membership of a team. While the transactional outcome of a win or a loss is likely to be experienced consistently by all members of the team, exceptions may occur. A member of a winning team may still feel a transactional loss if that individual's performance in competition was poor or incompetent: likewise, a member of the losing team may experience a transactional gain because of an exceptionally fine personal performance.

The question that needs to be addressed is whether the emotions experienced in winning and losing are different for different sports. This question can be answered empirically – the answer has important theoretical and methodological implications for reversal theory and research in sport psychology, as well as implications for practices in sport psychology and coaching. A more minor, but not inconsequential, methodological design consideration is the issue of obtaining equal numbers of winners and losers for statistical analyses in research using different sports. Many parametric statistical procedures either require equal numbers of participants in each group, or produce more reliable outcomes when numbers in different conditions are equal. In face-to-face competition, such as squash, every match produces a winner and a loser. If both players in a match agree to participate in the study, the numbers of winners and losers will be even. In team competitions, such as rugby, the paradigm has usually involved using one team of players who are assessed across a number of matches against different opponents. If the team wins and loses the same number of matches, then this is fortuitous for the researcher as it produces equal numbers in the win and lose conditions. There would be a problem for the researcher (but not for the team) if all matches were won: there would be problems all round if all matches were lost or drawn. The problem is similar in individual sports where there is a single winner and many losers in each competition: it is not possible to equalize groups of winners and losers without adopting some strategy to remove participants from the losing condition (e.g., randomly discarding participants, selecting 'worst' loser, or some other procedure).

## Type of Competition

Findings on the emotional effects of winning or losing have involved outcomes of 'real' competition in rugby (Kerr & van Schaik, 1995; Wilson & Kerr, 1999), gymnastics (Kerr & Pos, 1994), canoeing (Males & Kerr, 1996), and squash (Wilson & Phillips, 1995). A simulated squash tournament was used by Cox and Kerr (1989, 1990), and Kerr and Cox (1989, 1990) used a squash task of the number of hits on a designated target to elicit an outcome. Apart from possible qualitative differences in emotional outcome of the different types of sport (discussed in the preceding section), it is likely that real competitive situations will elicit more intense emotional reactions than simulated competition, training, or other type of sport performance.

## Research Design

Six of the seven studies have used a pre- and post-event repeated measures factor to measure emotional changes due to task performance and outcome. Where winning and losing outcomes are available, this forms an independent groups factor: this 2 × 2 (win/lose × pre-game/post-game) design allows the effect of game outcome to be clearly identified via the interaction involving post-game differences between groups. The design is very efficient and robust and is the most powerful research design available for use in a competitive context: it forms the basis of all the relevant studies, except Males and Kerr (1996).

Males and Kerr (1996) used a very different design in their study of canoeists in real competition conditions. This study used a single-case-study design with a correlational time series analysis of individuals' data across a full season of competition: pre-event emotion ratings were administered, but post-event data was via a structured interview. The single-case-study design is useful for coaching and for uncovering and improving performance; however, interpretation of causality in outcome is restricted and data collection is very time consuming and may need to be 'adjusted' to reduce intrusion.

## Measures of Emotion

The main instrument used to assess emotional tone has been the Telic State Measure (TSM) (Svebak & Murgatroyd, 1985). The TSM measures one's position with respect to the telic–paratelic pair of metamotivational states in terms of arousal avoidance, planning orientation, and serious–playful dimensions. The TSM measures the mechanism underlying the emotions, but does not identify the emotion actually experienced: from this perspective the resolution of the TSM is fairly coarse. For example, a high TSM score identifies the telic state, from which it is possible to experience any one of four different telic emotions (anxiety, anger, relaxation, placidity). Even if the TSM is used with a measure of felt arousal, the number of possible emotions is two (e.g., in high arousal, the telic emotions could be either anxiety or anger; in low arousal, the emotions could be either relaxation or placidity). The TSM does not provide for any measurement or inference about the eight transactional emotions. Because there are no state measures for the negativistic–conformist, mastery–sympathy, or autic–alloic pairs of metamotivational states, it has not been possible to explore or elaborate the full range of emotions in reversal theory using the TSM.

The Tension and Effort Stress Inventory (TESI) has been developed recently by Svebak (1993) and there is a state version assessing current emotional experience. The TESI includes ratings for the 16 individual emotions proposed in reversal theory. The strength of each emotion is measured directly, which avoids the need to infer or imply emotions via indirect metamotivational assessment using the TSM. Males and Kerr (1996) and Kerr and Svebak (1994) have used the TESI prior to competition and during participation, respectively. Wilson and Kerr (1999) used the TESI with rugby players to assess the emotional effects of winning and losing. Wilson and Phillips (1995) used a Mood Checklist (MC) which required squash players to select the strongest or salient emotion of the eight somatic and the eight transactional emotions to assess current emotional state.

It is important that measurement instruments used in the field in real sport competition can be completed quickly and cause minimal levels of intrusion on competitors. The TESI is fast and easy to complete and it can be repeated at a number of points during competition, as long as intrusion is not unacceptable. This type of comprehensive instrument allows for the full palate of reversal theory emotions to be considered and mapped directly. Instruments such as the TESI, or even the MC, present the researcher with powerful tools for the study and fuller understanding of emotions in sport.

## Timing of Measurements

Maximal internal experimental validity is achieved when emotional state measures are administered as close as possible to the event. Ideally, pre-game and post-game measurement should take place immediately (i.e., within minutes) before and after each game. The longer the time period, the larger the possibility of distortion of actual emotions experienced. Because of pre- and post-game procedures and requirements, the time immediately before and after games is unlikely to be available to be given over to research data collection. The researcher should be mindful of the likely effects of intervening events on the emotions and possible influence on validity of measurement.

One alternative to immediate measurement is to use a retrospective data collection procedure such as an interview or questionnaire. Males and Kerr (1996) used an interview to collect post-competition data. The technique allows for questions to be elaborated, issues to be pursued, and provides very rich data sets on individuals; however, the interview is expensive and time consuming and it is difficult to interview many players in the same session. Questionnaires are more constrained or restricted in the data that is collected, but the data is more uniform/consistent, which is important for statistical analysis and interpretation. The questionnaire is cost and time efficient and many players can be tested at the one time. Retrospective data collection is generally considered to be a methodologically suspect procedure because of the unknown influence of intervening events, of confounding, and of changes in mood state on the memory of past events and emotions.

# REVERSAL THEORY RESEARCH INTO WINNING AND LOSING

## Squash Competition

Wilson and Phillips (1995) studied 60 Australian male squash players playing in A, B, C, and D grade club pennant matches. There were 35 winners and 25 losers. Participants completed the Telic Dominance Scale (TDS) (Murgatroyd, Rushton, Apter, & Ray, 1978) and the Negativism Dominance Scale (NDS) (McDermott & Apter, 1988) 15 minutes before or after the match. Then, 2 to 3 minutes immediately before the match commenced, participants completed the TSM, a Mood Checklist (MC) which listed the eight somatic emotions (relaxation, anxiety, excitement, boredom, placidity, anger, provocativeness, sullenness) and the eight transactional emotions (pride, humiliation, modesty, shame, gratitude, resentment, virtue, guilt) (Apter, 1989) and required participants to choose the most relevant emotion from each group, and a Strength of Opponent Scale, a 7-point scale ranging from 'weaker' to 'stronger'. During the break following the second set of a best-of-five-sets match, the TSM and the MC were administered a second time. On completion of the match, the TSM and MC were again administered. Three 10-point scales – a Pleasantness Scale, a Satisfaction with Performance Scale, and a Closeness of Match Scale were also administered at this stage.

The results showed some clear differences between winners and losers:

1. *Telic State Measure*: A 2 group (win/lose) × 3 periods (pre-/during/post-match) ANOVA revealed a significant interaction, with winners and losers having similar TSM scores pre-match and during the match, but with winners having lower post-match TSM scores than losers. Winners also had a significantly lower post-match TSM compared to their TSM scores pre- and during match. Figure 3.1 illustrates this interaction.

2. On other scales, t-tests showed that winners had significantly lower post-match levels of dissatisfaction with performance, and higher levels of pleasantness than losers.

3. *Emotional responses*: The pattern of emotional responses of winners and losers provides a view of the dynamics of the differential emotional reactions involved. The MC ratings across the three measurement periods are shown in Figures 3.2 and 3.3, with frequencies expressed as percentages to facilitate comparison between the unequal number of winners and losers.

Pre-game somatic emotions were dominated by relaxation, excitement, and anxiety in both winners and losers. During play, anxiety and excitement

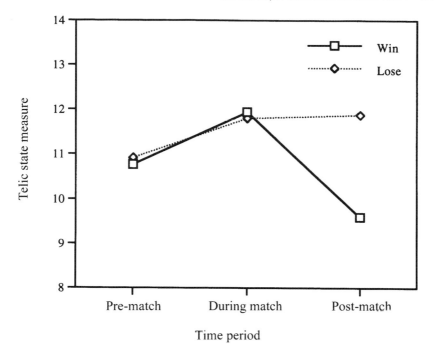

**Figure 3.1**    TSM scores at pre-match, match, and post-match for winners and losers in squash (from Wilson & Phillips, 1995).

were the dominant emotions experienced by both winners and losers; losers also experienced some moderate levels of anger at this stage, perhaps because play had not gone well. Post-match emotions were quite differentiated, with winners feeling relaxation and excitement and losers feeling anger and sullenness.

Transactional emotions showed high levels of both pride and modesty for both groups before the match. During the match, the eventual winners reported high levels of pride and modesty, while losers showed lower levels of pride and modesty; resentment was also salient for the losers at this stage. Post-match, winners continued to express pride and modesty, while the losers were reporting humiliation and shame with a reduction in level of modesty.

Because of a number of emotions with low or no endorsement, statistical analysis was performed by the Chi-squared test on the MC data categorized into dimensions described in reversal theory (Apter, 1989). As expected, pre-match emotions were very similar for the eventual winners and losers. Somatic emotions were significantly more conformist than negativistic and showed high rather than low hedonic tone, for both winners and losers; however, winners showed significantly more telic than

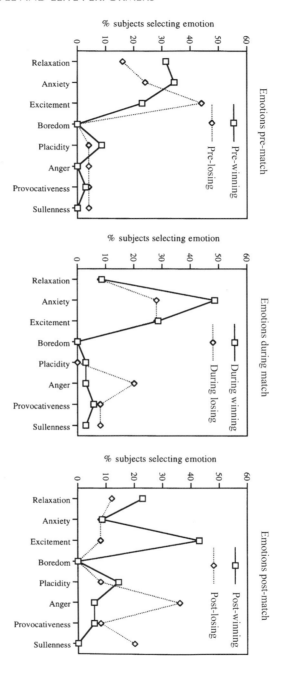

**Figure 3.2** Percentage of somatic emotions at pre-match, match, and post-match for winners and losers in squash (from Wilson & Phillips, 1995).

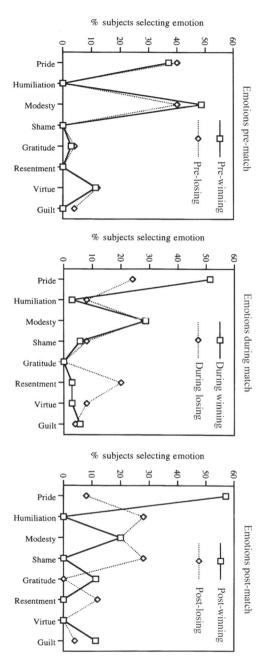

**Figure 3.3** Percentage of transactional emotions at pre-match, match, and post-match for winners and losers in squash (from Wilson & Phillips, 1995).

paratelic emotions, while losers showed no difference. Pre-match transactional emotions were identical for winners and losers: significantly more mastery than sympathy emotions, more high than low hedonic tone emotions, and no differences between gain and loss emotions (FTO).

Winners and losers were clearly differentiated on post-match emotions. For winners, post-match somatic emotions had significantly more high than low hedonic tone, were more conformist than negativistic, and more paratelic than telic, although this last difference was not significant. For losers, post-match somatic emotions were almost the opposite, with significantly more negativistic than conformist emotions, more telic than paratelic emotions, and with no difference between numbers of high and low hedonic tone emotions. For the post-match transactional emotions, winners showed significantly more mastery than sympathy emotions, more gain than loss emotions (FTO), and more high than low hedonic tone emotions. Losers also showed significantly more mastery than sympathy emotions, but showed more low than high hedonic tone emotions, and more loss than gain emotions (FTO), although this latter difference was not significant. Overall, losers changed from experiencing significantly more conformist and high hedonic tone transactional emotions pre-match to experiencing more negativistic and low hedonic tone transactional emotions post-match. Winners' emotional experience changed very little from pre-match to post-match. Mastery emotions were very significant and dominant across all stages of the match for both winners and losers.

## Competitive Rugby

In Wilson and Kerr (1999) data was collected from male Dutch rugby players from a first division team playing at the highest level of competition in Holland. The TESI and the Stress–Arousal Checklist (SACL) (Mackay, Cox, Burrows, & Lazzerini, 1978) were administered pre-game and post-game at four rugby games: two games were won, two were lost. A mixed between- and within-subjects design was used to analyse data, in which game outcome (win or lose) was the between-subjects factor and the within-subjects factor was time of testing (pre- and post-game). The TESI emotional ratings were grouped into the somatic emotions and the transactional emotions, and totals of the eight pleasant emotions (four somatic: relaxation, excitement, placidity, provocativeness; four transactional: pride, modesty, gratitude, virtue) and the eight unpleasant emotions (four somatic: anxiety, boredom, anger, sullenness; four transactional: humiliation, shame, resentment, guilt) were compiled to provide an overview of the level and direction of changes in hedonic tone experienced. The SACL stress and arousal measures were also grouped.

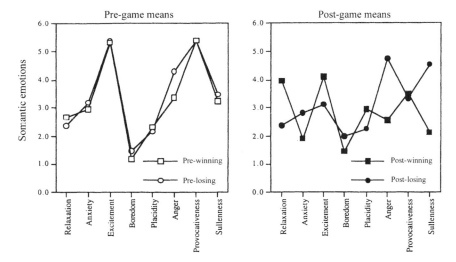

**Figure 3.4**   Effect of game outcome on somatic emotions in rugby (from Wilson & Kerr, 1999).

Somatic emotions are shown in Figure 3.4 and the results can be summarized as follows. None of the pre-game means for winning or losing were significantly different. The post-game emotions showed that winning produced higher scores than losing on the pleasant somatic emotions (relaxation, excitement, placidity, provocativeness) and lower scores than losing on the unpleasant somatic emotions (anxiety, boredom, anger, sullenness) and that these differences were significantly different for relaxation, anger, and sullenness. From pre- to post-game, both winning and losing produced significant reductions in excitement and provocativeness. Relaxation increased in the winning condition from pre- to post-game. With sullenness, winning decreased and losing increased the ratings from pre- to post-game.

Transactional emotions are shown in Figure 3.5. With reference to this figure, the following effects can be identified. None of the pre-game means for winning or losing were significantly different. The post-game means showed that winning produced higher scores than losing on the four positive transactional emotions (pride, modesty, gratitude, virtue) and lower scores than losing on the negative transactional emotions (humiliation, shame, resentment, guilt): these differences were significant for humiliation, shame, gratitude, and resentment. From pre-game to post-game, both conditions produced significant reductions in pride, and significant increases in humiliation, shame, and guilt. Gratitude and virtue increased in the winning condition from pre-game to post-game, while losing was associated with a significant decrease in virtue from pre-game to post-game and a non-significant trend ($p = 0.066$) for an increase in resentment.

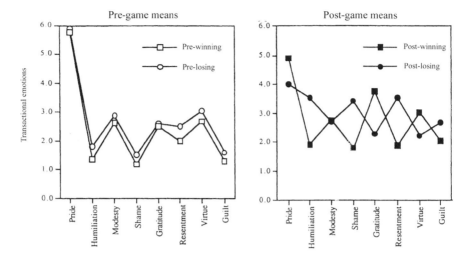

**Figure 3.5**   Effect of game outcome on transactional emotions in rugby (from Wilson & Kerr, 1999).

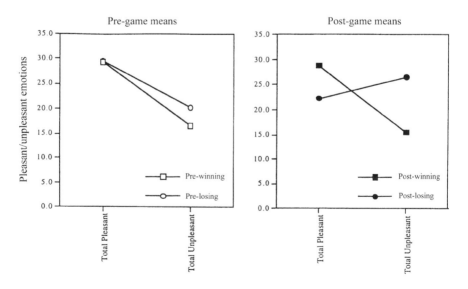

**Figure 3.6**   Effect of game outcome on total pleasant and unpleasant emotions in rugby (from Wilson & Kerr, 1999).

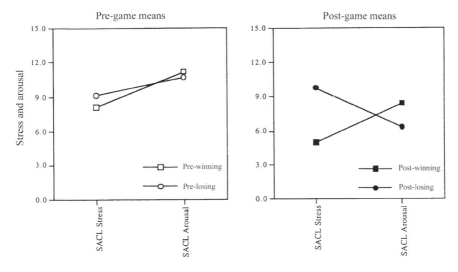

**Figure 3.7**   Effect of game outcome on SACL stress and arousal in rugby (from Wilson & Kerr, 1999).

Total pleasant/unpleasant emotions are graphed in Figure 3.6. The pre-game means for winning and losing were the same for pleasant emotions, but pre-game losers had more unpleasant emotions than pre-game winners. For post-game there were a number of significant differences: the total of the pleasant emotions was greater for winning than for losing; the total of unpleasant emotions was greater for losing than for winning. With losing, there was a reduction in total pleasant emotion and an increase in total unpleasant emotion from pre-game to post-game.

SACL stress and SACL arousal scores are shown in Figure 3.7. The pre-game means for winning and losing were the same for SACL stress and SACL arousal. Post-game there were a number of significant differences: SACL arousal was larger for winning than for losing; SACL stress was larger for losing compared to winning. With winning, there were reductions in both SACL stress and SACL arousal from pre-game to post-game; with losing, there was a reduction only in SACL arousal.

Findings for the rugby study can be summarized as follows:

1. All players showed the same pre-game emotions.
   - Somatic emotions were the pleasant paratelic emotions excitement and provocativeness.
   - Transactional emotions were dominated by the pleasant autic–mastery emotion pride.
2. There were marked post-game differences on the basis of game outcome.

- Winning produced the pleasant somatic emotions relaxation and excitement (but with excitement reduced from the level experienced at
  pre-game).
- In winning, the transactional emotions were marked by the pleasant sympathy emotions gratitude and virtue; the pleasant autic–
  mastery emotion pride was also present but was less than at pre-
  game.
- Winning produced less SACL stress and SACL arousal than the levels
  experienced at pre-game.
- Compared to losing, winning produced more pleasant and less unpleasant emotion or hedonic tone.
- Losing produced somatic emotions characterized by unpleasant negativism – anger and sullenness.
- In losing, the transactional emotions experienced were the unpleasant
  mastery and autic–sympathy emotions humiliation, shame, and resentment. Losing was also associated with a decrease in pride and a
  decrease in virtue.
- Losing produced a decrease in SACL arousal but no decrease in
  SACL stress, and less pleasant and more unpleasant emotion or
  hedonic tone.

The results were consistent with the Kerr and Svebak (1994) study of
recreational sports, including rugby, in that there was a pre-game to post-
game decrease in pleasant emotions and an increase in unpleasant emotions. However, while Kerr and Svebak found a decrease in relaxation and
an increase in excitement, the present study showed an increase in relaxation and a decrease in excitement. This difference is most likely to be the
effect of playing a truly competitive rather than recreational game of rugby
with a significant and meaningful outcome.

## Comparison of Emotional Responses in the Squash and Rugby Studies

In spite of the differences in the measurement instruments and the nature
of the emotion ratings, there are interesting similarities and differences
between the emotional profiles generated in the squash and rugby studies.
In squash, Figure 3.2 shows pre-match somatic emotions for both winners
and losers to be dominated by the conformist emotions relaxation, anxiety,
and excitement. In rugby, Figure 3.4 shows that the two strongest pre-game
somatic emotions were the paratelic emotions excitement and provocativeness. The post-game somatic emotions for winners were very similar for
squash and rugby: for squash, Figure 3.2 shows the pleasant conformist

emotions relaxation and excitement, while in rugby, Figure 3.4 shows the same two strongest emotions in winners – relaxation and excitement. Losers in both squash and rugby also experienced similar emotions. Figure 3.2 shows that, in squash, losers experienced the unpleasant negativistic emotions anger and sullenness; Figure 3.4 shows the same two unpleasant negativistic emotions – anger and sullenness – to be experienced by losers in rugby.

In squash, the transactional emotions in Figure 3.3 indicate that pre-match emotions were almost completely dominated by the two pleasant mastery emotions pride and modesty. In rugby, Figure 3.5 also shows pride to be clearly dominant, but with only moderate levels of modesty, and moderate levels of the two pleasant sympathy emotions virtue and gratitude. The post-game transactional emotions also indicated some similarities for winners and losers. In squash, Figure 3.3 shows that winners maintained the same dominant pleasant mastery emotions pride and modesty, whereas in rugby, Figure 3.5 shows that winners experienced pride and gratitude (a pleasant autic–sympathy emotion). In squash, Figure 3.3 shows that losers experienced humiliation and shame – two unpleasant mastery emotions; in rugby, it is evident from Figure 3.5 that, while losers felt moderate levels of humiliation and shame and also moderate levels of resentment (an unpleasant autic–sympathy emotion), surprisingly, losers also reported reasonably strong levels of pride (a pleasant autic–mastery emotion), which indicates that some players may have thought (perhaps under the guidance of a thoughtful coach) that they played well in the circumstances even though the match was lost.

Emotional differences between the eventual winners and losers began to emerge during the game. For squash players, Figure 3.2 shows that the winners mainly experienced the two somatic, high arousal conformist emotions of anxiety and excitement: the losers also experienced anxiety and excitement, but in addition they experienced moderate levels of anger (a high arousal, unpleasant telic–negativistic emotion). Figure 3.3 shows that the transactional emotions experienced by winners were the two pleasant mastery emotions pride and modesty. Losers also experienced pride and modesty, but they also experienced moderate levels of resentment, which is an unpleasant autic–sympathy emotion: some of the eventual losers were starting to feel sorry for themselves.

# RESEARCH SUPPORT FOR REVERSAL THEORY

The Wilson and Phillips (1995) and Wilson and Kerr (1999) studies provide consistent and confirmatory support for reversal theory predictions about emotional reactions during the playing of competitive sport and the emotional reactions to winning and losing outcomes in competitive sport. The extent of the agreement between reversal theory predictions and findings is impressive and will be described in this section: the notable disagreements between reversal theory predictions and findings will be highlighted and possible explanations will be pursued.

Prior to play in competitive sport, the predicted high arousal somatic emotions (excitement, provocativeness, anxiety, anger) were dominant: excitement and anxiety in squash; excitement and provocativeness in rugby, with a moderate level of anger. In squash there was also a high level of pre-match relaxation reported by the eventual match winners: this relaxation almost disappeared during match play. During match play, anger developed in the eventual match losers, possibly because things had already started to go wrong for some in this group. The high level of pre-match relaxation was most likely due to the pre-competition preparation by competitors, attempting to remain calm, relaxed, and mentally focused; for some competitors, relaxation may have been the salient choice of the eight somatic emotions. During play, the relaxation gave way to anxiety and excitement which was predicted from reversal theory.

The prediction of pleasant mastery transactional emotions (modesty, pride) prior to play was supported, as both the squash and the rugby players reported strong levels of pride and moderate levels of modesty. In rugby, moderate levels of gratitude and virtue (the pleasant sympathy emotions) were also present and this is consistent with reversal theory predictions. In squash, during the match, there was an unexpected emergence of resentment (the unpleasant autic–sympathy emotion to felt transactional loss) in the eventual match losers: the most likely explanation is that for some players in this group, things had already started to go wrong, which caused resentment in the transactional emotions and anger in the somatic emotions.

Competitive outcomes also produced patterns of emotions consistent with predictions from reversal theory. After winning, the somatic emotions predicted were the pleasant conformist emotions (excitement, relaxation): excitement and relaxation were the dominant emotions for both squash and rugby winners. The transactional emotions predicted after winning were the pleasant mastery emotions (modesty, pride) but could include the pleasant sympathy emotions (virtue, gratitude): squash winners reported high levels of pride and moderate levels of modesty; winning in rugby produced high levels of pride and gratitude and a moderate level of virtue. Winning produced consistent emotions with pleasant hedonic tone.

Losing was predicted to produce emotions with low hedonic tone. The somatic emotions after a loss were predicted to be the unpleasant negativistic emotions (anger, sullenness). A loss in squash produced high levels of anger and moderately low levels of sullenness; a loss in rugby produced high ratings of both anger and sullenness. The transactional emotions predicted for losing were the unpleasant mastery emotions (humiliation, shame) but could include the unpleasant sympathy emotions (resentment, guilt). The losers in squash showed moderate levels of humiliation and shame. In rugby, there were moderate ratings for humiliation, shame, and resentment, but there was also an unexpected and high rating for pride. This high rating for pride in a loss situation was not predicted by reversal theory, but could be explained if, for example, the players believed that they had played extremely well even though the game was lost. Such a belief could be instilled by the coach, by the applause or comments of spectators, or through some mutual understanding of team members concerning strength of opponents, bad luck, and so on: in this situation pride would be the appropriate emotional response.

The finding that pride is possible in the face of defeat is of great importance for coaches and sport managers who are charged with the responsibility of maintaining the personal morale and integrity of players and the *esprit de corps* of the team or group. This outcome raises the possibility of reducing some of the devastating negative consequences of losing by emphasizing positive aspects of performance during competition. While pride was found in losses in rugby, it was not a salient emotion to losing for squash players. The nature of the solitary 'one-on-one' competition in squash, and the lack of individual coaches or other support in squash tournaments, would make it extremely difficult to provide the same level of 'pride protection' for squash players as is available in team sports such as rugby.

The emotional states experienced prior to and during competitive sport and response to winning and losing are generally consistent with the predictions derived from reversal theory. Sport is entered into and performed in the pleasant mastery emotions and the high arousal somatic emotions dominate (although in squash some players experience pre-game relaxation): winning produces a range of pleasant emotional outcomes; losing mainly produces unpleasant/negative emotions.

# FUTURE DIRECTIONS AND DEVELOPMENTS IN RESEARCH

There are a number of directions in reversal theory research which still need to be explored. For example, the issue of the 'rewarding power' of winning and its role in keeping people competing or playing still remains to be answered. New approaches and developments may help to resolve this and other issues, and help to extend our knowledge about the emotional dynamics involved in sport and other endeavours. The following points are presented both as a type of 'wish list' and to target certain areas which are in need of attention.

## Technological Developments

The use of miniature video cameras/transmitters, miniature voice transmitters, compact data loggers, and telemetry devices is commonplace in commercial media and 'hi-tech' applications (e.g., 'stump-cam' in televised cricket, monitoring of physiology in astronauts), but the technology is currently very expensive and has practical/functional and technical limitations. This technology will become more affordable, more available, and more user-friendly with further development and the economies of scale that come with wider usage. Technological advances in miniaturization will facilitate monitoring and response recording across a range of different sports, from low mobility sports such as rifle shooting and archery to high mobility sports such as marathon running, sailing, or skiing. There are also many non-sporting applications, such as in gambling situations, meetings and interviews, driving, and the list goes on.

The use of this type of technology in future reversal theory research will provide a powerful tool which will permit events and data to be recorded in the field and in real time, to link emotional experience with actual events, or will allow a participant to respond to a target event or to respond to a probe stimulus initiated by a researcher at some distance from the participant.

In fact, a presentation by McLennan and Omodei (1995) illustrated the potential of this type of research in reversal theory. They used a lightweight head-mounted video camera to record the visual field of orienteers while orienteering. This video record was then later used to assist the individual orienteers to recall the experiences associated with their recorded actions. Powerful stimuli for the recall of moment-by-moment experiences are provided by video images taken from the individual's own perspective. This is just one example of the use of technological developments which could well play a very important role in future reversal theory research.

## Measurement Instruments

Field research, especially in reversal theory, is much in need of streamlined (i.e., short, unintrusive) and valid instruments for the measurement of metamotivational states and emotions.

As mentioned earlier, the TESI (Svebak, 1993), which measures all 16 emotions proposed in reversal theory, is one such instrument, and it is beginning to make a real impact in reversal theory research. The MC (Wilson & Phillips, 1995), an even briefer instrument than the TESI, which measures salient somatic and transactional emotions, is another.

There is also a pressing need for short and valid instruments to measure state dominance. The recently developed Motivational Style Profile (MSP) (Apter, Mallows, & Williams, 1998) provides an important development and extension in this area. It is the first instrument to allow the researcher to assess state dominance and state salience across all reversal theory states, and it is the only instrument which has addressed the measurement of dominance of the transactional emotions.

Cut-down versions of state and dominance instruments need to be developed for specific, less intrusive applications. Such customized instruments would facilitate use during sporting events, during play, and in other field research situations where intrusion of measurement and measurement reactivity must be minimized. For example, boredom is not a salient emotion during competitive sport or as a response to winning or losing: boredom could well be removed as an item for emotional assessment in these situations. In a similar way, a specific research question or manipulation may require only one dominant state to be assessed (e.g., mastery dominance) and a shorter and more precise or focused dominance test would greatly facilitate this type of research. However, the development of specialized cut-down tests for specific applications can occur only with a full understanding of the emotional dynamics involved. This requires careful and determined programmatic research using the full omnibus tests to obtain relevant data from the specific situations under investigation (see also Males, Chapter 5 in this volume).

## Physiological Arousal

Arousal is an important theoretical variable in reversal theory, in that felt arousal (Apter, 1989) is crucial in the moderation of the somatic emotions. The incorporation of changes in arousal is one of the real strengths of reversal theory which differentiates it positively from other explanations of emotions, including attribution theory. However, more empirical study is needed to verify the precise relationship between actual physiological arousal and felt arousal.

The relationships between physiological arousal and the type and intensity of emotions that are experienced are central to the integrity of reversal theory. However, these relationships have mainly been assumed by researchers, rather than being investigated as part of the research exercise by measuring physiological arousal levels, although Svebak (e.g., see Apter & Svebak, 1992, for a review) has incorporated measures of physiological arousal in his work, and one recent study of archery (Kerr, Yoshida, Hirata, Takai, & Yamazaki, 1997) monitored both physiological and felt arousal during performance. The investigation of the precise role of physiological arousal in emotional reactions can provide strong empirical support for at least part of the reversal theory structure.

There are other areas where the measurement of physiological arousal could provide empirical answers; for example, arousal preference (arousal seeking–arousal avoiding) and mood dominance, the relationship between arousal levels and performance in various sporting situations, as well as the quality/type of emotional experience. Another area is metamotivational state dominance and sport preference – for explosive (anaerobic) or endurance (aerobic) sports. For example, Kerr (1997) and Svebak (1996, see also this volume) report paratelic dominant individuals being drawn to explosive sports (e.g., baseball, basketball, cricket, soccer) and telic individuals being drawn to the endurance sports (e.g., cycling, long-distance running, rowing). The measurement of physiological arousal can answer important questions concerning differential arousal preferences and actual arousal levels of telic and paratelic participants across different sports.

At this stage of the development of reversal theory, whenever possible, actual physiology should be measured using appropriate psychophysiological techniques, in preference to making inferences or subjective estimates of levels of physiological arousal.

## Other Win/Lose Situations

Competitive sport arguably produces one of the simplest and most unambiguous types of outcome in terms of win or lose, gain or loss, and which are easily conceptualized within the structure of reversal theory for both somatic and transactional outcomes. There are other situations which also produce strong win/lose outcomes which could be analysed using reversal theory constructs and techniques. For example, gambling is an obvious candidate and some research has been reported using reversal theory constructs in this situation (Brown, 1988, 1991). Chess is another competitive situation which produces winners and losers, and strong emotional reactions (Griffin & O'Connell, 1997). If findings from different types of competition produce consistent results in terms of the emotional profiles to win and lose, this will extend, strengthen, and enrich reversal theory. Research on playing and winning and losing across different types of competitive situations with different requirements for physiological arousal will provide much needed generalizability of the patterns of emotional changes involved.

# SUMMARY

Strong emotions are evoked during participation in competitive sport and significant emotional consequences are attached to winning and losing. While various theoretical approaches have been applied to the investigation of emotional reactions in sport and the win/lose outcome, it is reversal theory that has provided the most useful and comprehensive theoretical and methodological framework for measuring and understanding these emotions. Methodological issues including research design, types of sporting competition, measurement instruments, and timing of emotional assessments have the potential to produce differences in outcomes between studies. The choice of appropriate methodology requires careful consideration by researchers to optimize the consistency and validity of findings.

Two investigations studying squash and rugby players displayed a consistent profile of emotions before and during play and in response to winning and losing. The findings obtained are consistent with predictions derived from reversal theory.

Developments in technology, the development of more precise measurement instruments, and greater emphasis on the measurement of actual physiological arousal are likely to extend the scope and usefulness of research in sport applications as well as in other situations where winning and losing are important issues. Reversal theory is well suited to describe, explain, and predict the emotional changes that are experienced as a result of these win/lose events and ultimately may help to understand the motivating or 'rewarding power' that drives competitive effort in sport, and in many of life's endeavours.

# REFERENCES

Apter, M. J. (1982). *The experience of motivation: The theory of psychological reversals*. London: Academic Press.

Apter, M. J. (1989). *Reversal theory: Motivation, emotion and personality*. London: Routledge.

Apter, M. J., Mallows, R. & Williams, S. (1998). The development of the Motivational Style Profile. *Personality and Individual Differences*, **24**, 7–18.

Apter, M. J. & Svebak, S. (1992). Reversal theory as a biological approach to individual differences. In A. Gale & M. W. Eysenck (Eds.), *Handbook of individual differences: Biological perspectives* (pp. 323–353). Chichester: Wiley.

Brown, R. I. F. (1988). Reversal theory and subjective experience in the explanation of addiction and relapse. In M. J. Apter, J. H. Kerr & M. P. Cowles (Eds.), *Progress in reversal theory* (pp. 191–211). Advances in Psychology series, 51. Amsterdam: North-Holland/Elsevier.

Brown, R. I. F. (1991). Gambling, gaming and other addictive play. In J. H. Kerr & M. J. Apter (Eds.), *Adult play* (pp. 101–118). Amsterdam: Swets & Zeitlinger.

Cox, T. & Kerr, J. H. (1989). Arousal effects during tournament play in squash. *Perceptual and Motor Skills*, **69**, 1275–1280.

Cox, T. & Kerr, J. H. (1990). Self-reported mood in competitive squash. *Personality and Individual Differences*, **11**, 199–203.

Griffin, M. & O'Connell, K. A. (1997, July). *Evidence for metamotivational reversals in elite chess players*. Paper presented at the 8th International Conference on Reversal Theory, University of East London, England.

Kerr, J. H. (1997). *Motivation and emotion in sport: Reversal theory*. Hove, UK: Psychology Press.

Kerr, J. H. & Cox, T. (1989). Effects of metamotivational dominance and metamotivational state on squash performance. *Perceptual and Motor Skills*, **67**, 171–174.

Kerr, J. H. & Cox, T. (1990). Cognition and mood in relation to the performance of a squash task. *Acta Psychologica*, **73**, 103–114.

Kerr, J. H. & Pos, E. (1994). Psychological mood in competitive gymnastics: An exploratory field study. *Journal of Human Movement*, **26**, 175–185.

Kerr, J. H. & Svebak, S. (1994). The acute effects of participation in sport on mood: The importance of level of 'antagonistic physical interaction'. *Personality and Individual Differences*, **16**, 159–166.

Kerr, J. H. & van Schaik, P. (1995). Effects of game venue and outcome on psychological mood states in rugby. *Personality and Individual Differences*, **19**, 407–410.

Kerr, J. H., Yoshida, H., Hirata, C., Takai, K. & Yamazaki, F. (1997). Effects on archery performance of manipulating metamotivational state and felt arousal. *Perceptual and Motor Skills*, **84**, 819–828.

Mackay, C. J., Cox, T., Burrows, G. C. & Lazzerini, A. J. (1978). An inventory for the measurement of self-reported stress and arousal. *British Journal of Social and Clinical Psychology*, **17**, 283–284.

Males, J. R. & Kerr, J. H. (1996). Stress, emotion, and performance in elite slalom canoeists. *The Sport Psychologist*, **10**, 17–36.

Martin, J. L. & Gill, D. L. (1991). The relationships among competitive orientation, sport-confidence, self efficacy, anxiety, and performance. *Journal of Sport and Exercise Psychology*, **13**, 149–159.

McAuley, E. & Duncan, T. E. (1989). Causal attributions and affective reactions to disconfirming outcomes in motor performance. *Journal of Sport and Exercise Psychology*, **11**, 187–200.

McAuley, E. & Duncan, T. E. (1990). Cognitive appraisal and affective reactions following physical achievement outcomes. *Journal of Sport and Exercise Psychology*, **12**, 415–426.

McAuley, E., Russell, D. & Gross, J. B. (1983). Affective consequences of winning and losing: An attributional analysis. *Journal of Sport Psychology*, **5**, 278–287.

McDermott, M. R. & Apter, M. J. (1988). The Negativism Dominance Scale (NDS). In M. J. Apter, J. H. Kerr & M. P. Cowles (Eds.), *Progress in reversal theory* (pp. 373–376). Advances in Psychology series, 51. Amsterdam: North-Holland/Elsevier.

McLennan, J. & Omodei, M. M. (1995, July). *Studying dynamic psychological phenomena in real-world settings*. Paper presented at the 7th International Conference on Reversal Theory, Melbourne, Australia.

Murgatroyd, S., Rushton, C., Apter, M. J. & Ray, R. E. (1978). The development of the Telic Dominance Scale. *Journal of Personality Assessment*, **42**, 519–528.

Reeve, J. (1992). *Understanding motivation and emotion*. Fort Worth, TX: Harcourt, Brace, Jovanovich.

Russell, D. & McAuley, E. (1986). Causal attributions, causal dimensions, and affective reactions to success and failure. *Journal of Personality and Social Psychology*, **50**, 1174–1185.

Spink, K. S. & Roberts, G. C. (1980). Ambiguity of outcome and causal attributions. *Journal of Sport Psychology*, **2**, 237–244.

Svebak, S. (1993). The development of the Tension and Effort Stress Inventory (TESI). In J. H. Kerr, S. Murgatroyd & M. J. Apter (Eds.), *Advances in reversal theory* (pp. 189–204). Amsterdam: Swets & Zeitlinger.

Svebak, S. (1996, October). *Optimal relations between biological, psychological and behavioural characteristics of competitive sport performers*. Paper presented at the 1st International Workshop on Motivation and Emotion in Sport: Reversal Theory, University of Tsukuba, Japan.

Svebak, S. & Murgatroyd, S. (1985). Metamotivational dominance: A multimethod validation of reversal theory constructs. *Journal of Personality and Social Psychology*, **48**, 107–116.

Vallerand, R. J. (1983). On emotion in sport: Theoretical and social psychological perspectives. *Journal of Sport Psychology*, **5**, 197–215.

Vallerand, R. J. (1987). Antecedents of self-related affects in sport: Preliminary evidence on the intuitive reflective appraisal model. *Journal of Sport Psychology*, **9**, 161–182.

Weiner, B. (1985). An attributional theory of achievement motivation and emotion. *Psychological Review*, **92**, 548–573.

Wilson, G. V. & Kerr. J. H. (1999). Affective responses to success and failure: A study of winning and losing in competitive rugby. *Personality and Individual Differences* (in press).

Wilson, G. V. & Phillips, M. (1995, July). *A reversal theory explanation of emotions in competitive sport*. Paper presented at the 7th International Conference on Reversal Theory, Melbourne, Australia.

# 4

# Verbal Protocols and Structured Interviews for Motives, Plans, and Decisions in Golf

**Ian P. Purcell**

*Northern Territory University, Australia*

## INTRODUCTION

The competitive pressures of sport are related to the coping efforts of elite athletes (Hardy, Jones, & Gould, 1996; Madden, 1995). The success of these athletes in managing their stress and emotion during competition is associated with the achievement of their goals (Gould, Eklund, & Jackson, 1992a, 1992b; Jones & Hardy, 1990; Orlick & Partington, 1988; Rotella & Lerner, 1993). Some technically skilled performers are able to excel under the challenges of sporting contests to produce exceptional performances, while others appear to wilt under its manifest pressures to perform well below their best. The psychological skills of elite athletes to deal with competitive stressors and the intervention strategies to optimize their

*Experiencing Sport: Reversal Theory.* Edited by J. H. Kerr.
© 1999 John Wiley & Sons Ltd.

mental approach are important issues for scientific investigation. The comprehensive approach of reversal theory to motivation, stress and emotion is a major direction for this research.

Early research with reversal theory was largely connected to the investigation of the telic–paratelic metamotivational states (Kerr, 1993). An important advance was the exploration of the four metamotivational state pairs and their associated emotions in a series of case studies with elite slalom canoeists (Males & Kerr, 1996; Males, Kerr, & Gerkovich, 1998). More recently, two group-based, multimethod studies of golfers have complemented this research (Purcell, 1999). Quantitative and qualitative data were collected to determine the relationship of the complete set of metamotivational states in the decision making and performance of highly skilled and successful golfers. This chapter will focus primarily on the qualitative approach of the first of these studies. Initially, the chapter will consider the nature of skilled performance in golf. The previous research into the psychological characteristics of elite golfers will be reviewed. Secondly, it will evaluate the qualitative methods of concurrent, think-aloud reports and retrospective, structured interviews for the investigation of metamotivational states. The next section will examine the qualitative results of a non-adversarial, stroke play study of metamotivation, stress, and emotion. The implications of this research for the understanding of skilled performance, the strengths and limitations of think-aloud and structured interview methods for reversal theory investigations and some directions for future research will be treated in the final section.

# PSYCHOLOGICAL AND TECHNICAL SKILLS OF ELITE GOLFERS

Golf involves a unique combination of physical skill, mental concentration, course management, judgement and decision making (Newell & Foston, 1995). It is a complex, self-paced skill which requires over 10 years of 'deliberative practice' to achieve expertise (see Ericsson, 1996). An understanding of golf's task demands is enhanced by a classificatory scheme which considers motor skills along an open and closed continuum (Arnold, 1986). The golf swing is a closed skill. It is performed in a relatively predictable environment which allows for the advance planning of the motor response. Golfers are required to examine the features of a course, select a club, determine the appropriate place to aim the ball, and then to perform a smooth swing to execute a movement to achieve their goal. The cognitive-perceptual and motor components exhibited by golfers are consistent with an information-processing approach to motor performance (see Schmidt, 1991). This approach has had a major impact upon the understanding of skilled performance in sport (Kremer & Scully, 1994; Wrisberg, 1993).

Elite golfers are expected to demonstrate a high level of technical and psychological skill in competitive settings. In a professional tournament, these golfers are on the course for over four hours in each round, but only spend an overall time of about two minutes actually hitting the golf ball. Under these conditions, their thoughts and emotions have every opportunity to facilitate or harm their performance. The experience of Greg Norman, winner of two British Opens, at the United States Masters at Augusta, in 1996, is an example of the crucial role which mental factors can play in golf. Norman led this tournament by six shots going into the final round, but performed well below his usual standards to finish second. Norman has high levels of technical ability to execute his motor skills, but the mental aspects of competition were almost certainly related to his disappointing performance on the final day. Raymond Floyd, winner of the United States PGA, Open and Masters titles, has claimed that the mental aspects of golf become increasingly important after a specific skill level has been reached. He stated:

> Once you have a swing or a stroke that works reasonably well, your mental and emotional approach becomes ninety five percent of the package that determines how well and how consistently you score.
>
> (Floyd & Dennis, 1992, p. 19)

The role of psychological factors has been studied to determine the differences between successful and less successful golfers (McCaffrey & Orlick, 1989; Thomas & Over, 1994) and the peak performances of highly skilled golfers (Cohn, 1991). McCaffrey and Orlick (1989) interviewed touring and teaching professionals to identify the psychological factors associated with golf excellence. The reports of the touring professionals about the factors associated with mental excellence included the establishment of clear goals, practice and tournament plans, shot-by-shot focus, concentration strategies, and the recognition and preparation to cope with pressure situations. The comparison group of teaching professionals was found to be less sophisticated than the touring professionals in their application of these mental factors. A study by Cohn (1991) asked a sample of professional and highly skilled amateur golfers a number of open, semi-structured questions for the recall of their best performance. Physical and mental relaxation, lack of conscious thoughts during the golf swing, a goal-directed focus on the present shot, high levels of confidence, and positive feeling states were found to be characteristic of peak performance. Thomas and Over (1994) developed a questionnaire to assess the component skills of golf in low and high-handicap players. These components were psychological skills and tactics, psychomotor skills, and golf involvement. They found that the higher skilled golfers (lower handicaps) invested more effort in preparing mentally, were more committed to golf, had greater automaticity in their psychomotor skills, and reported fewer negative thoughts and emotions. These characteristics of successful performers and their peak performances in golf are consistent with the evidence regarding the role of mental factors for elite athletes in other sports (see Hardy, Jones, & Gould, 1996; Williams & Krane, 1993).

The relationship of playing statistics and prize money has also been used to determine the role of mental skills in golf. Rotella and Boutcher (1989) examined this information for players on the United States Professional Golfers Association Tour. They found that these statistics were more useful for predicting the stroke average than the earnings of these golfers. Scoring average, birdies divided by greens in regulation, and fairways hit were significant variables associated with earnings, but these factors could account for only a little over half of the variance in the monetary measure. Rotella and Boutcher (1989) suggested that the playing statistics did not reflect the importance of psychological factors for the placings of golfers in tournaments. Some players were able to make the important shots in pressure situations to improve their finishing position, while others seemed less able to do so. Rotella and Boutcher (1989, pp. 96–97) were prompted to ask:

> What do we really know about human emotions and how they influence golf performance? Do we know which emotions, if any, can be useful, and which, if any, are counterproductive? . . . Is being serious on the golf course the best way to think or are golfers better off having fun? Are these two ways of thinking necessarily in opposition to one another? . . . Is there one right way to think? Sport psychologists will have to determine the optimal way of thinking for each individual and then to analyse these individual thinking patterns to assess whether it should be the same for every player.

The motives and emotions associated with golf achievement have relevance for sport psychologists interested in reversal theory. The telic–paratelic metamotivational states are directly concerned with the oppositional qualities of serious-mindedness and playfulness. These states are also associated with a person's goal-directedness and sensation-orientation. Reversal theory also postulates a number of other metamotivational states of importance for the understanding of golf. The collection of information about negativistic–conformist, mastery–sympathy, and autic–alloic metamotivational states is also likely to increase the knowledge about motivation and emotion in this sport. These states reflect rule-breaking and rule-adherence, competitiveness and cooperation, and self-concern and other-concern, respectively. The metamotivational states and their related somatic and transactional emotions have been described extensively in reversal theory-related texts (see Apter, 1989; Kerr, 1997). The mapping of the combinations of meta-motivational states in the decision making and performance of golfers is a new avenue for reversal theory research in sport.

# QUALITATIVE METHODS FOR REVERSAL THEORY RESEARCH

Qualitative methods have received increasing attention for psychological research into the experiences of athletes in sport settings (Jackson, 1995; Locke, 1989). For example, Gould and Krane (1992) stated a rationale for the use of qualitative methodologies for studies of the arousal–stress–performance relationship in sport. To describe the positive aspects of qualitative research, Gould and Krane (1992, p. 138) said:

> The strength of the qualitative approach is that it allows the subject to describe in his or her own detailed words the naturally occurring events that surround the phenomena of interest. The qualitative approach may be especially useful in identifying new variables and relationships in unexplored areas or in obtaining in-depth assessments of athlete's emotions and cognitions.

A qualitative approach has advantages for the investigation of sporting questions from the perspective of reversal theory. The collection of verbal data from elite athletes can provide the depth and richness of information for a better understanding of their mental states. It also helps to determine whether the experiential aspects of sport behaviour are consistent with the phenomenological structures of reversal theory. Huberman and Miles (1994) describe qualitative research along a continuum of 'loosely' to 'tightly' designed studies. These studies differ in their concern with exploratory or confirmatory issues and the use of inductive and/or deductive analyses. Krane, Andersen, and Strean (1997) emphasized the importance for sport researchers to acknowledge the descriptive or theoretical character of their qualitative approach. Many of the qualitative studies in sport have adopted the 'bottom-up' approach of inductive content analysis (e.g., Gould, Tuffey, Udry, & Loehr, 1996; Scanlan, Ravizza, & Stein, 1989) and/or grounded theory methodology (e.g., Côté, Salmela, Baria, & Russell, 1993). In contrast, reversal theory's *a priori* theoretical framework offers a 'top-down' approach for a deductive analysis of the contents of experience. Despite reversal theory's primary accordance with confirmatory analyses, there is also scope to use inductive methods for the exploration of the links between metamotivation, emotion, and skilled performance.

# INFORMATION PROCESSING, MOTIVATION, AND AFFECT

Strean and Roberts (1992) advocated the expansion of the cognitive and infor-mation-processing approach with the inclusion of affective variables in exer-cise and sport research. This lack of concern with motivational and affective functioning is exhibited by many of the theories of human skill and performance. A large number of these theories have minimized or neglected the influence of motivation and emotion in skilled performance. In a review of this literature, Glencross (1993) examined a number of models of human skill, and concluded:

> One further comment should be made, and this relates to the inadequacies of all the models reviewed in addressing issues of motivation and the impact that personality and affective factors can have upon performance. Indeed, the sport psychologist usually sees these factors as his or her major concern, the single major issue in the applied setting. It is timely that models of human skill and performance address these affective factors as an integral part of skill learning and performance, not as separate factors, too often ignored or assumed not to be relevant by those interested in studying human skill. (p. 252)

The sport-related research of reversal theory can be enhanced by the application of qualitative methods to examine the influence of motivation, emotion, and cognition in models of skilled performance. For example, consideration needs to be given to the metamotivational states which sur-round the cognitive processes of decision making and the execution of motor responses. Svebak and Murgatroyd (1985) recognized the bistable nature of metamotivational systems and the role of psychological reversals for this processing of information. They stated:

> Reversal theory is unique in suggesting that individuals will reverse between these two states or modes of information processing and that such a reversal is related to a number of psychological conditions, namely satiation, con-tingency, and frustration. (p. 108)

A model of sport performance will be more sophisticated if it includes the motivation which occurs in a sporting task as well as the cognitive procedures for its skills. Think-aloud reports and structured interviews are two methods for investigating this matter from the perspective of reversal theory. The following sections will consider these methods.

# THINK-ALOUD PROTOCOLS FOR MENTAL EVENTS

Think-aloud protocols enable the recording of concurrent or retrospective verbal reports about task performance (Ericsson & Simon, 1980, 1993;

Svenson, 1989). Nisbett and Wilson (1977) were critical of the use of verbal reports in psychological research.* They reviewed evidence which showed that individuals were often unaware of the factors which influenced their responses, and frequently used post-hoc theories to construct plausible explanations to account for their behaviour. In a response to this criticism, Ericsson and Simon (1980, 1993) developed a model of protocol generation to justify the collection of verbal reports. Following this model, the collection of information is restricted to verbalizations in focal attention, which assumes that the processing is under conscious control. Using this method, the instructions for think-aloud reports are designed to trace a person's thoughts in the absence of attempts by the respondent to explain his or her cognitive processes. It assumes that think-aloud reports are concerned with the products, not the structures or mechanisms of thinking. The mental structures and processes must be inferred from the reports by the researcher.

Theoretical and applied questions are relevant when considering the implementation of think-aloud protocols in reversal theory research in sport. A continuous record of an athlete's thoughts has advantages for identifying the mental states which are operative at various times throughout performance. This positive feature must be tempered to some degree by the actual data which is elicited. Gilhooly (1986) found individual differences in the quality and quantity of think-aloud data with consistencies in the verbalization of 'rich' or 'sparse' amounts of information. The potential for limited responses in some individuals presents some difficulties for the acceptance of their reports. However, the inclusion of practice activities can reduce this problem by facilitating the provision of more extensive accounts by individuals (Ericsson & Simon, 1993).

The nature of think-aloud instructions influences the possible inferences that can be made from verbal data (Ericsson & Simon, 1993; Svenson, 1989). Generally, the instructions are designed to avoid the respondent's interpretation of mental events in task performance. This reflects an attempt to elicit the contents of thought which are central to conscious experience. It constrains the exploration of motives and emotions to the extent to which they appear as verbalizations in focal awareness. In contrast, reversal theory regards subjective experience as essential to the understanding of a person's behaviour in a given context. It examines the 'structures of experience', not the 'structures within experience' which rests on a distinction between the 'form' and 'content' of experience (see Apter,

---

* The use of verbal data in psychological research has been and still is a controversial topic. There are major ontological and epistemological issues involved which could not be dealt with in this chapter. The interested reader is directed to Henwood and Pigeon (1992) for an introduction to these important questions.

1989, p. 4). This theory encompasses the higher order metamotivational states of experience, not a cognitive construction *per se*, and recognizes that the form of these states mostly occurs outside of conscious awareness.

The relationship of the contents of consciousness to changes in metamotivational systems is an important issue for the viability of think-aloud protocols in reversal theory. Reversals occur as a result of contingent events, satiation or frustration (Apter, 1982, 1989). The reversal process involves three sequential components which lead to a shift from one metamotivational state to another. Apter (1982, p. 317) stated:

> First of all there is the 'reversal proper' from one metamotivational system to the opposite member of its pair. Secondly, the newly operative metamotivational system must acquire a 'content'. Thirdly, this 'content' suggests, and typically leads to, action.

The role of 'content' was also recognized as having the potential to act as a contingent event to precipitate a reversal. This function was described by Apter (1982, p. 317) as an 'inversion' of the first of the three steps in the reversal process. This suggests the potential value of cognitive-behavioural methods such as self-talk and action routines for the maintenance of appropriate mental states in task performance. Previous research has indicated the relevance of psychological strategies for performance in golf and other sports (Boutcher, 1990; Boutcher & Crews, 1987; Crews & Boutcher, 1986; Van Raalte, Brewer, Rivera, & Pepitas, 1994). Using observational records and self-report responses, Van Raalte *et al.* (1994) found that the self-talk of tennis players was related to their performance outcomes. A content analysis of their self-reports revealed the higher order categories of self-motivation, calming, and strategic thinking for positive self-talk. Negative self-talk included negative thoughts, fear of losing, and self-instruction. Kerr (1993) stated that a function of pre-performance routines in sport was to establish the appropriate metamotivational states for competition. Professional golfers have been found to be highly consistent in their pre-shot routines (Boutcher, 1990; Boutcher & Crews, 1987; Crews & Boutcher, 1986). Purcell and Kerr (1995) stated that these pre-shot routines in golf were important for the instigation of appropriate metamotivational states and the maintenance of preferred levels of experiential variables such as felt arousal. Think-aloud protocols provide access to information about these cognitive-behavioural factors in sport performance and a chance to explore their possible action as contingent events. The identification of irregularities or inconsistencies in cognitions and behaviours may also help to explain intra- and inter-individual variations in psychological states.

Previous studies with the think-aloud method in sport have been carried out for baseball (McPherson, 1993, 1994) and orienteering (Johansen, 1991). McPherson (1993) examined the knowledge structures of expert and novice baseballers in a simulated batting task. She used a model of protocol structure to examine the condition-action links in their decision making. The elite orienteers in Johansen's (1991) study were asked to report their mental activities while performing a 3.5 kilometre course with eight controls. The verbal data was coded into a pre-existing scheme with four different categories: planning, registration/navigation, control work, and time loss. Johansen (1991) also interviewed the orienteers after they had listened to a tape recording of their concurrent report.

The studies of McPherson (1993) and Johansen (1991) were designed to examine the cognitive factors in problem-solving contexts. A recent study has used think-aloud reports and structured interviews to examine the role of cognition, motivation and emotion in the skilled performance of golfers (Purcell, 1999; Purcell, Kerr, & Pollock, 1996). It compared the cognitive skills as well as the motivational and emotional states of highly skilled and lesser skilled golfers during nine holes of non-adversarial stroke play. The information-processing approach and the theory of psychological reversals were the guiding theoretical frameworks for this research. Both quantitative and qualitative data were collected. The methods and qualitative results will be described in the following sections.

# STROKE PLAY IN NON-ADVERSARIAL CONDITIONS

The psychological characteristics of elite and high-handicap golfers were examined in a non-adversarial, stroke play format (Purcell, 1999; Purcell, Kerr, & Pollock, 1996). These golfers played a round of nine holes at The Vines Country Club, near Perth. The sample consisted of 15 high-skill (mean age = 25.8 years, handicap = 1.87) and 15 low-skill (mean age = 33.8, handicap = 22.47) male amateur golfers. Elite players of the current or previous state amateur representative squads in Western Australia formed the high-skill group. The low-skill group were volunteers from three golf clubs who met specific criteria for participation. These golfers had handicaps between 20 and 28, more than five years of playing experience, and were aged between 20 and 45 years. The last two criteria were requirements for all of the golfers in the research. The participating golfers were also expected to have played The Vines golf course on between 5 and 25 occasions as part of a process to standardize the level of course familiarity between the skill groups.

After an orientation to the equipment and procedures, the golfers spent 30 minutes warming up on the practice fairway. After this, data was collected as each golfer played nine holes in the author's presence. Firstly, a think-aloud procedure was implemented to determine each golfer's naturally occurring thoughts. The prior practice of this procedure was conducted on the practice fairway to support appropriate verbalization. A cassette recorder (Model: Sony TCM-S68V) was attached to the belt of each golfer and a microphone was connected to the lapel. Think-aloud protocols were collected at the two par 5s (first and ninth holes) on The Lakes Nine at The Vines. Secondly, brief structured interviews were conducted after these two holes to supplement the think-aloud data. These retrospective interviews were conducted to ask the golfers specific questions about their goals, plans, and decisions. They were used to obtain more detailed responses about these factors as well as to cross-validate the information which emerged in the think-aloud reports. Finally, after playing each of the nine holes, the golfers also completed a self-report questionnaire, the Tension and Effort Stress Inventory (TESI) (Svebak, 1993; Svebak, Ursin, Endresen, Hjelmen, & Apter, 1991), which asked them to rate the 16 emotions related to reversal theory. Some additional items were added from the Telic State Measure (TSM) (Svebak & Murgatroyd, 1985) for the measurement of felt and preferred arousal. Only some aspects of the results from the think-aloud protocols and retrospective interviews are discussed in this chapter.

# THE ANALYSIS OF VERBAL REPORTS

The interactive model of Huberman and Miles (Huberman & Miles, 1994; Miles & Huberman, 1994) was used to analyse the think-aloud protocols. The subprocesses in this model are data reduction, data display, and conclusion drawing/verification. Data reduction consists of a cycle of inductive identification and deductive verification to create order in raw, unstructured data. The think-aloud protocols were managed with the software program QSR NUD.IST 4.0. This program facilitates the on-line storage, analysis, and retrieval of textual information (Richards & Richards, 1994). The benefits of QSR NUD.IST for qualitative analysis of sport-related data have been outlined in Gorely, Gordon, and Ford (1994) and more particularly for reversal theory research in this domain (Purcell, 1996). The program's hierarchical organization was useful for coding the sequences of thoughts to represent the concepts and facilitate the building of categories for golf decision making and performance.

The information-processing approach was a guiding framework in the construction of higher and lower level categories to represent the structures and processes in golf. Ripoll (1991) distinguished between the concepts of 'understanding' and 'action' in motor performance. This distinction supported the use of a think-aloud method in golf, since the decision-making and action-execution components are relatively independent in self-paced skills. Moore and Stevenson (1991) outlined a sequence of stages in the selection and execution processes of the skilled movement of golfers. Boutcher (1990) described the components of the self-paced, pre-performance routines of highly skilled golfers. These orienting ideas influenced the formation of preliminary categories in the index system for representing the verbal data. Information-processing operations can be represented as a flow diagram with each processing stage divided into its subprocesses (Kimchi & Palmer, 1986; Massaro & Cowan, 1993). The model of Miles and Huberman (1994) stated that the subprocess of data display involves a summary of the information to clarify its meaning. An example of such a representation of the temporal flow of events and processes in the contents of verbal material is the time-oriented display. This form of flow diagram was chosen to show the individualized and group-based representations of the temporal sequence for golf-related events.

# A MODEL OF GOLF PERFORMANCE

The index system was commenced with a tentative labelling of coding units to identify the golf-related concepts. A sentence or a phrase (broken with a pause) was found to constitute the most effective unit for coding purposes. The labelling resulted in the description of thought sequences at a conceptual level. As coding continued, the number of conceptual labels increased and these often reappeared in the transcripts of other golfers. The emergence of relationships among the concepts indicated their groupings into higher order categories. For example, the perception of environmental cues frequently occurred in the protocols of golfers. Their decision making often considered the trouble spots such as sand bunkers and water hazards. These concepts were given a label and numerical code of trouble/hazards. As the content of each document was further examined, other cues such as hole number, par, length and layout also emerged. These factors were grouped by a process of induction into the lower categorical level of course features. The category of course features was later grouped with climatic factors within the higher order category of context/conditions. The entire process involved the flexible application of inductive and deductive analyses which included the function to redefine a concept or category to a more general or specific label (if necessary).

A general model was constructed using the coding procedures to show the concepts, categories, and components of golf performance. This model is shown in Figure 4.1. It represents four components: planning activities, pre-motor execution, motor skill execution, and post-motor execution. Planning activities involve the preparation for performance, which included the elements of strategic thinking and goal setting. In the pre-motor execution component, the higher order categories of context/conditions, shot analysis, club selection, and action preparation were identified.

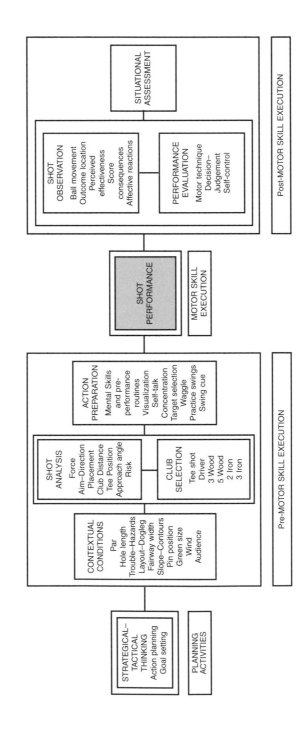

**Figure 4.1** Information-processing model of golf decision making and performance

Golfers were found to consider the relevant conditions on the course. The cues in the performance environment influenced the processing of information for club selection and tactical considerations such as the direction and flight-shape of the shot. The activities of action preparation included mental skills such as self-talk, visualization, and kinaesthetic coupling. Following the execution of a motor response, golfers often observed their shot, evaluated their performance, and assessed their next shot.

## STABILITY AND CHANGE IN MENTAL PHENOMENA

The identification of intra- and inter-individual differences in the contents of think-aloud reports is important for reversal theory. These reports provide a window into consciousness to examine the mental events which are associated with sport performance. A comparison of the thought sequences of the same golfer at different holes permits the stability and change in his mental operations to be assessed. Any observed changes in typical performance patterns are possibly related to the antecedents or consequences of psychological reversals. The intrusion of unexpected events in the sequence of cognitive activities may also help to identify the contingent events responsible for changes in mental state. The exploration of the think-aloud data was undertaken to chart the ongoing contents of conscious experience, uncover the emotions and associated states of meta-motivation, and determine the events which appeared to trigger changes in psychological state. In the following sections, individual and group comparisons of verbal responses in categories of golf performance will be examined. Further, the use of schematic event sequence diagrams for intra- and inter-individual differences in mental phenomena and the significance of motivational and emotional content for reversal theory will be outlined.

## INDIVIDUAL AND GROUP COMPARISONS

A sample of the contents of the think-aloud reports of an elite and a high-handicap golfer are shown in Tables 4.1a and 4.1b, respectively. These were taken as representative examples of their groups for comparative purposes. Table 4.1a shows that the elite golfer (HS16)* considered the actual

---

* The golfers were given identification letters to indicate whether they were highly (HS) or lesser (LS) skilled. The accompanying number represents the unique position of each performer in each group. The LS and HS golfers were numbered from 01 to 15 and 16 to 30, respectively.

**Table 4.1a**   The coding of an elite golfer's thought sequence for the tee shot on hole 1

| Raw data in coding units | Concepts and categories |
|---|---|
| It's a par 5. | Course Conditions/Hole Features/Par |
| 466 metres to the flag. | Course Conditions/Hole Features/Hole Length |
| Chance for a birdie if I can get in a good position on the fairway with my tee shot. | Course Management/Plans–Goals/Strategic |
| Slight dogleg with bunkers 220 metres on the right side. | Course Conditions/Hole Features/Layout–Dogleg Course Conditions/Hole Features/Trouble–Hazards |
| There's a little wind coming over my right shoulder. | Course Conditions/Climate/Wind |
| I'll take a three wood and draw the ball. | Club Selection/Club Choice/Three Wood Shot Analysis/Decision Elements/Flight–Shape |
| I'll start it out inside the bunker. | Shot Analysis/Decision Elements/Aim–Direction Action Preparation/Mental Skill/Object–Target Relations |
| It should leave me with a chance of getting on in two. | Course Management/Plans–Goals/Strategic |
| Let's go. | Action Preparation/Mental Skills/Self-talk |
| See the shot. | Action Preparation/Mental Skills/Visualization |
| A couple of practice swings. | Action Preparation/Mental Skills/Kinaesthetic Association/Swing Practice |
| I'll take that feeling into the ball. | Action Preparation/Mental Skills/Kinaesthetic Association/Swing Feel |
| Nice and smooth. | Action Preparation/Mental Skills/Kinaesthetic Association/Swing (Cue Words) |
| That's come back into the centre of the fairway. | Shot Observation/Ball Movement/Position |
| It looks like it's in good position from here. | Shot Observation/Perceived Effectiveness/Positive |

**Table 4.1b** The coding of a high-handicap golfer's thought sequence for the tee shot on hole 1

| Raw data in coding units | Concepts and categories |
|---|---|
| One gets a bit anxious on the first tee. | Course Conditions/Other Factors/1st Hole–Anxiety |
| People are looking and there's always the problem of hitting a good shot. | Course Conditions/Other Factors/Audience<br>Action Preparation/Self-Talk/Negative Thinking |
| It's a par 5. | Course Conditions/Features/Par |
| Get out the driver. | Club Selection/Club Choice/Three Wood |
| From the blue markers it's 460 metres. | Course Conditions/Hole Features/Hole Length |
| No wind. | Course Conditions/Climate/Wind |
| Concentrate on the shot. | Action Preparation/State Description–Management/Focus–Concentration |
| Get my grip right. | Action Preparation/Motor Technique/Grip |
| Aim for the middle of the fairway. | Shot Analysis/Decision Elements/Aim–Direction |
| Get my feet in line with the direction I'm aiming. | Action Preparation/Mental Skills/Object–Target Relations |
| Put it out on the fairway. | Course Management/Plans–Goals/Tactical–Immediate Shot |
| Don't swing too fast. | Action Preparation/Motor Technique/Swing |
| Oh, shit! | Shot Observation/Affective Reaction/Adverse Feeling |
| It's run along the ground. | Shot Observation/Ball Movement–Location/Trajectory |
| Thank goodness it's stayed out on the fairway. | Situation Assessment/Current Position/Acceptable |
| It's gone about 150 metres and straight down the middle. | Shot Observation/Ball Movement–Location/Trajectory<br>Shot Observation/Ball Movement–Location/Direction |
| I think I was squeezing the club too tight and hit down on the ball. | Performance Evaluation/Motor Technique |

distance to the bunkers, a particular target, and the shape of his tee shot. Table 4.1b reveals that the high-handicap golfer (LS13) also considered the wind conditions, but his planning was more general, with the objective of hitting the ball into a central position on the fairway. This lesser skilled golfer reported the technical aspect of his swing, but this did not occur for the elite golfer. This finding is likely to indicate an earlier stage of motor skill acquisition, in comparison to the automatic and effortless swing which emerges with expert performance. The high-handicap golfer also exhibited a negative description of his swing tempo. In contrast, the elite golfer used cue words to programme the swing tempo and instigate the movement. Following the execution of the shot, there were other important differences in the reports of the two golfers. The high-handicap golfer experienced a negative affective reaction to his tee shot and attempted to examine the technical factors contributing to a suboptimal performance. The elite player observed his tee shot and commented on its apparent effectiveness. These verbal responses were typical of the two groups, as will be further demonstrated with the group-based comparisons.

A group-based comparison was also conducted to examine the frequency of concepts and categories in the verbal reports of elite and high-handicap golfers. This skill-based comparison was complicated, since the golfers were playing their balls from various locations (after the tee shot) which resulted in different problems to be solved for their continued perfor-mance. The tee shot was standardized for all performers, so it was decided to limit the skill-group comparisons to the preparation and execution of this specific shot. The reports of elite golfers showed higher frequencies of conditional cues (e.g., par, hole length, bunkers) and elements of shot analysis (e.g., direction, flight-shape). These golfers were also found to have a greater usage of higher order mental skills in their action prepara-tion. Reports about technical factors related to the golf swing (e.g., grip, body position) were more prevalent in high-handicap golfers. A conserva-tive approach was taken to the interpretation of these skill-based dif-ferences. The rationale for this analytic approach will be considered in a later examination of the advantages and limitations of verbal reports.

# MENTAL EVENT SEQUENCES

Schematic event sequence diagrams were constructed to examine the intra- and inter-individual differences in the mental activities of elite and high-handicap golfers. Figure 4.2 shows a representative case from each of the groups. Each case is related to the tee shots on the par-5 holes (1 and 9). The thought sequences are summarized with relevant higher and lower order codes from the index system. The actual thoughts associated with

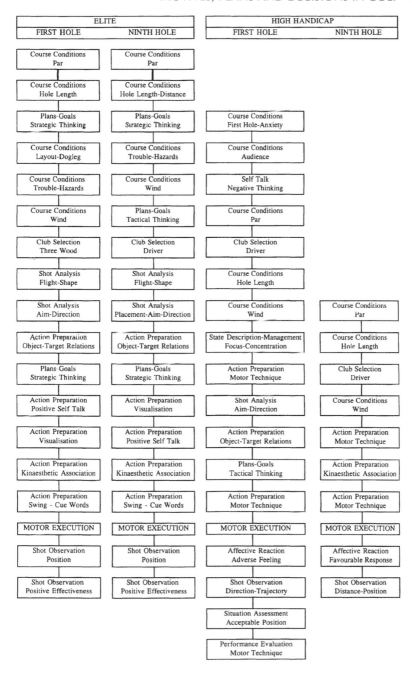

**Figure 4.2**  Schematic event sequence diagrams for the tee shot of an elite and a high-handicap golfer at the first and ninth holes

one of the tee shots (hole 1) are provided in Tables 4.1a and 4.1b. There are several important points to be made from these diagrams. Firstly, the sequence of mental activities was highly consistent for the elite golfer on holes 1 and 9. This golfer perceived features of the hole, considered a strategy, selected a club, followed a pre-shot routine and observed the effectiveness of his shot. Although not shown in the diagram, this golfer also made a further assessment of his position when he approached the ball on both of these holes. It was typical of elite golfers to delay a final appraisal of a shot's merits until they had assessed the lie, trajectory, and distance for their next shot. The high-handicap golfer showed less consistency, as reflected in the qualitative and quantitative nature of his responses. Different elements appeared across the two holes and hole 9 contained more content. At the first hole, this golfer reported anxiousness and the need to concentrate on his shot, but this did not occur at the ninth hole. Different technical aspects of performance were also considered for the two tee shots. Grip and alignment were reported on the first tee, whereas grip and head position were considered on the ninth. Negative and positive affective reactions were also reported for shot outcome at the first and ninth holes, respectively. In contrast, the reports of the elite golfer showed a more rational approach to performance. These cases are concrete examples which reflect the similarities and differences in the thought sequences of the two groups. Generally, the content and structure of the verbal protocols for the elite golfers were more consistent. The intrusion of extraneous factors that impinged upon performance appeared less frequently in their verbal accounts.

## MOTIVATIONAL AND EMOTIONAL CONTENT

The construction of a performance model provided the framework for considering the operation of mental events in golf. As part of this process, the decomposition of think-aloud protocols revealed the thought sequences in the focal attention of golfers. Table 4.2 shows the major motivational and emotional categories of practical significance for reversal theory. The existence of planning-ahead and goal-directed thoughts in the think-aloud reports indicated the operation of the telic state. There were 19 reports of strategic planning in the think-aloud protocols of the elite golfers and 8 in those of the high-handicap golfers. This longer term planning centred around the consideration of an attacking or defensive approach to reach the green in two or three shots, respectively.

The information collected from post-hole interviews raised some questions about the validity of think-aloud protocols to assess the intentional nature of performance. These retrospective interviews suggested that plans

**Table 4.2**   Frequency of motivational and emotional categories in think aloud reports of elite and high-handicap golfers

| Higher and lower order categories | Elite (high skill) | | High handicap (low skill) | |
|---|---|---|---|---|
| | Frequency tee shot only (holes 1 and 9) | Total frequency All shots | Frequency tee shot only (holes 1 and 9) | Total frequency All shots |
| Plans and goals* | | | | |
| Strategic-planning ahead | 19 | | 8 | |
| Pre-shot arousal and emotion | | | | |
| State description | 4 | 9 | 15 | 26 |
| Management procedure | 13 | 21 | 4 | 10 |
| Pre-shot self-talk | | | | |
| Positive outlook/ confidence | 12 | 27 | 7 | 18 |
| Negative view/self-doubt | 4 | 11 | 12 | 25 |
| Affective reaction to shot outcome | | | | |
| Favourable response | 4 | 12 | 3 | 16 |
| Adverse feeling | 3 | 7 | 8 | 25 |

* Strategic-planning ahead was only calculated for the tee shot.

and goals were operative, but not always verbalized in concurrent reports. Further, on those occasions when planning was reported in concurrent reports, it was often limited to a brief statement of purpose. For example, Table 4.1a shows that the elite golfer stated, 'Chance for a birdie if I can get in a good position on the fairway with my tee shot.' The reliance on a reductionist approach *per se* also restricts the discovery of the pattern of relationships among the various facets of golf performance. This implies that a think-aloud report also needs to be examined holistically to determine its meaning beyond a division into elemental units.

# GOALS, PLANS, AND DECISIONS

Goals, plans, and decisions were found to be interrelated in the think-aloud reports and retrospective interviews of elite golfers. Strategic plans were general outlines that were conditional upon the characteristics of a hole, the prevailing climatic conditions, the effectiveness of motor execution, and the next shot's requirements. In a retrospective interview, one of the elite golfers (HS17) described the conditional nature of his planning for the first hole:

> The plan for the tee shot was to try to attack the hole and get there in two because of the wind direction and that sort of thing. The second plan comes into action where you lay up and pitch and you one putt for a birdie. When I was on the tee I was actually just thinking about the tee shot but prior to that I was thinking that if I do hit a good tee shot I may have the opportunity to go for the second but that's all in the future and as soon as you've thought that could happen you have to go back and work on your original tee shot. You have to set the ball in play before you think about what to do next.

The alternative attacking or defensive strategies in these flexible plans could change during the performance on a particular hole. The elite golfers might take an attacking strategy into a particular hole, but an unfavourable lie could result in a change to a more defensive strategy. These golfers also indicated lower level goals in their reports, but these were embedded within their higher order goals. Examples of lower level goals were keeping the ball on the fairway and focusing on one shot at a time. The adoption of a particular strategy was related to risk assessment and the likely impact of a tactical decision on scoring. A flexible, conditional form of planning of an elite golfer (HS27) with a goal-directed focus during the motor execution is shown in the following quote:

> My plan was to keep the ball in play. I knew I wouldn't get there in two with the wind coming left to right and into me. So I played the hole to try to knock my second shot as close as I could to set myself up for my third shot. However, I always put this out of my mind when I'm playing each shot. It's there but I could come unstuck if I think about it when I have to hit the present shot. It's important to have a general plan but to stay focused on the shot you're playing.

The retrospective interviews showed that flexible plans were adopted by a majority of elite golfers. In contrast, almost half of the high-handicap group had minimal or non-existent planning on the par-5 holes. These golfers appeared to react to unfolding circumstances rather than considering their response to possible eventualities. A smaller number, three for the first and five for the ninth hole, expressed a fixed plan which did not consider the various contingencies for their next shot. From the perspective of reversal theory, the plans and goals expressed in the think-aloud and retrospective reports of these golfers were indicators of the telic state. An extensive account of skill-based differences in the plans, goals and decisions of the golfers can be found in Purcell, Kerr, and Pollock (1996).

## METAMOTIVATIONAL ASSESSMENT

The states of metamotivation were sometimes indicated by the expression of emotion in the think-aloud protocols. The pre-shot emotional states, as well as the affective reactions to shot execution, were two situations when emotions were often described. The golfers made general comments about the pleasantness or unpleasantness of their experience for pre- and post-motor execution. For example, a high-handicap golfer (LS06) stated for his tee shot on hole 1:

> Getting reasonably comfortable over the ball. Look at the ball. Looks like I got the middle of the fairway. I'll have that shot. It's pleasing. Looks like I got the middle of the fairway. I'm not sure. It's a four hundred and thirty eight metre, par five. I've hit it about one hundred and seventy metres.

Another description of hedonic tone was given by an elite golfer (HS28) for his tee shot on the same hole:

> First hole. Two hundred and twenty metres to the bunkers. Into a fairly strong breeze. Use a three wood to draw the ball back into the centre. It's a three shot – par five. There's no point in hitting the driver 'cause I can't get on for two. Three wood will allow me to hit the fairway with confidence. See the shape of the shot. Couple of practice swings. Set up. Easy. Oops! Maybe not. Not happy at all with that. That's dead. It's gone right in the gunga. It's not good in here. Glad this isn't a tournament. Jesus. Think I've got it. Ah, Jesus. Yep. Take an unplayable. Um, I'm pissed off about it but I'll get on with it. I now have a three iron to lay up short of the water.

Specific emotions were also expressed in the thinking-aloud of the golfers. The salience of the telic–conformity state combination was suggested by a predominance of relaxation, anxiety, or related concepts in these reports. Three high-handicap golfers reported being anxious on the first tee. Seven of the welite and 10 of the lesser skilled players referred to relaxation or calmness in the reports of their tee shots during the two holes. This prevalence figure is deceptive, because the content of these reports was different for the two groups. Table 4.2 shows the frequency of verbal responses in the higher order category of pre-shot arousal and emotion. Examination of the lower order categories reveals that the high-handicap golfers reported more frequent descriptions of their state of arousal or emotion in the pre-shot period. In contrast, the elite players reported more frequent management strategies for these variables. A check of the actual transcripts showed that the high-handicap golfers were more likely to mention relaxation in an attempt to regain control of their emotions, while the elite golfers were reporting the elements of a routine to manage their performance state.

Although present in both groups, negative emotions were more prevalent for high-handicap than elite golfers. Table 4.2 reveals that the lesser skilled golfers were more likely to report unpleasant affective responses after their tee shot than elite golfers. Negative reactions were expressed on 25 occasions in the high-handicap group for their golf shots on these holes.

The elite group reported only seven. It should be noted that the high-handicap group played more shots than the elite golfers, but even after correcting for this factor, the relationship was maintained. Table 4.2 also suggests that the two skill groups were comparable in the frequency of reported positive affect as a consequence of motor performance.

The highly and lesser skilled groups both reported frustration as a consequence of their shot-making when they did not achieve their goals. The shot outcome was identified as a major contingent event which was likely to be linked to the stability or disruption of metamotivational and emotional states. The lesser skilled players were more likely to hit poor shots and, as previously shown, their behavioural and mental skills were less structured to cope with these performance errors. The descriptions of varying degrees of anger and the use of expletives as a result of inaccurate motor responses were indicators of telic-negativism. For example, a high-handicap golfer (LS01) expressed a negative reaction for his second shot on the first hole:

> I've just put that into the bush. Not a very good shot. I was probably standing too close. No, too far away from the ball and toed it off the end of the club. The next shot is going to be a tap out onto the fairway. I'll probably drop a couple of shots. It's not worth looking for. I should play a provisional. I didn't feel comfortable. That was what it was. I'll have a quick look to see if I can find it but I don't like my chances. I'm disappointed with that shot. I'll play a shot from up here.

Negative affect was also expressed by a high-handicap golfer (LS03) for his tee shot on the first hole:

> First hole. Don't try and force it too much. Just up there in three. It'll be right. Typical start. It's off to the right. Went in just about here somewhere. If it is I'm in trouble. Got myself in a bad position here. A lot of scrub. I'll just have to take another one off the fairway. I'm in deep trouble and pretty annoyed about it. I've lost that one.

This golfer (LS03), in a retrospective report of the same shot, indicated the stress or pressure which often occurs with poor play:

> Off the blue tees. It's a bit longer. It's a par five. The wind was blowing into my face so it's going to be a long hole. Um, my first drive went off to the right which is fairly well expected on the first hole but I went off a bit far there. I took a penalty and then I tried to bring it back onto the fairway but that didn't work too well. I put myself under pressure by not getting back on the fairway. And when I finally did that I was still having shots on the fairway which weren't in good positions. It was only the last two putts that were reasonable.

Telic–negativism was described more frequently by high-handicap golfers. Despite this, the following example was chosen to show that it can also happen to the best of golfers. The selected extracts were taken from the concurrent report of an elite golfer (HS19) on the ninth hole. This report shows how a golfer's mental state can be revealed in his ongoing thoughts. He stated for his tee shot:

> Par five. Four hundred and fifty metres. Water on the left and the traps on the right. Fairly big landing area. Into the wind. Unreachable in two. I'm hitting driver. It's not a long par four but the conditions are tough. I won't get on in two but I want to get some distance off the tee. Pick out the line I want to hit my shot on. Aim at that tree through the fairway. See the shot. Practice swings. Um. From now on I'm trying to focus on that point and forget about everything else. Put a good swing on it. Aahh! That one's in the water. It's in the water that one. A little bit annoyed. Angry with that shot. It was a shockin' golf swing.

This golfer then took a one-shot penalty before hitting his third shot into a good position. Thinking-aloud for the fourth shot, he said:

> Getting my distance to the green. One hundred and sixty one take nine. So I've got one hundred and fifty two into the breeze. It's right between a five and a six. Still haven't thought about the shape of the shot I want to hit. Starting to think about that now. What sort of shot I want to hit in there. I could hit a hard, low six iron and keep it under the wind or I could try and hit a smooth five. A hard six isn't normally an option because I think it would balloon up into the wind too much. I'll go with the five. The wind seems a little stronger. Starting to think about how hard I want to hit this five iron. Wind's picking up more and more. I'm gonna hit a draw in there. Go through my routine. Aahh! Tried to hit it low. Got ahead of it and hit a big hook. Absolutely shocking golf shot. I'm a little bit angry about the way I've played the hole.

In a post-hole interview, the elite golfer summarized his experience of this hole. It demonstrates the anger which can arise from uncertain club selection and poor execution of the motor response. He stated:

> I was thinking it was a par five with some water on the left and the traps on the right. There's a lot of space to get the ball into play. I couldn't get on in two but I wanted to get some distance off the tee. I picked out the line for my shot, visualized the shot and experienced the feeling of striking the ball. I put a poor swing on the ball and it went into the water. That made me angry. I took a drop and then played an iron into a better position on the fairway. I paced out the distance to the flag. It was one hundred and fifty-two into the wind. It was tricky 'cause I was caught between a five and a six and I was in two minds about the shot I should hit. I went to hit a draw with a five iron which I turned over and hit a shocker. I rushed my chip shot and I misread my putt. Ended with a double which made me think about throwing my club.

The preceding discussion shows that the nature and context of an emotion is often available in verbal reports for the assessment of metamotivation. These exploratory analyses of think-aloud reports and retrospective interviews were supportive of reversal theory research into skilled performance. The extracts that have been presented show the role of telic–conformity and telic–negativism in the performance of elite and lesser skilled golfers. Frustration was also identified as likely to induce psychological reversals. Further, the elite golfer's more highly structured approach to performance may make him less susceptible to the impact of inappropriate changes in psychological state. The final section will summarize the implications of these findings, evaluate the use of think-aloud and structured interview methods for reversal theory studies and consider some directions for future research.

# RECOMMENDATIONS AND CONCLUSIONS

This non-adversarial stroke play study has contributed to the understanding of skilled performance in golf. It suggested the salience of somatic metamotivational states in this sport. The somatic emotions relaxation, anxiety, and anger were the state descriptions most frequently reported by the golfers. These reflected the telic–conformist and telic–negativistic metamotivational state combinations. The operation of these states of metamotivation has implications for the strategies which golfers use to optimize their performance. Kerr (1993, 1997) has given an extensive treatment of the implications of reversal theory for interventions to improve performance. A general principle of intervention is to ensure that a sportsperson manipulates the internal and external conditions of performance to modulate arousal and psychological reversals. The salience of the telic state would indicate the importance of creating a set of performance conditions for low arousal states of relaxation. Purcell (1996) has suggested that an important factor in attaining appropriate states of metamotivation and emotion in golf is the development of pre-performance routines. The role of the telic state in golf performance requires further investigation.

The non-adversarial conditions of the stroke play study were likely to have established a motivational climate which lessened the impact of transactional factors. The golfers may have been competing against themselves or the course, but the interpersonal element was missing in their performance environment. Further research is recommended to determine the role of adversarial conditions in the promotion of transactional metamotives. This issue is currently being investigated in a match play competition with quantitative and qualitative methods (Purcell, 1999). The second of these studies is attempting to complement the exploratory research reported in this chapter with a move to a deductive approach *per se*. Post-match interviews have been conducted to target the metamotivational states and emotions which are operative for winning and losing golfers in specific decision incidents. The plan is to code each golfer's verbal responses for their 'fit' within reversal theory's four metamotivational state pairs and then to determine the relationship of these states with match outcome and decision effectiveness.

The structural phenomenological basis of reversal theory influences the treatment of think-aloud data. The two major approaches – decompositional and holistic analyses – have different strengths and limitations for delineating the mental states of this theoretical perspective. The golf performance model was based primarily upon a segmentation of verbal data into coding units. This strategy demonstrated a greater sophistication in cognitive-behavioural skills in elite golfers and an increased consistency in their mental and behavioural activities. The reduction of these reports to a sequence of mental activities also identified the functional and structural factors in the maintenance or change of psychological state. The role of frustration, due to a failure to attain goals and/or the inadequate outcomes of motor execution, was identified as a likely agent for the occurrence of psychological reversals in golf. Despite the benefits of dividing the verbal material into discrete units, there are some problems with this approach.

One difficulty concerned the coding of verbal responses into relevant categories for the model of golf performance. For some coding units, it was essential to examine the surrounding text to ensure the valid and reliable classification of these responses. For example, the category of pre-shot arousal and emotion subsumed the lower order categories of state description and management procedures (see Table 4.2). Some of the elite golfers mentioned their emotional state, but this was a feature of self-talk in their pre-shot routine. The significance of this could have been overlooked without considering the context of this verbal content. This problem concerns the decontextualization of content which can occur with a reductionistic approach to verbal protocols.

Another important question in the analysis of think-aloud data is the ascription of a performer's intentions and motives. Aanstoos (1983, 1989) claimed that the intentional nature, as well as the significance of experience, is better accessed by examining think-aloud reports as a whole, rather than by dividing them into discrete segments. In this golf research, it was assumed that the motivational and emotional contents of consciousness would emerge in think-aloud data. This assumption underpinned the assessment of metamotivational state, as well as the identification of potential antecedents and consequences of psychological reversals. The think-aloud data was found to mark the likely internal and external events for changes in mental state, but it provided only limited access to the experiential meaning of a situation. It was often difficult to categorize the contents of think-aloud protocols into metamotivational states without the inclusion of a holistic interpretation, as well as access to additional information such as retrospective interviews. This outcome may have resulted from the nature of the specific domain under investigation and/or the set of task instructions, which placed tight restrictions on the reporting of thought processes. Karlsson (1989) claimed that the reflective nature of decision making is not always captured in a process-tracing method such as thinking aloud. He observed that a person may fluctuate between levels of self-consciousness and situational immersion while they are making a decision. Using an empirical phenomenological approach, Karlsson (1989) recognized a major constraint of the think-aloud method for an experiential approach to performance. He stated:

> A concurrent, think-aloud protocol contains a gap between the thinking and the utterances of the thoughts. Not only is it impossible for the subject to pronounce aloud all thoughts, but thinking may have a different structure than speaking, which follows certain grammatical and syntactical rules. My point is that the object of analysis for the researcher is the subject's protocol and not the subject's original experience. (p. 56)

The use of retrospective interviews was designed to augment the think-aloud reports to investigate the factors which contribute to performance. Plans, goals, and decisions were targeted for investigation because it was assumed that they formed a fundamental aspect of golf performance. There were occasions when these factors received limited verbalization or no attention at all in the think-aloud reports. The post-hole interviews enabled the standardized questioning to indicate whether these factors had actually been considered and, if so, to give the golfers an opportunity for an in-depth response concerning their thinking on these matters. The plans of golfers were considered to reflect their goals and to influence their choice of decision-based actions. Retrospective think-aloud reports and structured interviews are recommended when the task demands of a sport or the importance of a competitive event are associated with the intrusiveness of concurrent reports. It is suggested that, when concurrent reports are possible, they are conducted in conjunction with retrospective interviews to gather in-depth information about the intentional nature of behaviour. The restricted data which occurs as a result of the propensity of some athletes to limit the verbalization of their thoughts, even with training, can be overcome with the inclusion of additional methods.

Another issue concerns the limitations of a think-aloud report for the assessment of sport skills. Abernethy, Thomas, and Thomas (1993) supported the validity of verbal reports for the understanding of the response selection component, but they questioned their value for the motor execution component of skilled performance. The automatic nature of a well-practised motor skill reduces the likelihood of its direct access via conscious processes. This consideration supports the caution which was earlier recommended for the quantification of skill-based differences in verbal reports. For example, the think-aloud reports indicated that the elite golfers had a consistent, pre-shot set of cognitive and behavioural routines to support their skilled performance. Seven of the elite golfers reported visualization in their concurrent reports, but this psychological skill did not appear in any of the reports of the high-handicap golfers. In post-game questioning, 11 elite golfers reported using visualization. This discrepancy in the contents of concurrent and retrospective reporting may indicate an automatic function of this psychological skill which resulted in its omission from conscious processing. There are also concerns about verbal reports for planning and decision making. Course familiarity and experience may also result in the development of rapid condition–action links which eliminate the need for deep thinking about an appropriate course of action. This implies that an understanding of the processes and structure of decision making may be more trustworthy for non-routine events or situations. Notwithstanding these issues, the think-aloud reports led to the construction of a performance model and indicators of the nature of mental events with increasing levels of skill.

In conclusion, think-aloud data has some limitations, but these should not detract from its potential benefits for reversal theory research. Thinking aloud exhibits motivational and emotional content which allows for inferences about prevailing metamotivational states, as well as contingent events for the reversal process. However, it needs to be supplemented with techniques such as structured interviews to assess the full range of metamotivational states, as well as to identify the triggers for reversals during performance. Further, the decomposition of a think-aloud protocol is necessary, but not sufficient for the investigation of reversal theory. A verbal report should also be examined in a holistic fashion to access the changes which occur in mental phenomena over time.

# ACKNOWLEDGEMENTS

This chapter is part of the author's doctoral research. The research was conducted with the supervision of Prof. John Kerr of Tsukuba University, Japan, and Dr. Clare Pollock of Curtin University, Australia. The coding of the verbal reports was completed with the valuable assistance of Darin Cairns. The non-adversarial golf study was supported by a grant from the

Applied Sports Research Program of the Australian Sports Commission. The author also gratefully acknowledges the cooperation of The Vines Country Club and the participation of the golfers in this research.

# REFERENCES

Aanstoos, C. M. (1983). The think-aloud method in descriptive research. *Journal of Phenomenological Psychology*, **14**, 150–190.

Aanstoos, C. M. (1989). The structure of thinking in chess. In A. Giorgi (Ed.), *Phenomenology and psychological research* (pp. 86–117). Pittsburgh: Duquesne University Press.

Abernethy, B., Thomas, K. T. & Thomas, J. T. (1993). Strategies for improving understanding of motor expertise (or mistakes we have made and things we have learned!!). In J. L. Starkes & F. Allard (Eds.), *Cognitive issues in motor expertise* (pp. 317–356). Amsterdam: North-Holland/Elsevier.

Apter, M. J. (1982). *The experience of motivation: The theory of psychological reversals*. London: Academic Press.

Apter, M. J. (1989). *Reversal theory: Motivation, emotion and personality*. London: Routledge.

Arnold, R. K. (1986). Taxonomies of motor skills. In L. D. Zaichkowsky & C. A. Fuchs (Eds.), *The psychology of motor behaviour. Development, control, learning and performance* (pp. 13–27). New York: Mouvement.

Boutcher, S. H. (1990). The role of preperformance routines in sport. In J. G. Jones & L. Hardy (Eds.), *Stress and performance in sport* (pp. 231–245). Chichester: Wiley.

Boutcher, S. H. & Crews, D. J. (1987). The effect of a pre-shot routine on a well-learned skill. *International Journal of Sport Psychology*, **18**, 30–39.

Cohn, P. J. (1991). An exploratory study on peak performance in golf. *The Sport Psychologist*, **5**, 1–14.

Côté, J., Salmela, J., Baria, A. & Russell, S. J. (1993). Organising and interpreting unstructured qualitative data. *The Sport Psychologist*, **7**, 127–137.

Crews, D. J. & Boutcher, S. H. (1986). An exploratory observational analysis of professional golfers during competition. *Journal of Sport Behaviour*, **9**, 51–58.

Ericsson, K. A. (1996). *The road to excellence. The acquisition of expert performance in the arts sciences, sports and games*. Hillsdale, NJ: Erlbaum.

Ericsson, K. A. & Simon, H. A. (1980). Verbal reports as data. *Psychological Review*, **87**, 215–251.

Ericsson, K. A. & Simon, H. A. (1993). *Protocol analysis. Verbal reports as data* (Revised Ed.). Cambridge, MA: Bradford Books/MIT Press.

Floyd, R. & Dennis, L. (1992). *From sixty yards in. How to master golf's short game*. New York: Harper Collins.

Gilhooly, K. J. (1986). Individual differences in thinking-aloud performance. *Current Psychological Research and Reviews*, **5**, 328–334.

Glencross, D. J. (1993). Human skill: Ideas, concepts and models. In R. N. Singer, M. Murphey & L. K. Tennant (Eds.), *Handbook of research on sport psychology* (pp. 242–253). New York: Macmillan.

Gorely, T., Gordon, S. & Ford, I. (1994). Nudist: A qualitative data analysis system for sport psychology research. *The Sport Psychologist*, **8**, 319–320.

Gould, D., Eklund, R. C. & Jackson, S. (1992a). 1988 USA Olympic wrestling excellence I: Mental preparation, precompetitive cognition, and affect. *The Sport Psychologist*, **6**, 358–382.

Gould, D., Eklund, R. C. & Jackson, S. (1992b). 1988 USA wrestling excellence II: Competitive cognition and affect. *The Sport Psychologist*, **6**, 383–402.

Gould, D. & Krane, V. (1992). The arousal–athletic performance relationship: Current status and future directions. In T. S. Horn (Ed.), *Advances in sport psychology* (pp. 119–141). Champaign, IL: Human Kinetics.

Gould, D., Tuffey, S., Udry, E. & Loehr, J. (1996). Burnout in competitive junior tennis players: II. Qualitative analysis. *The Sport Psychologist*, **10**, 341–366.

Hardy, L., Jones, G. & Gould, D. (1996). *Understanding psychological preparation for sport. Theory and practice of elite performers*. Chichester: Wiley.

Henwood, K. L. & Pigeon, N. F. (1992). Qualitative research and psychological theorising. *British Journal of Psychology*, **83**, 97–111.

Huberman, A. M. & Miles, M. B. (1994). Data management and analysis methods. In N. K. Denzin & Y. S. Lincoln (Eds.), *Handbook of qualitative research* (pp. 428–444). Thousand Oaks, CA: Sage.

Jackson, S. A. (1995). The growth of qualitative research in sport psychology. In T. Morris & J. Summers (Eds.), *Sport psychology: Theory, application and issues* (pp. 575–591). Brisbane: Wiley.

Johansen, B. T. (1991). Self-report data for 'Think Aloud' technique during orienteering. *Scientific Journal of Orienteering*, **7**, 48–56.

Jones, G. & Hardy, L. (1990). Stress in sport: Experiences of some elite performers. In G. Jones & L. Hardy (Eds.), *Stress and performance in sport* (pp. 247–277). Chichester: Wiley.

Karlsson, G. (1989). Rules and strategies in decision making: A critical analysis from a phenomenological perspective. In H. Montgomery & O. Svenson (Eds.), *Process and structure in human decision making* (pp. 51–64). New York: Wiley.

Kerr, J. H. (1993). An eclectic approach to psychological interventions in sport: Reversal theory. *The Sport Psychologist*, **7**, 400–418.

Kerr, J. H. (1997). *Motivation and emotion in sport. Reversal theory*. Hove, East Sussex: Taylor & Francis.

Kimchi, R. & Palmer, S. E. (1986). The information processing approach to cognition. In T. J. Knapp & L. C. Robertson (Eds.), *Approaches to cognition: Contrasts and controversies* (pp. 37–77). Hillsdale, NJ: Erlbaum.

Krane, V., Andersen, M. B. & Strean, W. B. (1997). Issues of qualitative research methods and presentation. *Journal of Sport and Exercise Psychology*, **19**, 213–218.

Kremer, J. & Scully, D. (1994). *Psychology in sport*. London: Taylor & Francis.

Locke, L. F. (1989). Qualitative research as a form of scientific enquiry in sport and physical education. *Research Quarterly for Exercise and Sport*, **60**, 1–20.

Madden, C. (1995). Ways of coping. In T. Morris & J. Summers (Eds.), *Sport psychology. Theory, application and issues* (pp. 288–310). Brisbane: Wiley.

Males, J. R. & Kerr, J. H. (1996). Stress, emotion and performance in elite slalom canoeists. *The Sport Psychologist*, **10**, 17–36.

Males, J. R., Kerr, J. H. & Gerkovich, M. M. (1998). Metamotivational states during canoe slalom competition: A qualitative analysis using reversal theory. *Journal of Applied Sport Psychology*, **10**, 185–200.

Massaro, N. & Cowan, N. (1993). Information processing models: Microscopes of the mind. *Annual Review of Psychology*, **44**, 383–425.

McCaffrey, N. & Orlick, T. (1989). Mental factors related to excellence among top professional golfers. *International Journal of Sport Psychology*, **20**, 256–278.

McPherson, S. L. (1993). The influence of player experience on problem solving during batting preparation in baseball. *Journal of Sport and Exercise Psychology*, **15**, 304–325.

McPherson, S. L. (1994). The development of sport expertise: Mapping the tactical domain. *Quest*, **46**, 223–240.

Miles, M. B. & Huberman, A. M. (1994). *Qualitative data analysis: An expanded source book* (2nd Edn.). Thousand Oaks, CA: Sage.

Moore, W. E. & Stevenson, J. R. (1991). Understanding trust in the performance of complex automatic sport skills. *The Sport Psychologist*, **5**, 281–289.

Newell, S. & Foston, P. (1995). *How to play golf*. London: Anness.

Nisbett, R. E. & Wilson, T. D. (1977). Telling more than we can know. Verbal reports on mental processes. *Psychological Review*, **84**, 231–259.

Orlick, T. & Partington, J. (1988). Mental links to excellence. *The Sport Psychologist*, **2**, 105–130.

Purcell, I. P. (1996, October). *The qualitative analysis of phenomenological structures in sport-related data.* Paper presented at the 1st International Workshop on Motivation and Emotion in Sport: Reversal Theory, Tsukuba, Japan.

Purcell, I. P. (1999). *Expertise, decisions and emotions in the performance of male golfers.* Unpublished doctoral dissertation, Curtin University of Technology, Perth, Australia.

Purcell, I. P. & Kerr, J. H. (1995, July). *Expertise and psychological reversals. Solving the puzzle through golf.* Paper presented at the 8th International Conference on Reversal Theory, Melbourne, Australia.

Purcell, I.P., Kerr, J. H. & Pollock, C. M. (1996). Plans, decisions and emotions in golf. *Coaches Report of the Applied Sports Research Program.* Canberra: Australian Sports Commission.

Richards, T. J. & Richards, L. (1994). Using computers in qualitative research. In N. K. Denzin & Y. S. Lincoln (Eds.), *Handbook of qualitative research* (pp. 445–462). Thousand Oaks: Sage.

Ripoll, H. (1991). The understanding-acting process in sport: The relationship between the semantic and sensorimotor visual function. *International Journal of Sport Psychology*, **22**, 221–250.

Rotella, R. J. & Boutcher, S. H. (1989). A closer look at the role of mind in golf. In A. J. Cochran (Ed.), *Science and golf: I. Proceedings of the First World Scientific Congress of Golf* (pp. 93–97). London: Sponsforth.

Rotella, R. J. & Lerner, J. D. (1993). Responding to competitive pressure. In R. N. Singer, M. Murphey & L. K. Tennant (Eds.), *Handbook on research on sport psychology* (pp. 528–541). New York: Macmillan.

Scanlan, T. K., Ravizza, K. & Stein, G. I. (1989). An in-depth study of former elite figure skaters: I. Introduction to the project. *Journal of Sport and Exercise Psychology*, **11**, 54–64.

Schmidt, R. A. (1991). *Motor learning and performance. From principles to practice.* Champaign, IL: Human Kinetics.

Strean, W. B. & Roberts, G. C. (1992). Future directions in applied sport psychology research. *The Sport Psychologist*, **6**, 55–65.

Svebak, S. (1993). The development of the Tension and Effort Stress Inventory (TESI). In J. H. Kerr, S. Murgatroyd, S. & Apter, M. J. (Eds.), *Advances in reversal theory* (pp. 189–204). Amsterdam: Swets & Zeitlinger.

Svebak, S. & Murgatroyd, S. (1985). Metamotivational dominance: A multimethod validation of reversal theory constructs. *Journal of Personality and Social Psychology*, **48**, 107–116.

Svebak, S., Ursin, H., Endresen, I., Hjelmen, A. M. & Apter, M. J. (1991). Back pain and the experience of stress, effort and moods. *Psychology and Health*, **5**, 307–314.

Svenson, O. (1989). Eliciting and analysing verbal protocols in process studies of judgement and decision making. In H. Montgomery & O. Svenson (Eds.), *Process and structure in human decision making* (pp. 65–81). Chichester: Wiley.

Thomas, P. R. & Over, R. (1994). Psychological and psychomotor skills associated with performance in golf. *The Sport Psychologist*, **8**, 73–86.

Van Raalte, J. L., Brewer, B. W., Rivera, P. M. & Pepitas, A. J. (1994). The relationship between observable self-talk and competitive junior tennis player's match performances. *Journal of Sport and Exercise Psychology*, **16**, 400–415.

Williams, J. M. & Krane, V. (1993). Psychological characteristics of peak performance. In J. M. Williams (Ed.), *Applied sport psychology* (pp. 137–147). Mountain View, CA: Mayfield.

Wrisberg, C. A. (1993). Levels of performance skill. In R. N. Singer, M. Murphey & L. K. Tennant (Eds.), *Handbook on research on sport psychology* (pp. 61–72). New York: Macmillan.

# 5

# Individual Experience in Slalom Canoeing

Jonathan R. Males

*University of Nottingham and Sporting Bodymind Ltd., England*

## INTRODUCTION

Reversal theory attempts to explain a broad sweep of experience and provide meaning for much that is paradoxical and inconsistent within the human condition. It gives individual phenomenology a primary role, yet at the same time offers a complex and predetermined structure that is posited to apply to all people in all situations. This chapter will review the range of research methodologies used in early reversal theory studies before describing a research programme (Males & Kerr, 1996; Males, Kerr, & Gerkovich, 1998) that has attempted to combine quantitative and qualitative approaches within a naturalistic environment. The methodological and theoretical concerns with this research will also be examined.

## REVERSAL THEORY SPORT RESEARCH: A CRITICAL VIEW

Early published reversal theory research (see Kerr, 1997, for a comprehensive review) can be categorized into two approaches: those that explored

*Experiencing Sport: Reversal Theory.* Edited by J. H. Kerr.
© 1999 John Wiley & Sons Ltd.

motivational preference, and those that measured a range of indices before and after physical activity or sport participation. The first category of studies, and also the earliest to be published, typically used the Telic Dominance Scale (TDS) (Murgatroyd, Rushton, Apter, & Ray, 1978). Dominance scores were related to the level of participation in sport (recreational, serious amateur, and professional) by Kerr (1987), who found that telic dominance increased with the 'seriousness' of participation. The telic dominance of novice, average, and expert (Kerr & Cox, 1988), and winning versus losing squash players (Cox & Kerr, 1989) was also examined, but no significant differences between groups in the two studies were identified. Kerr and Svebak (1989) identified a relationship between preference for risk or safe sports and the arousal-avoidance dimension of the TDS, a finding replicated and extended by Kerr (1991), who found that participants in sports such as surfing and sailboarding were generally lower in arousal avoidance and in overall telic dominance (i.e., more paratelic) than participants in such sports as weightlifting or marathon running. Svebak and Kerr (1989) also noted a preference for explosive sports such as baseball in paratelic dominant individuals. Using the Negativism Dominance Scale (NDS) (McDermott & Apter, 1988), Vlaswinkel and Kerr (1990) tested their hypothesis that a tendency to conformity would be found in team sport participants and to negativism in risk sport participants, but the conformist–negativistic dimension was found to be unrelated to participation in either risk or safe, and team or individual sports with elite level performers. Later, Braathen and Svebak (1992) found that talented teenage Norwegian male risk sport athletes scored significantly higher on reactive negativism than female athletes competing in risk sports.

These studies used methodologies that were originally developed in sport psychology to test conventional trait personality theories. A relationship between questionnaire scores and some aspect of participation or performance was tested by application of correlation or regression statistics. The fact that relationships did occur, such as sport preference matching arousal-seeking preference, provided face validity for reversal theory constructs such as the telic–paratelic dimension, yet the results offered little insight into the actual experience of participants when they participated in their sport and did not address whether this was consistent with or in contrast to their dominance.

Early reversal theory sport studies were also limited by the lack of a robust instrument that assessed the complete range of metamotivational preferences and dominance. While the TDS addresses the telic–paratelic dimension, and the NDS the conformist–negativistic dimension, they give no indication of either of the transactional state dimensions. The isolation of any metamotivational state ignores the important conceptual point that at any given moment of an individual's experience, the full combination of somatic and transactional states are thought to be operative. The same applies in terms of metamotivational preference. Paratelic–negativistic sporting experiences (e.g., ignoring a high wind warning to go surfing in a storm) are phenomenologically very different from activities that provide a paratelic–conformist experience (e.g., playing touch football). A published and validated dominance measure covering all four metamotivational states and their combinations became available recently (Apter, Mallows, & Williams, 1998).

The second category of research used state measures completed before and after real sporting activities. These self-report measures included the TDS, the Telic State Measure (TSM) (Svebak & Murgatroyd, 1985), the Stress–Arousal Checklist (SACL) (Mackay, Cox, Burrows, & Lazzerini, 1978) and the Tension and Effort Stress Inventory (TESI) (Svebak, 1993; see also Svebak, Ursin, Endresen, Hjelmen, & Apter, 1991). For example, Kerr and Cox (1988, 1990) explored the affective responses of male novice, average, and skilled squash players who were set a series of target performance tasks in a standard squash court. The TSM and SACL were completed prior to the first and after the second task. While this study did not identify a direct relationship between metamotivational dominance or state and performance, it did point to differences in the way skilled squash players perceived the affective demands of the task. A second study (Cox & Kerr, 1989, 1990) extended this research by means of three simulated squash tournaments so that affective responses could be determined under ecologically valid conditions. Among other questionnaires, the TSM and SACL were administered to players before and after each of four tournament games. A post-hoc separation of participants into most and least successful players led to the creation of a pool of seven winners and seven losers. The only significant group difference in telic state scores occurred among losers after the second game, significantly more of whom were in the paratelic than the telic state. In general, a greater number of winners than losers were in the telic state before and after the tournament. A clear pattern emerged in the arousal discrepancy scores of winners and losers. Winners' scores remained relatively constant and at a low level across all games while the losers' scores increased as the tournament progressed. This may be taken to indicate different perceptions of stress by the two groups, an interpretation supported by the SACL scores. These indicated that winners experienced high and constant levels of arousal across all games and throughout the tournament. By comparison, the losers' arousal scores dropped significantly from game 3 onwards. This was considered to be the critical game, after which the losers' chances of improving their tournament positions were slim. The SACL stress scores were also of interest. Winners' stress scores displayed a pattern of game-by-game reductions, while losers' stress scores remained at a high level at the conclusion of each game.

Sport research also addressed less overtly competitive situations. In a field study, participants completed the SACL and the TSM before and after completing a weekly outdoor run of varying distance and intensity as part of a physical education programme (Kerr & Vlaswinkel, 1993). Arousal, as measured by both questionnaires (TSM, SACL), increased in both male and female participants after running. Runners' scores were categorized into fast and slow groups on the basis of recorded times for each run. Arousal discrepancy scores were significantly lower for fast male and female runners, as were SACL stress scores. Fast runners also started their sessions with lower levels of felt arousal and ended with higher levels of felt arousal than slow runners. This finding echoes the low arousal discrepancy score of winning squash players in Cox and Kerr's (1989) study and suggests that the ability to regulate arousal, or at least to feel comfortable with a given level, is important for good sport performances.

Finally, Kerr and Svebak (1994) pointed to the influence of the type of sport on players' mood changes. Easy running, basketball, and rugby were considered to vary in the degree of antagonistic physical interaction (API), and TESI results indicated that while all these activities led to increased arousal, their effect on negative mood varied. Rugby, the high API sport, led to a decrease in positive mood and an increase in negative mood pre- to post-exercise, while easy running, low in API, led to a reduction in negative mood.

However, these 'pre-post' studies could only measure change in self-reported arousal and mood at a relatively coarse level of detail. All were group-based studies, so comparisons were made not between individuals but between groups, for example, squash tournament winners versus losers, fast versus slow runners, rugby players versus basketball players. Pre-post measurement also meant that there was no way of checking for emotional or motivational changes between the measurement points. However, the colour preference changes identified throughout the course of a cross-country run (Kerr & Vlaswinkel, 1993) did give credence to Apter's (1982) claim that individuals will experience a range of meta-motivational states that may change rapidly.

In summary, early reversal theory sport research could be seen as somewhat limited because it relied on questionnaires and focused on a restricted range of metamotivational possibilities.

# COMBINING QUANTITATIVE AND QUALITATIVE METHODOLOGY

Given the limitations outlined above, the problem remained of trying to improve the application of reversal theory to form a deeper understanding of competitive sport performance. Three factors seemed critical: that the studies should take place during real, elite level competition, that the research should focus on individuals as well as groups and, finally, that qualitative rather than quantitative methods should take precedence. Although Kerr's squash studies included a specially staged tournament that was by all accounts realistic, it was still a one-off special event that to some extent may have lacked the consequences and emotional investment that comes with real, high-profile events. The use of real competitors necessitated a move away from experimental manipulation and group-based statistical analysis. Instead of a large group size and concomitant statistical power, it seemed preferable to use a case study approach that provided details of individual changes over time, but would also allow group patterns (if apparent) to be identified. Finally, qualitative methods were required to uncover the individual participant's detailed experience and add to the relatively static 'snap-shots' provided by questionnaires.

The first phase of research employing the combined use of qualitative and quantitative approaches began at the end of 1992 with a group of world-ranked British slalom canoeists (Males & Kerr, 1996; Males, Kerr, & Gerkovich, 1998) and extended over the next few years to the team sports of lacrosse and volleyball (Males, 1996). The programme has therefore covered both individual and team sport at an elite level. The overall purpose was to extend the scope of previous research (reviewed briefly above) and to examine the influence of reversal theory-based factors such as tension stress and arousal discrepancy on performance as well as mapping the experience of participants in reversal theory terms. The slalom studies will be discussed in detail in the next sections of this chapter as they are representative of the approach used with the other sports.

# THE CANOE SLALOM STUDIES

The research programme was a collection of individual case studies based on nine male slalom canoeists who were tracked throughout a full competitive season, beginning with early local events, moving to national team selection trials, and culminating with the World Championships. Each canoeist completed the TESI before he raced and was then interviewed at the conclusion of each event. The participants were committed athletes who took their sport seriously. Only one had full-time employment and the rest had delayed study and careers in order to train full time. All had competed internationally, three were members of the 1992 Olympic team, and five were World Championship or World Cup medal winners. They were ranked in the top 10 and were the main contenders for the four places on the British national team to contest the 1993 World Championships. Three went on to win individual and team medals in this event, the most successful-ever showing by their team. The mean age was 25.2 years at the commencement of the study, and the average length of experience in the sport was 10.1 years.

# PART 1: QUANTITATIVE METHODOLOGY

The Tension and Effort Stress Inventory (TESI) State version (Svebak *et al.*, 1991) was selected because, in addition to indexing internal (bodily) and external stress, it addresses all 16 primary emotions from reversal theory. Respondents are asked to estimate the degree to which any of the 16 emotions are being experienced. Eight somatic emotions relate to the perception of felt arousal, and eight transactional emotions relate to the consequences of interactions with others. The pleasant somatic emotions are relaxation, excitement, placidity, and provocativeness; the unpleasant somatic emotions are anxiety, boredom, anger, and sullenness. The pleasant transactional emotions are pride, modesty, gratitude, and virtue; the unpleasant transactional emotions are humiliation, shame, resentment, and guilt. Each emotion is posited to be the consequence of a particular metamotivational combination and the individual's current experience of important variables like felt arousal or felt transactional outcome.

Earlier reversal theory sport study results (e.g., Kerr & Cox, 1991) had pointed to the importance of arousal discrepancy as correlate of both tension stress and performance, so the TESI was modified by the addition of the 'felt arousal' and 'preferred arousal' scales from the TSM (Svebak & Murgatroyd, 1985). An arousal discrepancy score can be calculated as the absolute difference between these two scores. The modified TESI was therefore a fusion of two state measures that had previously been applied in reversal theory research (Kerr & Cox, 1988; Kerr & Vlaswinkel, 1993; Kerr & Svebak, 1994).

The research design (see Males & Kerr, 1996) was based on research which used time-series analysis to monitor changes in individual behaviour and symptoms following clinical intervention (Mueser, Yarnold, & Foy, 1991). Unlike conventional time-series analysis (Box & Jenkins, 1970), this type of analysis does not require a large number of data points and can be used to contrast as few as two data points. There are several advantages to this type of case study over more traditional A–B–A–B single subject designs (Bryan, 1987). Firstly, the method of analysis used here takes into account possible serial dependency effects by incorporating an autocorrelation function that indicates the degree to which data points are correlated with each other (Gottman & Glass, 1978). Secondly, it allows the magnitude of changes to be assessed statistically rather than by visual inspection of a graph. Visual inspection may lead to inappropriate conclusions due to small changes being overlooked, or seemingly large changes being too readily accepted as significant. Finally, traditional A–B–A–B designs require the introduction and removal of specific interventions. This would clearly be inappropriate in a natural competitive environment, and in any case the purpose of the study was to explore, rather than create change.

Raw scores from the modified TESI were first converted to ipsative z-scores to provide standardized scores for each canoeist which were then subjected to a time-series analysis using the procedure described by Mueser *et al.* (1991; see also Males & Kerr, 1996). This calculation was carried out separately for each canoeist's TESI item scores and the critical difference score was used to compare items from best and worst performances. This analysis therefore took into account the degree of autocorrelation between item scores and allowed the difference between any pair of scores (that is between any two events) to be assessed in terms of significance or otherwise.

The findings indicated that, among slalom paddlers generally, levels of unpleasant emotions (TESI) were found to be consistently lower than levels of pleasant emotions (TESI) (see also Kerr & Svebak, 1994), but there were no important changes across performances. The majority of canoeists also had a similar pattern for stress (TESI), effort (TESI), and felt arousal (TSM) scores, with zero or low levels of arousal discrepancy (TSM) before all their best performances. Males and Kerr (1996) highlighted the contrasting profiles of two individual canoeists (F and G), both national team members and Olympic competitors, at their best and worst performances, and these are examined in the next section.

## Canoeist G

Canoeist G achieved his season's best performance at the World Championships and his poorest at a local event. His emotion scores did show a greater variation than canoeist F, but only scores on *anger* revealed a significant difference between best and worst performance.

He reported his highest levels of internal and external stress prior to competing at the World Championships. This might have been expected prior to such an important event. Internal effort scores were greater than internal stress scores, whereas scores on external effort were considerably less than external stress scores (see Figure 5.1a). It may have been that canoeist G's internal or bodily state was more important to him than

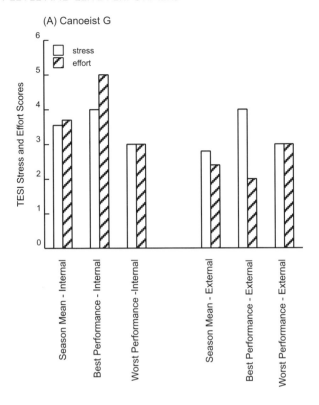

**Figure 5.1a**    TESI stress (tension-stress) and effort (effort-stress) scores for canoeist G (from Males & Kerr, 1996)

external considerations. His efforts to cope (effort-stress) were therefore directed towards dealing with bodily stress.

Canoeist G's felt arousal level (TSM) before his worst performance (at a local event) was significantly lower than that reported at his best performance in the World Championships, even though he would have preferred a level of felt arousal similar to his seasonal average (see Figure 5.2).

## Canoeist F

Canoeist F performed best in a local canoeing event in front of his home crowd, just after his selection for the national team. His worst performance was at the World Championships. Perhaps surprisingly, there were no significant differences between TESI emotion scores for any emotion before best and worst performances. In fact, he reported the majority of his emotion scores at similar levels (11 out of 16).

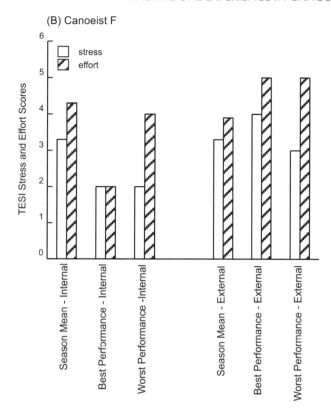

**Figure 5.1b**    TESI stress (tension-stress) and effort (effort-stress) scores for canoeist F (from Males & Kerr, 1996).

His internal stress score was matched by his internal effort score, but was below his mean score for the season at his best performance. Conversely, here his external stress score was higher than his mean score for the season and his external effort score even higher. His worst performance, at the World Championships, revealed stress scores similar to those recorded at his best performance, but here both internal and external effort scores were higher than the respective stress scores (see Figure 5.1b).

Both felt and preferred levels of arousal (TSM) were higher than his seasonal average before his worst performance at the World Championships (see Figure 5.2). This may have been due to canoeist F *trying harder* and may have been related to his desire for a higher than average felt arousal level at the same event (Males & Kerr, 1996). This proposal appeared correct, as a discrepancy was also obtained which indicated that effort-stress exceeded tension-stress.

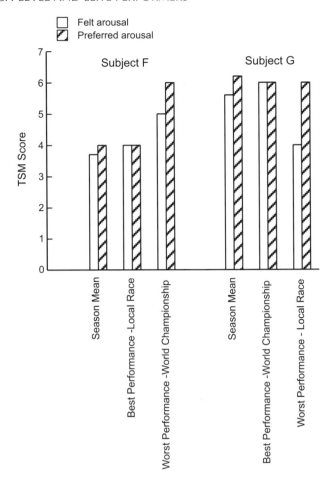

**Figure 5.2**   Felt and preferred arousal scores (TSM) for canoeists F and G (from Males & Kerr, 1996)

It is noteworthy that both G and F experienced a mismatch between preferred and felt arousal levels before their worst performances and both had zero arousal discrepancy scores before their best performances (see Figure 5.2).

# PART 2: QUALITATIVE METHODOLOGY

Other areas of reversal theory research have made effective use of structured and semi-structured interviews, and the methodology developed by

O'Connell, Cook, Gerkovich, Potocky, and Swan (1990) was adapted for this programme. A prepared interview schedule was designed to elicit specific phenomenological information from each participant (see case vignettes below). The interview was then analysed using the Metamotivational State Coding Schedule (MSCS) (O'Connell *et al.*, 1990; Potocky, Cook, & O'Connell, 1993).

The author carried out all post-event interviews and was present at all events in his capacity as a national team coach. He was also a former international canoe slalom competitor with a detailed understanding of the demands of the sport. Participants were given a guarantee of confidentiality and an assurance that information gathered in interviews would not be passed on to other coaching staff or used for team selection purposes. Participants knew they were free not to be interviewed and several exercised this right at different stages of the research programme.

In most cases, the interviews took place on the same day as the event, often within an hour of the conclusion of the race. The remainder of interviews occurred within the next 24 hours. Each interview lasted between 20 and 45 minutes, depending on the participant's availability and other demands within the competitive environment. Inevitably, the duration and depth of interviews varied, but this was considered an unavoidable factor in field research of this kind. As a result of variations in the availability of each athlete and his selection or non-selection in the national team, which influenced which international events he attended, a complete set of nine interviews was obtained for three canoeists. These three were the most successful of the entire group, gaining selection to compete in the World Championships. The remainder were interviewed on at least four occasions and a total of 50 interviews were completed.

## APPLYING THE MSCS

All tape-recorded interviews were transcribed and the transcriptions checked for accuracy before coding using a modified version of the MSCS. O'Connell and her colleagues originally developed this procedure to classify the reported experience of relapsed and ex-smokers (O'Connell *et al.*, 1990; Potocky *et al.*, 1993). Content validity of the MSCS was established through independent review by four individuals who were well-versed in reversal theory, including the theory's originator Michael Apter. Sport events fulfil the main requirements identified by Potocky *et al.*, (1993) for the successful application of the MSCS; they can be clearly pinpointed in time and involve intense emotional experience.

The coding process first involved the identification of coding units, defined as distinct periods of time in a given environment during which the participant reported a single goal and experienced only one combination of metamotivational states. A change in environment, a different objective, or a change in reported emotional experience constituted a change in coding unit. A typical interview contained between five and seven coding units. A separate coding sheet listing predetermined criteria was used for each coding unit.

The first section required the coder to decide whether the participant was in the telic or paratelic state by first identifying whether a goal was present, and if so what it was. The coder then examined the text, paying particular attention to the type of adjectives used, and rated each of a set of phenomenological descriptors on a scale of 1 to 3, where 1 indicated that the characteristic was not present or barely identifiable, 2 indicated that the characteristic was present, and 3 indicated that it was both present and strong. The telic–paratelic descriptors were: *job to do, fun to do, result oriented, thinking ahead, sensation-present oriented, activity with important consequences, activity enjoyable in itself, trying to accomplish something important, and under pressure*. Subjective assessments using a scale of low, medium, and high were then made of the degree of felt significance and felt arousal. Hedonic tone was rated as pleasant, neutral, or unpleasant. Finally, the four somatic emotions of *boredom, calmness, excitement*, or *anxiety* were rated using the 1 to 3 scale described above.

A similar process was then used for the negativistic–conformist dimension. The first decision addressed whether or not the participant reported awareness of a particular rule or rule system in place. This was usually assumed, given the canoeist's participation in a well-structured race environment with established competition rules. Next was an assessment of a further set of descriptors: *stubborn, being difficult, rebellious, angry, guilty, wanting to break rules, and wanting to follow rules*. The final judgement was of the level of perceived negativism, based on the degree to which the participant expressed either contentment at following the rules or a desire to rebel. Any expression of anger was taken as a cardinal sign of negativism.

The mastery–sympathy dimension required a primary judgement on the participant's perception of the situation, whether it was seen in terms of a competition, trial or struggle (mastery) or harmony, unity, sensitivity (sympathy). The mastery descriptors were: *strong, self-disciplined, aggressive, weak, indulgent, and wimpish*. The sympathy descriptors were: *sensitive, caring, insensitive, and uncaring*. Finally the autic–alloic dimension required a decision on the source of the participant's 'self tone', that is whether he placed primary importance on his own or others' well-being. The final decision addressed whether the participant felt he was gaining or losing in the situation and whether that felt pleasant or unpleasant.

After all coding units were completed, the results were transferred to a summary sheet that also contained basic contextual information about the race performance and the interview. A preliminary sample of 15 interviews, some 30% of the data, was analysed. An independent coder, highly experienced in the methodology, then coded the same selection blind to the outcome of the first coding. The process of discussion and reconciliation recommended by O'Connell *et al.* (1990) was used to produce a specific coding protocol for this sample. The inter-rater reliability for each of the primary coding decisions was tested by the kappa statistic (Cohen, 1960). As these were all in excess of the 0.70 cut-off commonly recommended (Schweigert, 1994), the coding process was considered reliable. The remaining interviews were then analysed using the newly established protocol.

# FINDINGS

Firstly, individual coding units from across the nine events were sorted into *pre-event, during race, between runs* and *post-race* categories to identify possible patterns in the canoeists' experience of metamotivational state combinations throughout the competitive period. The coding units were totalled for each of the four possible somatic and four possible transactional state combinations and converted to percentages. As the number of

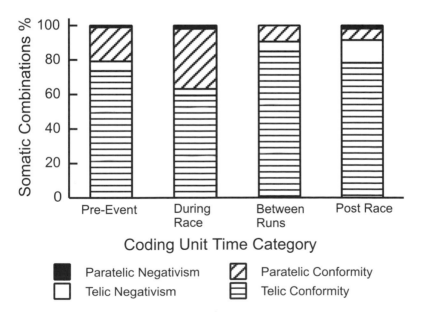

**Figure 5.3** Proportion of somatic metamotivational state combinations reported pre-event (*N* = 103), during race (*N* = 57), between runs (*N* = 32) and post-race (*N* = 70) (from Males, Kerr, & Gerkovich, 1998).

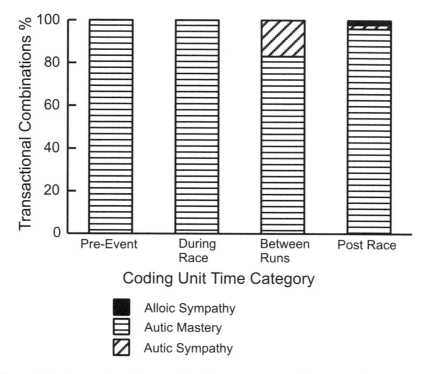

**Figure 5.4** Proportion of transactional metamotivational state combinations reported pre-event (*N* = 103), during race (*N* = 57), between runs (*N* = 32) and postrace (*N* = 70) (from Males, Kerr, & Gerkovich, 1998).

individual coding units varied within each category, percentages were used to standardize the comparison. The most frequently operative somatic state combination at any stage of competition was telic–conformity at 75% and over for the *pre-event, between runs*, and *post-race* categories. During the race, the proportion was different, with the telic–conformity category reduced to just under 60% and paratelic–conformity increasing to 35% of the total (see Figure 5.3). Figure 5.4 shows in striking fashion that, of the transactional states, autic–mastery was by far the most frequently coded operative state combination for all four competition categories. The percentages reached 100% for the *pre-event* and *during race* categories, were over 95% in the *post-race* category, and it was only in the *between runs* category that autic–sympathy, with over 16% of the coding units, made an impact on the overall transactional state pattern. The proportions of operative metamotivational states are surprisingly consistent, given the fact that the percentages of coding units were the result of individual interviews.

As reversal theory emphasizes the importance of individual experience, the following three case vignettes (from material collected in the Males & Kerr, 1996 and Males, Kerr, & Gerkovich, 1988 studies) are presented in order to demonstrate the variety of individual responses to the competitive environment. Some information from the TESI results is also mentioned, but the emphasis is on providing cxamples of the post-race interview material and the corresponding reversal theory interpretation. Note that the canoe slalom events comprised two races over two days with each race involving two runs down the slalom course. The interviewer's questions or comments are in italics, the participant's comments are in bold print.

# CASE VIGNETTES

## 1: Canoeist D

| INTERVIEW TRANSCRIPT | REVERSAL THEORY INTERPRETATION |
|---|---|

In the first vignette, canoeist D's TESI scores indicated that he experienced no discrepancy between his felt and preferred arousal levels at any races, a finding that, in conjunction with no reported unpleasant emotions, suggests very low levels of tension stress. The first excerpt was reported at event 2 and the strong tclic orientation of the comments are in stark contrast to participant C's (case vignette 2) paratelic orientation at the same race.

*Anything else that you think is important about your performance today?*
**No I enjoyed it, I've been doing a lot of racing the last couple of weekends and travelling, so for me the challenge was to stay with a good performance because I've been a bit tired, and I didn't really want to get on here and be off the pace and demoralised because I was tired. I wanted it to be worthwhile, we've come a long way out of the way to come here just to do two runs today, two tomorrow, and it's been worthwhile. I feel like I've achieved my goal in that sense, so it's been worth coming because we could have just gone back to France. I made a point of coming up to practise for the selections, so I guess no matter what happens tomorrow I'm on target for a few months time so it's been worthwhile.**

The performance goal-oriented comments in terms of a job to be done and the satisfaction and pleasure associated with goal achievement, alongside the preparation and planning elements, point to the telic state being operative, probably in conjunction with the autic and mastery states. It is assumed that the conformist state is also operative as, in turning up and competing in official competition, complying with the rules is a necessity.

| INTERVIEW TRANSCRIPT | REVERSAL THEORY INTERPRETATION |
| --- | --- |

The next exchange was recorded in a different interview after event 6, following participant D's selection to compete in the World Championships.

*Did you have a particular goal for the race?*
**Yeah, I was looking for a good result, a good race and not just your average, steady outcome, . . . I feel I'm getting closer to the Worlds. Selection [events] I didn't do quite so well as I could have, so I was quite motivated for a result.**
*And the result you got – was that what you wanted?*
**Yeah, I mean I was happy to win, obviously – I was pleased with that outcome. I think as I paddled two clean runs, it was quite a technical course so I was pleased with that outcome. Maybe could have picked up a little bit of time here and there but, on the whole, I was quite pleased – I felt pleased that, feeling the way I had felt before – I had come here and done what I came to do, you know. I made an effort to come and do this race, been doing a lot of races, and I felt that following from selection it was good, psychologically, to come and do a good performance and actually to win it, it made me feel quite good – so I was pretty pleased with the outcome.**

These comments illustrate how this race, like the event described above, had a meaning and importance above and beyond itself. After previously achieving the goal of being selected for the national team, he was focused on the outcome of the race and its role as preparation for future, even more important events at the World Championships. He emphasized his pleasure and satisfaction at the attainment of his objectives rather than on the experience of competing. He was also pleased with (and perhaps proud of) his 'two clean runs' over quite 'a technical course'. In terms of felt transactional outcome, he had mastered a relatively difficult course. The autic and mastery states are also likely to have been operative and salient.

*And the way you were looking at the race – were you looking forward to it as something that was enjoyable or more that it was something you needed to do to get it out of the way?*
**I think that, because I was feeling a bit tired generally beforehand, I think it was because I was committed to the race. I suppose I was saying to myself 'well you're here – do the best, do the job as it were'. The worst thing in this situation is to resign and not commit yourself fully to it because you don't feel great and sometimes when you feel tired and lethargic that's a sign of anxiety, so I think I was trying to focus on being committed to do the job because I was here and I made the decision to come here and I wanted the outcome so it wasn't – like get this out of the way and say, well it's not a problem.**

Canoeist D also provided a good example of how the autic-mastery states combined with telic-conformity in a slightly different way. In this excerpt, still from event 6, he described how it was important 'not to wimp out' but to control his own feelings of fatigue and lethargy in order to achieve important goals. His comments about the danger of 'not committing' suggests that if autic–sympathy were combined with telic–conformity, the competitor could lack the necessary determination to race effectively, instead just 'getting it over with'.

| INTERVIEW TRANSCRIPT | REVERSAL THEORY INTERPRETATION |
|---|---|

*So it was a serious thing. You made the effort to get here and . . .*

**Yeah, you know, get on and do it. Don't wimp out as it were and not pull hard because you don't feel like pulling hard or you can't be bothered because really the outcome here isn't that important. It doesn't decide anything for anybody particularly, but a good result makes you feel better than a bad result and if you've got the power to make the difference, why not go for a good result.**

Looking at these interview comments overall, it might be concluded that canoeist D exhibited a consistent telic–conformity–autic–mastery state combination throughout each event. This metamotivational pattern was typical of the majority of canoeists when competing.

## 2: Canoeist C

| INTERVIEW TRANSCRIPT | REVERSAL THEORY INTERPRETATION |
|---|---|

*Did you have a goal for this race?*

**I didn't really no, I didn't know I was racing until this morning, bit of confusion in the entries and what was going on so it was a bit of a rushed job this morning, I didn't prepare real well.**

*Now let's talk about what happened just before your first run. Can you give me three words to describe how you were feeling just before your first run?*

**Pretty relaxed, pretty happy, uh, another word, uh, sort of we were joking around a lot, – I don't know if you'll put that down or not (laughs).**

*I'll just write down what you say (laughs). Is that the way you wanted to feel?*

**No I think I should have been a bit more focused in.**

*And the way you were feeling was it pleasant or unpleasant?*

**No it (was) pretty pleasant, it was cool.**

*What was the most important thing on your mind?*

**Um, what you mean, in the actual . . . ?**

*Just before the race.*

**I dunno I don't have a lot on my mind, uh no I don't remember.**

*Was it like the race was a job you had to do, or was it something you really enjoyed because it was fun?*

Canoeist C did not organize his entry to this event until the day of the race, a sign of a lack of planning and strategic goals and a generally paratelic approach to this race.

| INTERVIEW TRANSCRIPT | REVERSAL THEORY INTERPRETATION |
|---|---|

**No it was just fun.**
*Were you planning ahead or just taking things as they came along?*
**Uh, on my first run I was just taking it as it came along, I didn't really prepare much.**
*Now, what about the time between your runs. You said before that you came back here?*
**Yeah the basic thing was I wasn't focusing on the race so I thought I'd better come back to the van, took a sleep, got myself away from messing around.**
*What was the most important thing on your mind? How would you describe it?*
**Well not quite sure really, just trying to get myself in the state of mind where, like that I'm usually like, which I didn't normally have to make an effort to do, just coming away from (the crowd) focusing on what I have to do.**
*When you say you get focused does that mean getting more serious about what you do or doesn't that describe it?*
**Not serious, I think it's like excited in the right way, like know what I mean? Like messing around (in the cafe) is a good laugh, so 'excited' but focusing that excitement on the right things, like I wasn't . . . (doing that before).**
*Yeah I know its hard to get words for it, so rather than just stuffing around it was like taking that energy and taking it towards the course?*
**Yeah, yep.**
*Where do you focus it on, or to?*
**I think you come down, I get myself to a familiar relaxed state which I'm sort of familiar with when I race, then I think I go into a race, I get a bit nervous but I can convert that excitement quite easily, that sort of happens naturally, know what I mean?**
*Yeah.*
**I don't really have to make an effort to do that, but today I had to make an effort to get myself away from, so I could get like a state I was familiar with so I could build on it for my second run.**

His comments here about 'fun' and 'taking it as it came along' point to C being in the paratelic state prior to the first run, which, although enjoyable, lacked the concentration and focus (related to control and mastery in terms of his skills and the demands of the slalom course) he wanted.

After the first run, one of C's poorest of the season, he decided that a change was necessary before the second run. This involved moving away from the crowded cafe where most of the canoeists were sitting, chatting, joking, eating, and drinking coffee. This paratelic–alloic–sympathy–oriented environment was warm, comfortable and removed from the detail of the competition. Canoeists tended not to talk seriously about the race while inside the cafe, although by walking outside they could easily watch the race, check scores and so on. C, an experienced performer, realizing that he had performed badly and was not in his usual pre-race state of mind, chose to spend some time alone and try and change his mental state.

When alone in the quiet self-contained environment of his van he concentrated on mental preparation. He induced the telic state by first taking a sleep and relaxing (a telic act in itself) before deliberately increasing the significance and importance of the event and his participation in it (by this stage the autic and mastery states would have also been operative). This led to increased arousal and nervousness which he could then 'turn into excitement' by reversing back to the paratelic state.

INTERVIEW TRANSCRIPT

REVERSAL THEORY
INTERPRETATION

*And you turn the nervousness into
excitement?*
**Yeah, I find that happens uh not long
before my run, like twenty minutes.**
*Did something different happen before
your first run?*
**I didn't think. I didn't have the
nervousness.**
*So because you didn't have the nervousness
you didn't have the excitement?*
**That's right, like I was happy and that but
it wasn't like the excitement of a race.**
*So what about your second run then?*

**Yeah I got more excited about it, like the
way I wanted to.**
*So did you end up feeling the way you
wanted to feel?*
**Yeah I felt pretty focused in.**
*Was it a job you had to do, or was it
something you really enjoyed because it
was fun?*
**No I never find it a job I have to do I
always find it pretty fun, I like being in the
competition situation.**
*What about during the second run, did
anything change once you had started?*
**No that went quite well, I was quite happy
with my second run.**

*During the run, or at the end or both?*
**During, again I was a bit disappointed at
the end cause I got a couple of touches,
but during the run like, I only considered
them afterwards.**

These additional comments from C
confirm that usually before
performing a telic to paratelic
reversal occurs which characterizes
his normal pre-competitive mental
state, i.e., pleasant paratelic high
arousal ('excitement'). On this
particular occasion (prior to the first
run) the customary reversal did not
occur. As a result he was forced to
take action and use his experience
and skill to induce the necessary
reversal and the state of mind that
he prefers prior to white water
slalom performance.

C's focus was on the present
moment and trying to master the
gates on the slalom course rather
than on the consequences of the
race and there was no comparison
with others. He confirms his answers
to earlier questions by describing his
mental state as enjoyable and that
competition is fun and a challenge.
This is representative of a
metamotivational combination of
paratelic-autic-mastery. (Presumably
C had to follow the competition
rules while performing therefore it
might be assumed that the
conformist state was the fourth part
of his operative metamotivational
combination.)

Canoeist C ignored his gate
penalties until the race was over,
then experienced disappointment
suggesting a paratelic to telic
reversal when the consequences of
his performance were realized. His
basic time for the second run was
much better than for the first run
and very competitive in comparison
with other canoeists' times.
Unfortunately his basic time was
marred by the addition of time
penalties incurred at two gates.

## 3: Canoeist E

| INTERVIEW TRANSCRIPT | REVERSAL THEORY INTERPRETATION |
|---|---|

Participant E reported the widest variety of metamotivational state combinations throughout the study. Like the other participants, he rarely reported significant arousal discrepancy scores, but his internal and external effort scores were always greater than reported stress. The following example from event 6 is included because it illustrated an occasion when the pattern of metamotivational shifts differed from normal, particularly from the first run of this race, which was his best performance of the season. The event took place in front of his 'home crowd' and the external effort score was the highest of the season. He misjudged his preparation time for his second run and found himself with only 15 minutes to prepare instead of his customary half an hour.

**I left it a little bit sharp, a little bit late and I wasn't really focused in on exactly what I was doing. I tried to make that effort – I had fifteen minutes to get ready, to get warmed up and do the thing, . . . basically I used it as an exercise to keep cool just with fifteen minutes to go and like, normally while I'm getting changed I tend to listen to music or something like that without really thinking too deeply into it but that's what I was trying to do – focus in like I would when I was on the water because I was trying to catch everything up a little bit.**

**When I actually got on the start line I felt quite all right. I was quite hungry to race, to go hard at it – but maybe I risked it more . . . I didn't have that same air of caution as I did [on first run] – like when you're coming into gates then normally I would ease off just a little bit to make sure that I've got the boat in control and that it is where I want it, whereas on the second run I was trying to keep paddling all the time – keep everything going all the time so that if it did come off, then I would be two, three seconds clear.**

Because of the shorter time (perhaps experiencing some anxiety as a result), he skipped his normal strategy of listening to loud rock music, apparently deliberately designed to induce the paratelic state and increase pleasant felt arousal. (A post-interview check confirmed that it was loud rock music that he usually listened to.) Instead he engaged in a telic-oriented strategy to reduce or, at least, not to increase arousal levels ('an exercise to keep cool'). The mastery state was also likely to have been operative as he spent the time 'focusing in' on his performance. This 'focusing' would normally have occurred on the water after the earlier increase in pleasant arousal. When he arrived at the start line his state of mind was satisfactory and he felt 'quite hungry to race'. However, in spite of not following his usual strategy, he did not feel under-aroused on the start-line (perhaps because of the rush to get ready and/ or the failure of his strategy to 'keep cool'), but this led to a different, more reckless approach to the run that was categorized by the interview coders as a state combination of paratelic–negativism and autic–mastery.

| INTERVIEW TRANSCRIPT | REVERSAL THEORY INTERPRETATION |

The first few gates of this run were 'better than my first' but he incurred a penalty at gate seven.

**That broke my concentration a little bit – I got a penalty on [gate] seven and dropped low and I thought 'oh shit – out of the window' and I started to evaluate really. For that sort of, one second, after you have made a mistake you are thinking about the mistake and not where you should be going next and things like that – what happened then is that I lost the run of the boat a little bit – I started to eddy out a little bit and it just sort of had an avalanche effect sort of thing.**
*So what was happening to your mood as these mistakes were building up?*
**I was getting a bit blasé towards the end really, as soon as I had taken the five – as soon as I took the penalty, then I knew that I wasn't going to win with the penalty . . .**
*So then, how did you feel at the end after that run?*
**Pissed off really . . . I wanted to feel . . . that . . . I was seen as a more consistent paddler and that I can do it when it matters and I didn't do that on the second run and I was pissed off with that – okay I had this good first run but I had a shit second run, and I felt that maybe it [my performance] could have been perceived as a flash in the pan.**

The penalty at gate seven led to a paratelic to telic reversal and the experience of telic tension stress as a result of high levels of felt arousal.

The telic state continued after the run finished, however by then the negativistic state was also operative and the high levels of felt arousal became expressed in feelings of anger ('pissed off') associated with a telic–negativistic state combination. The realization that he had not fulfilled his own and others' expectations was indicative of autic–mastery tension stress because of his perceived loss in felt transactional outcome. Instead of experiencing a sense of pride from a second good performance (not a flash in the pan), he may have been feeling somewhat humiliated.

It is likely that the unusual metamotivational state pattern prior to his second run hindered his performance by not allowing him to spend sufficient time in a pleasant paratelic high arousal state. As a result, he was unable to concentrate on the race as an enjoyable challenge – in his words, 'to be offensive rather than defensive'.

The qualitative data supports Apter's (1982) contention that reversals in metamotivational state are likely to occur for a number of reasons, including fatigue and external contingencies. For example a contingent event, such as an error within a run, typically triggered a paratelic to telic reversal. This was marked by an increased orientation towards the future and specifically consideration of the implications of the error on the final result, and accompanied by negative self-talk indicative of the experience of unpleasant emotion, especially anxiety.

# PARATELIC PROTECTIVE FRAMES

The athletes in this study were all elite performers who devoted substantial effort to their sport and, as mentioned above, only one was in full-time employment and most had delayed study or career options in order to devote sufficient time to their preparation. Most of them would describe their occupation as 'sportsperson'. Nearly all had carefully planned training programmes and yearly schedules, well-prepared plans for race days and clearly defined goals. Many spoke of the challenge of achieving their goals and the pleasure that came from doing so successfully. Yet, despite this telic orientation, both telic and paratelic states were reported throughout all stages of a competition. When experiencing the telic state and high felt arousal, participants reported tension stress in the form of unpleasant anxiety and pressure. At these times, their coping efforts involved the use of breathing and visualization techniques to reduce the unpleasant high arousal.

In other cases, canoeists were clearly paratelic and simply enjoyed the 'buzz' of racing, eagerly anticipating the pre-event feelings and experiencing these as exciting and pleasurable. For example, participant C described his sensations just before and during event 1 as being 'pretty high all the way, it was good'. Others used specific strategies that seemed to be designed to engender a paratelic experience around their participation in major events. These strategies included reducing the importance of the event by 'putting it into perspective compared to the rest of my life', listening to loud rock music to in order to 'arouse emotions and feel more aggressive', concentrating on aspects of technique and 'in the moment' awareness rather than dwelling on the future results, self-talk to reinforce process rather than outcome goals, and distraction by chatting to other competitors or officials. The use of these strategies supports Kerr's (1993) contention that some strategies used by athletes to ensure their preferred state of mind result in changes in their metamotivational state.

These strategies are also an example of what Apter (1992) has described as attempts to create a paratelic 'frame of experience'. Paratelic frames may be based on a perception of confidence, or a sense of distance from real physical or emotional harm. Apter (1992) developed this model to explain participation in a wide range of high-risk sports and activities, but it may also be the case that they occur during competitive sport. Although the risk of physical harm in slalom canoeing is relatively low for these highly skilled athletes, competitors may risk emotional harm and a threat to self-esteem should they under-perform. The overall motivation for participation was often paratelic – the canoeist simply enjoyed racing. This then reversed to telic seriousness around specific events, which in turn allowed increased significance and therefore potentially greater goal satisfaction.

The increased significance also increased felt arousal, which was then converted via the paratelic frame into excitement. Without the paratelic frame, participation in major events could be unpleasant because high felt arousal would be experienced as telic tension stress, and frightening because failure would represent a threat to self-esteem and personal meaning.

# ADDITIONAL POINTS

In terms of the qualitative component of this study, some writers contrast positivistic with naturalistic research paradigms (e.g., Lincoln & Guba, 1985), while others point to a more pragmatic approach that incorporates whatever methods seem most appropriate (Patton, 1990). The current study was pragmatic in that positivistic elements (e.g., a predetermined theoretical structure and the establishment of coder reliability and protocols) coexisted with naturalistic elements (e.g., a naturally occurring research environment and acceptance of experiential reports).

Silverman (1994) suggests that it is inappropriate to consider conventional notions of reliability and validity in qualitative research and Lincoln and Guba (1985) recommend the examination of naturalistic data for trustworthiness – the extent to which data is credible, transferable, dependable, and conceivable. The credibility of this study is strengthened by its nine-month duration and repeated interviews. However, negative case analysis, one of the most important methods of determining credibility, is complicated by the nature of reversal theory. It is a general and all-encompassing theory, so 'negative cases' are easily explained through the mechanism of reversals.

The transferability of the study's results is dependent on the extent to which there are underlying patterns of competitive experience that apply across a range of sports. The findings are consistent with many of the basic premises of reversal theory. They describe the range of metamotivational states experienced during slalom competition and illustrate how individuals have their own patterns of metamotivational reversals. These findings now clearly demand to be tested in a variety of sports at a range of skill levels. Dependability and conceivability are both enhanced by the application of the MSCS which provided a clear audit trail and the potential for cross-checking.

Like all qualitative data, the material presented in this study was a subjective construction created by the interaction between the participant and the intentions and responses of the interviewer (Siedentop, 1989). Unlike interpretational studies which developed thematic structures of experience (e.g., Kreiner-Phillips & Orlick, 1993), this study created data and applied it to a predetermined structure. As such, the nature of the questions oriented the participants towards areas of interest and tended to steer them away from other seemingly unrelated areas. Because of the bipolar structure of reversal theory, many of the questions were phrased as 'either–or' choices that could restrict the participant's options, yet such questions were deemed necessary by Potocky *et al.* (1993) because an open-ended interview frequently did not reveal appropriate detail. Kvale (1994) argues that questions of this type do not reduce the reliability of interviews so long as their orientation is made explicit, allowing the reader to evaluate their influence on findings. Krane, Andersen, and Strean (1997) point out that most qualitative sport psychology research is carried out by researchers with pre-existing theoretical notions, even when they use an interpretational approach.

Another factor to be considered is the relationship between the participants and the interviewer, who in this study held a unique position. A valid concern is the extent to which participants could have responded to him variously as a researcher, as a coach, or as a confidant. In each case, the social context will have contributed to the participants' willingness and ability to provide an accurate account of their experiences. In positivistic research, the interviewer–participant relationship is treated as a variable to be controlled so as not to bias the data, whereas more contemporary approaches recognize that this relationship, the social context, and the nature of the findings are inextricably linked (Silverman, 1994). In this study, the strong relationship between the interviewer and participants met Eklund's (1993) key recommendations for successful field research: the interviewer developed trust and rapport with the participants over an extended period of contact, had an in-depth understanding of the specific sport environment, and established a mode of access at a range of events. Against this must be weighed the limitation that the interviewer's pre-existing knowledge of the competitive situation and reversal theory interrupted the possibility of a more naive appreciative enquiry that would have produced different responses from participants (Bushe & Bushe, 1991).

## CLOSING COMMENTS

All research methods used in psychology have their limitations and can be criticized from one point of view or another. The study reported in this chapter utilized both quantitative and qualitative techniques and sought to maximize the advantages and minimize the disadvantages associated with each approach. This dual approach has provided a much richer picture of the metamotivation and emotion involved in high-level slalom canoeing than could have been achieved by the independent use of either approach. It allowed important information to be obtained not only about the experience of the canoeists as a group at a series of events over a competitive season, but also about individual canoeists' experience at these events. This study built on previous arousal discrepancy and tension stress findings, for which it provided support, and underlined the importance of skills that elite athletes have (most of the time) for manipulating metamotivational states at competitions.

Reversal theory is a phenomenological theory about individual experience and it was only through the interviews that the details of metamotivation as the canoeist coped with problems or experienced the successes and failures of competitive slalom canoeing became apparent. The dual approach, using both quantitative and qualitative methods, is recommended where possible for future reversal theory sport research.

# REFERENCES

Apter, M. J. (1982). *The experience of motivation: The theory of psychological reversals*. London: Academic Press.

Apter, M. J. (1992). *The dangerous edge*. New York: Free Press.

Apter, M. J., Mallows, R. & Williams, S. (1998). The development of the Motivational Style Profile. *Personality and Individual Differences*, **24**, 7–18.

Box, G. E. P. & Jenkins, G. M. (1970). *Time series analysis: Forecasting and control*. San Francisco: Holden-Day.

Braathen, E. T. & Svebak, S. (1992). Motivational differences among talented teenage athletes: The significance of gender, type of sport and level of excellence. *Scandinavian Journal of Medicine and Science in Sports*, **2**, 153–159.

Bryan, A. J. (1987). Single subject designs for evaluation of sport psychology interventions. *The Sport Psychologist*, **1**, 283–292.

Bushe, G. R. & Bushe, V. (1991). *Attending to others: interviewing for insight*. Vancouver, BC: Discovery & Design Inc.

Cohen, J. (1960). A coefficient of agreement for nominal scales. *Educational and Psychological Measurement*, **20** (1), 37–46.

Cox, T. & Kerr, J. H. (1989). Arousal effects during tournament play in squash. *Perceptual and Motor Skills*, **69**, 1275–1280.

Cox, T. & Kerr, J. H. (1990). Self-reported mood in competitive squash. *Personality and Individual Differences*, **11** (2), 199–203.

Eklund, R. C. (1993). Considerations for gaining entry to conduct sport psychology field research. *The Sport Psychologist*, **7**, 232–243.

Gottman, J. M. & Glass, G. G. (1978). Analysis of interrupted time-series experiments. In T. R. Kratochwill (Ed.), *Single subject research: Strategies for evaluating change* (pp. 197–235). New York: Academic Press.

Kerr, J. H. (1987). Differences in the motivational characteristics of 'professional', 'serious amateur' and 'recreational' sports performers. *Perceptual and Motor Skills*, **64**, 379–382.

Kerr, J. H. (1991). Arousal-seeking in risk sport participants. *Personality and Individual Differences*, **12** (6), 613–616.

Kerr, J. H. (1993). An eclectic approach to psychological interventions in sport: Reversal theory. *The Sport Psychologist*, **7**, 400–418.

Kerr, J. H. (1997). *Motivation and emotion in sport: Reversal theory*. Hove, UK: Psychology Press.

Kerr, J. H. & Cox, T. (1988). Effects of metamotivational dominance and metamotivational state on squash task performance. *Perceptual and Motor Skills*, **67**, 171–174.

Kerr, J. H. & Cox, T. (1990). Cognition and mood in relation to the performance of a squash task. *Acta Psychologica*, **73** (1), 103–114.

Kerr, J. H. & Cox, T. (1991). Arousal and individual differences in sport. *Personality and Individual Differences*, **12** (10), 1075–1085.

Kerr, J. H. & Svebak, S. (1989). Motivational aspects of preference for and participation in risk sports. *Personality and Individual Differences*, **10**, 797–800.

Kerr, J. H. & Svebak, S. (1994). The acute effects of participation in sports on mood. *Personality and Individual Differences*, **16** (1), 159–166.

Kerr, J. H. & Vlaswinkel, E. H. (1993). Self-reported mood and running. *Work and Stress*, **7** (3), 161–177.

Krane, V., Andersen, M. B. & Strean, W. B. (1997). Issues of qualitative research methods and presentation. *Journal of Sport and Exercise Psychology*, **19**, 213–218.

Kreiner-Phillips, K. & Orlick, T. (1993). Winning after winning: The psychology of ongoing excellence. *The Sport Psychologist*, **7**, 31–48.

Kvale, S. (1994). Ten standard objections to qualitative research interviews. *Journal of Phenomenological Psychology*, **25**, (2), 147–173.

Lincoln, Y. S. & Guba, E. G. (1985). *Naturalistic inquiry*. Newbury Park, CA: Sage.

Mackay, C. J., Cox, T., Burrows, G. C. & Lazzerini, A. J. (1978). An inventory for the measurement of self-reported stress and arousal. *British Journal of Social and Clinical Psychology*, **17**, 283–284.

Males, J. R. (1996, October). *A comparison of pre-competitive mood and stress in elite male lacrosse and volleyball players*. Paper presented at the 1st International Workshop on Motivation and Emotion in Sport: Reversal Theory, Tsukuba, Japan.

Males, J. R. & Kerr, J. H. (1996). Stress, emotion and performance in elite slalom canoeists. *The Sport Psychologist*, **10**, 17–36.

Males, J. R., Kerr, J. H. & Gerkovich, M. (1998). Metamotivational states during canoe slalom competition: A qualitative analysis using reversal theory. *Journal of Applied Sport Psychology*, **10**, 185–200.

McDermott, M. R. & Apter, M. J. (1988). The Negativism Dominance Scale (NDS). In M. J. Apter, J. H. Kerr & M. P. Cowles (Eds.), *Progress in reversal theory* (pp. 373–376). Advances in Psychology series, 51. Amsterdam: North-Holland/Elsevier.

Mueser, K. T., Yarnold, P. R. & Foy, D. W. (1991). Statistical analysis for single case designs: Evaluating outcome of imaginal exposure treatment of chronic PTSD. *Behaviour Modification*, **15**, 134–155.

Murgatroyd, S., Rushton, C., Apter, M. J. & Ray, C. (1978). The development of the Telic Dominance Scale. *Journal of Personality Assessment*, **42**, 519–528.

O'Connell, K. A., Cook, M. R., Gerkovich, M. M., Potocky, M. & Swan, G. E. (1990). Reversal theory and smoking: A state-based approach to ex-smokers' highly tempting situations. *Journal of Consulting and Clinical Psychology*, **58**, 489–494.

Patton, M. Q. (1990). *Qualitative evaluation and research methods*. London: Sage.

Potocky, M., Cook, M. R. & O'Connell, K. A. (1993). The use of an interview and structured coding system to assess metamotivational state. In J. H. Kerr, S. Murgatroyd & M. J. Apter (Eds.), *Advances in reversal theory* (pp. 135–150). Amsterdam: Swets & Zeitlinger.

Schweigert, W. A. (1994). *Research methods and statistics for psychology*. Pacific Grove, CA: Cole Publishing Company.

Siedentop, D. (1989). Do lockers really smell? *Research Quarterly for Exercise and Sport*, **60** (1), 36–41.

Silverman, D. (1994). *Interpreting qualitative data*. London: Sage.

Svebak, S. (1993). The development of the Tension and Effort Stress Inventory (TESI). In J. H. Kerr, S. Murgatroyd & M. J. Apter (Eds.), *Advances in reversal theory* (pp. 189–204). Amsterdam: Swets & Zeitlinger.

Svebak, S. & Kerr, J. H. (1989). The role of impulsivity in preference for sports. *Personality and Individual Differences*, **10** (1), 51–58.

Svebak, S. & Murgatroyd, S. (1985). Metamotivational dominance: A multimethod validation of reversal theory. *Journal of Personality and Social Psychology*, **48**, 519–528.

Svebak, S., Ursin, H., Endresen, I., Hjelmen, A. M. & Apter, M. J. (1991). Back pain and the experience of stress, efforts and moods. *Psychology and Health*, **5**, 307–314.

Vlaswinkel, E. H. & Kerr, J. H. (1990). Negativism dominance in risk and team sports. *Perceptual and Motor Skills*, **70**, 289–290.

# 6

# Links between Motivational and Biological Factors in Sport: A Review

Sven Svebak

*The Norwegian University of Science and Technology, Norway*

## INTRODUCTION

A capacity for long-term planning and goal-directed behaviour is essential in the development of excellence in sport, and the biological substrate for these motivational functions in the brain resides within the frontal lobes. This capacity may be exclusively taken care of by the individual and thus be part of a personality profile. It may also be taken care of by a surrounding team of supporters and coaches who compensate for a lack of these talents in the promising athlete. However, these psychosocial prerequisites for sport excellence cannot work unless they are supported by biological processes that involve the skeletal muscles. The bio-psycho-social interrelationship in metabolic activation is cultivated to become a major source of

*Experiencing Sport: Reversal Theory.* Edited by J. H. Kerr.
© 1999 John Wiley & Sons Ltd.

excellence in the elite athlete, and it may even define level of enjoyment in low-level sport performers. It is the purpose of this chapter to explore the nature of some such relationships in particular groups of sports.

Goal-directed behaviour and planning orientation have been defined in reversal theory as characteristics of the telic state, as opposed to impulsivity and action orientation that are key characteristics of the paratelic state. Ideas on the relevance of these so-called metamotivational states for sport preference as well as excellence will be at focus. This is not to downgrade the significance of less well-researched psychobiological relations with the other pairs of metamotivational states defined in reversal theory (mastery versus sympathy, conformity versus negativism, autic versus alloic; see Apter 1982, 1989). Related psychobiological studies will be reviewed briefly. They focus on the relationship between sport preference, biological process and the telic versus paratelic states. The studies were initiated from the perspective of reversal theory, and they involve recreational as well as competitive sport. Several studies focused upon particular electromyographical response characteristics of skeletal muscles in perceptual-motor model situations in the laboratory. Findings from these studies are presented within a broader context of personality to bring out implications for understanding exercise preferences, enjoyment of sport, psychobiological sources of success in particular types of competitive sport, as well as the potential for exercise in maintaining good health and in the rehabilitation of alcohol-abusing individuals.

## SOME BASIC IDEAS

Social comparison is at focus in competitive sport. Teenage high-level sport performance has become extremely competitive in recent years. The commercial side of modern high-level sport performance involves powerful extrinsic motivational rewards (monetary, heroic public image) which may play a significant role in achievement motivation by stretching the biological potential to its ultimate limit during competition. The joint effect of extrinsic and intrinsic sources of motivation are likely to define the often marginal differences in time, force or distance needed to distinguish between success and failure in modern high-level sport performance, whereas this is not at focus in low-level sport and non-competitive physical exercise.

The intimate association between motivation and movement was acknowledged several thousand years ago, as is implicit in the term *motivation* which is derived from the Latin word *motivus* (movement). The related word *movere* simply means to induce movement. Motivation is a central component of personality. Kaplan, Sadock, and Grebb (1994) defined personality as 'the totality of emotional and behavioral traits that characterize the person . . . ' (p. 731). This definition left motivational and cognitive components of personality out of focus. It fails to capture the most significant aspect of personality when studying excellence in sport, which means it will not work well within sport and perhaps not even within psychiatry. The close relationship between motivation and emotion has been acknowledged in the Latin origin where the analogy to physical movement implies that emotions are 'movements' of the mind, if not also of the body. Both motivational and emotional processes are intimately dependent upon biological mechanisms involved in metabolic activity, and the field of sport provides numerous examples of the close relations between movement, motivation and even extremely intense emotional experience and display.

A multivariate approach is capable of testing the interrelationship and relevance of many independent factors that may operate to define excellence and enjoyment in a particular sport. The multifactorial approach, therefore, can bring out patterns of constellations that are unique to individual sports as opposed to team sports, or to endurance sports (e.g., long-distance running) as opposed to explosive sports (e.g., sprint). Some of the studies cited below reflect the distinction between amateur and competitive sports, as well as individual versus team sports. Taken together, these studies present a triangulation of methodological approaches in research, including (1) experimental psychophysiology, (2) survey, and (3) qualitative interviewing. This methodological triangulation has shed light upon a set of theoretical assumptions on relations between (a) *biological composition*, (b) *motivational characteristics* of the individual, and (c) *choice of sport*. Some assumptions about specific constellations of characteristics

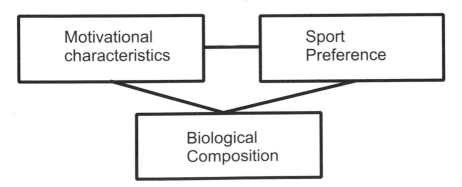

**Figure 6.1**   A schematic illustration of the triangular relation between factors that may, or may not, fit together and that, therefore, define the potential for enjoyment in physical exercise and success in competitive sport (from Svebak, 1990)

within these three domains are proposed to optimize enjoyment and competitive success in sport. Other constellations are suggested as cases of mismatch with dysfunctional outcome.

The basic elements in the triangular relationship that can present with pairwise match or mismatch are shown in Figure 6.1 (see Svebak, 1990, for a more detailed account). One example of a mismatch between one pair of elements in Figure 6.1 would be the individual who is biologically (genetically) talented for performing a kind of sport that is different from the one that is actually performed (the right side of the triangle in Figure 6.1). For example, a genetically determined predominance of aerobic fibres may be present in the leg muscles, and the individual's choice of sport is weightlifting. It is assumed that this individual will experience, intuitively, that there is no fun in trying to develop skills in weightlifting. Displeasure will be provoked more intensely if ambitions are to achieve excellence. Being forced to continue provokes displeasure, frustration, and negativistic opposition.

Another example of a mismatch is the telic dominant individual who habitually avoids situations that provoke high levels of felt arousal because they give rise to anxiety rather than excitement. A discrepancy is present when this individual chooses a sport with arousal-boosting elements of danger or threat of physical damage, such as downhill skiing (upper side of the triangle in Figure 6.1).

A third class of mismatch concerns discrepancies between motivational and biological dispositions (the left side of the triangle in Figure 6.1). For example, a child may have established a predominance for planning ahead (which has facilitated frontal lobe processing). On the biological side, in contrast, the child's skeletal muscles are genetically structured with a predominance of fast-twitch fibres, which are ideally suited for explosive short bursts of high force on impulse. The choice of an endurance sport like marathon, for example, which takes some planning to complete as well as tolerance for monotony, would match the motivational characteristics, while being at odds with genetic disposition. Endurance sports may be preferred on psychological grounds by a child, for example in order to be with friends who enjoy endurance sport performance, while genetically the skeletal muscles abound in fast-twitch fibres ideally suited for short bursts of high force. The biological talent is then again at odds with the choice. In general, when biological talents are not matched with psychological characteristics, there is an increased risk of frustration with any kind of sport activity; one type or other of motivational mismatch with muscular demands is likely to be the outcome. As in the first example, the salience of frustration increases with pushing hard to achieve excellence.

Reversal theory has defined four pairs of opposite motivational states of consciousness, as indicated earlier. Figure 6.2 includes one characteristic from each of two pairs of states which have been applied in empirical

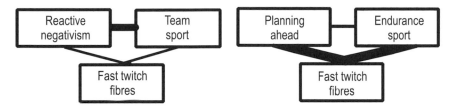

**Figure 6.2**    Two illustrations of hypothesized triangular mismatch between specific factors that define a risk of low enjoyment, frustration, and poor performance in sports (thick lines represent pairs at mismatch)

research (so-called reactive negativism (negativism) versus conformity, and planning ahead (telic) versus impulsivity (paratelic); see e.g., Apter & Smith, 1985).

Three examples of discrepancies have been introduced into Figure 6.2 to bring out ideas on more complex relations between pairs of metamotivational opposites and biological and behavioural dimensions. These distinctions are between (1) fast- versus slow-twitch fibres in skeletal muscles (implied in both panels), (2) team versus individual sports (implied in the left panel), and (3) explosive versus endurance sports (implied in the right panel). Of course, these distinctions present simplified perspectives on striate muscles as well as on types of sport and motivational states. However, they are introduced because they may help to bring out the structure of the argument in the simplest possible way.

The left panel defines a person who is dominated by reactive negativism (i.e., the inclination to respond with anger to frustrations and provocations induced by some other person), and is also a player of a team sport (e.g., soccer). This person is at constant high risk of responding with anger or sullenness due to frustrations provoked by poor performance by other members in his or her team and/or by superior performance in the opposing team. Although adrenaline may be boosted by anger, and thus help facilitate muscular metabolism, the social strain on the team from such negativistic behaviour may override the beneficial metabolic effects and cause reduced performance of the team as a whole. If the dominantly negativistic style of responding to frustrations cannot be treated to cause more time to be spent in the conformist state, this person should shift to some individual sport and take advantage of the potential for improved performance that may be provoked by increased adrenaline with reactive negativism. The distinction between endurance (slow-twitch) and explosive (fast-twitch) muscle fibre dominance may be of less importance in this sport (soccer) because both biological talents can add to the success of a team, provided the player is occupying a position on the field where performance demands are in concert with the biological talent.

There is a need to explore the significance of such discrepancies when counselling individuals who are physically inactive and who find it difficult to become involved in regular physical exercise. One aim of this kind of research is to make people involved in physical education and competitive sport become more sensitive to individual differences in psycho-bio-behavioural constellations of significance for enjoyment or frustration in exercise and sport. It should be an obvious human right for every child to support his or her ego-development by exploring a range of possibilities for finding intrinsically rewarding ways to be physically active with exercise or sport as a socializing agent. No child should be misled into believing that he or she is not capable of being physically active. It is likely that such misconceptions are solely the consequence of a more or less random mismatch between exposure to a narrow range of culturally acceptable or available sports and the psychobiological characteristics of that child.

# EARLY FINDINGS ON PSYCHOLOGICAL CONSEQUENCES OF SPORT PERFORMANCE

It is an old assumption that different types of sport attract different personality types and may even induce addiction in some individuals (see Taylor, Sallis, & Needle, 1985, for an early review). Henry (1941) and Harlow (1951) were among the first to study sport-specific personality types. One conclusion from their research was that body builders suffer from masculine inadequacy. More recent evidence by Thirer and Greer (1981) failed to support this view. Personality differences have also been suggested between team and individual sport performers (Schurr, Ashley, & Joy, 1977). Team sport athletes were found to be more anxious, dependent and extroverted than were individual sport athletes, thus suggesting a predominance of telic and conformist states. Performers of team sports with a marked element of antagonistic interaction (basketball, football, soccer) were more independent and scored higher on measures of ego-strength than did performers of so-called parallel sports (volleyball, baseball), thus suggesting a bias towards autic and negativistic dominance. There is a pattern of weak support for personality profile differences among performers of different sports when traditional measures of personality, such as the Cattell 16-PF test, have been used.

More success has been achieved with a sport-specific motivational orientation. One example is Gavin (1988), who distinguished performers of different sports according to their profiles from responding to items on seven personality dimensions: (1) sociability, (2) spontaneity, (3) discipline, (4) aggressiveness, (5) competitiveness, (6) mental focus, and (7) risk taking. The typical golfer was described as sociable, competitive, and mentally focused, and with little spontaneity and discipline. The typical body builder was described as high on aggressiveness and discipline, whereas the typical long-distance runner scored high on discipline but low on spontaneity, mental focus, and risk taking. Downhill skiing, in contrast, appeared to attract people with high spontaneity, competitiveness, and risk taking, as well as low scores on discipline. One robust early finding appears to be that elevated behavioural vigour and low depression characterize the successful athlete (Morgan, 1980).

Pargman (1986) presented an extensive review and analysis of motivational factors in sport. His orientation focused upon motivational styles that related to the telic state (goal or consequence orientation). More recently, achievement goal theory (Nicholls, 1989) has been the major theoretical focus in motivational sport psychology, and a distinction has been made between ego- versus task-involvement. The former implies social comparison, whereas the latter involves improving one's own achievement. Recent evidence suggests that elite athletes tend to score high on measures of both motivational orientations (Duda & White, 1992; Roberts & Ommundsen, 1996). Duda (1993) suggested that there is a relationship between these motivational trait-based processes and stress responses in sport performance that has not yet been explored. However, when looking at these approaches from the perspective of reversal theory, both ego- and task-involvement are facets of the telic state because they are consequence oriented rather than activity oriented. There is a risk in this biased orientation to motivation in sport of downgrading the fact that, at least for some people and in some sports, the activity is performed mainly for the fun that it provides in itself. This means that physical exercise and competitive sport may sometimes be performed within motivational states indistinguishable from those that prevail in play (see Kerr, 1997; Svebak & Stoyva, 1980). Without this distinction between serious-mindedness and fun, studies of stress responses in sport performance may not provide much psychobiological meaning.

Another side of this early research and bias towards achievement goal perspectives in current sport research is the lack of assumptions about underlying biological mechanisms that may be implicated in explaining why these personality traits or states may relate to successful sport performance. If such relations are more than just circumstantial, there must be a range of mediating mechanisms to account for the transactions between personality, behaviour, and biological processes, and these mechanisms must be biological in nature because sport performance is inherently biologically anchored in the coordination of sensory-motor control and related metabolic activation. Moreover, these processes would have no personal or social meaning unless there is a motivational and social embedding. Psychophysiology is one scientific field that offers the technology and methodology to explore ideas on some of the mediating mechanisms that may be implicated in sport-related enjoyment and excellence.

# MEDIATING MECHANISMS

A major proportion of the research on mental effects of physical exercise has been oriented to aerobic sports in general and to jogging in particular. The mediating mechanisms involved in the mental effects of taking part in such sports are still not well known. Speculations have been made and have focused on the role of self-hypnosis, as well as increased norepinephrine and endorphin release in the central nervous system. These changes have been proposed to account for the so-called 'runner's high' (a trance-like state of hedonia during or right after periods of long-distance running). Callen (1983) reported that more than two-thirds of 424 subjects who had been running for more than one year and for an average of 50 kilometres per week experienced the phenomenon of runner's high. However, other mechanisms may be of greater importance in less peculiar mental effects of aerobic sport and in other types of sport (see Steinberg & Sykes, 1985, for an early critical evaluation of the role of endorphins in effects of sport). It is likely that there is a range of mediating mechanisms, involving major pathways in the interaction of the central nervous system with the metabolic activation in skeletal muscles (pyramidal and extrapyramidal neural pathways from the brain cortex and sub-cortical areas, respectively, to skeletal muscles, sympathetic and parasympathetic autonomic nervous system, including the sympathetic adreno-medullar catecholamine axis, the hypothalamic–hypophyseal–adrenocortical endocrine pathway, the hypophyseal control of thyroxine release, etc.). Some of the significant biological mechanisms may reside in membrane electrolyte permeability of skeletal muscle cells as well as within the muscle fibre, such as in the mitochondrial density and ability to burst elements of the Krebs' cycle (see Reilly, Secher, Snell, & Williams, 1990). There is no point in psychosocial activation of mediating mechanisms if it makes no difference at the cellular level of skeletal muscle metabolism.

Most of the triangular relationships that can be imagined along this chain of reasoning have not as yet been studied. Furthermore, the most significant mediating mechanisms may be different in nature across different types of sport. Some of them may be genetically defined, like the muscle fibre composition of skeletal muscles, whereas others may be more open to effects of practice and incentives, like synaptic electrochemical impulse transmission. The identification of such differences may shed light upon the optimal choice of sport in health promotion and secondary intervention, as well as be of help in the cultivation of high-level athletic achievement.

# A CLOSER LOOK AT THE BIOLOGICAL CONTEXT

The importance of biological talent for excellence in sport has long been acknowledged and is not a controversial issue in high-level sport performance. Some of these talents are genetically determined characteristics of the skeletal muscles themselves and include the proportion of fast versus slow twitch fibres. Others may relate more to characteristics of the metabolic and circulatory systems. Some talents may even be determined by characteristics of the central nervous system transmitter-related pathways and be reflected in the capacity of the brain to activate and modulate the peripheral biological systems of crucial importance in high-level sport performance.

Adaptive changes in skeletal muscles, as well as in the neuromuscular junction and motor neurons, follow regular exercise. Large doses of endurance training induce increased concentration of myoglobin, glycogen, and triglyceride stores, slow twitch fibre hypertrophy, as well as the improved ability to oxidize fats and carbohydrates. In contrast, the more significant effects of sprint training upon skeletal muscles involve increased ATP–PC system enzyme activities as well as hypertrophy of fast-twitch fibres, with some hypertrophy of slow-twitch fibres. The proportion of fast versus slow twitch fibres seems to remain essentially unaffected by type of exercise and at all dose levels.

High-level endurance athletes show bradycardia (decreased heart rate) and an increased stroke volume when resting. They also show increased haemoglobin content and blood volume, which are both of importance in the transport of oxygen. However, increase in blood volume is essentially due to increase in amount of plasma and is, therefore, of particular significance to the transportation of deep body heat by blood that is flushed out to the peripheral layers of the body and dissipated into the environment with support of the calorie-dependent evaporation of sweating. Endurance training at submaximal levels results in a marked reduction of blood lactic acid, as compared with a relatively moderate reduction of blood lactic level among sprint trainees (Fox, 1984).

Some physiological changes in response to high-level exercise involve sex differences. Although amenorrhea has been documented in approximately one-third of performers of long-distance running, swimming, and among performers of gymnastics during their competitive seasons, menstruation itself seems to have a less detrimental effect upon performance, although individual differences are substantial. One example is the seemingly greater incidence of amenorrhea among females with late onset menarche who had not experienced pregnancy (Dale, Gerlach, & Wilhite, 1979).

Distribution of fibre types throughout the skeletal muscles seems to be more genetically defined and more stable than anything else in the biology of sport. For this reason, fibre composition of skeletal muscles may be of particular significance to the psychobiology of sport and can put up a powerful biological barrier to intended effects of motivational change when it is at mismatch with this biological disposition. This fact is not without theoretical significance, because the latent biological talent, due to fibre type composition, may or may not be optimized by a particular type of motivational characteristic, or may be affected by the choice of a sport that is not in concert with biological composition and/or motivational characteristics, as indicated above in Figures 6.1 and 6.2.

The important implication of fibre composition is that skeletal muscle energy systems relate to fibre composition and have long been acknowledged as important in sport. The ATP–PC (anaerobic or phosphagenic) and LA (lactic acid) systems are of particular significance to the high-level athlete in sports such as golf (95%), short-distance track and field (98%; 100 and 200 m sprint), volleyball (90%), wrestling (90%), and gymnastics (90%). The $LA–O_2$ (combined lactic acid and aerobic) energy systems dominate in high-level performance of only a few sports, including medium-distance running and swimming (65%; 800m and 200m respectively). The $O_2$ (aerobic) energy system is of particular significance to high-level performance of cross-country skiing and marathon running (95%). These differences between types of sport are illustrated in Table 6.1. One should keep in mind that elite performers of endurance sports score around 70 on tests of maximum oxygen consumption (ml per kg per minute), whereas untrained young adults may score well below 30.

**Table 6.1** Predominance of energy systems in different types of high-level sport performance given as percentages (ATP–AC = phosphagen system; LA = lactic acid system; $O_2$ = aerobic system)

| Sports | Type of energy system | | |
| --- | --- | --- | --- |
|  | ATP–PC/LA | LA–$O_2$ | $O_2$ |
| Track and field 100 m | 98 | 2 | – |
| Golf | 95 | 5 | – |
| Gymnastics | 95 | 5 | – |
| Volleyball | 90 | 10 | – |
| Wrestling | 90 | 10 | – |
| Running 800 m | 30 | 65 | 5 |
| Swimming 200 m | 30 | 65 | 5 |
| Cross-country skiing | – | 5 | 95 |
| Marathon | – | 5 | 95 |
| Recreational sports | – | 5 | 95 |

(Modified from Fox & Mathews, 1974)

# MOTIVATIONAL STYLES AND SPORT PREFERENCES

Arousal seeking is one of the defining features of the paratelic state. This phenomenon relates to the concept of sensation seeking proposed by Zuckerman (e.g., 1983). Rowland, Franken, and Harrison (1986) reported males high on sensation seeking to prefer particular sports such as snooker, water-skiing, and racquetball. In contrast, males low in sensation seeking reported preferences for sports like jogging and hiking. Accordingly, females high in sensation seeking frequently reported preferences for sports like white-water rafting and windsurfing, as contrasted with preferences among females low in sensation seeking who listed preferences for sports like sailing and ballet.

Kerr and Svebak had three Australian samples complete the Telic Dominance Scale (TDS) (Murgatroyd, Rushton, Apter, & Ray, 1978) and Barratt Impulsiveness Scale (BIS) (Barratt, 1985). Scores were computed for serious-mindedness, planning orientation, and arousal avoidance (TDS) as well as for cognitive, non-planning, and motor impulsivity (BIS). Scores were related to sport preferences according to independent classification of 'telic sports' and 'paratelic sports'. Their findings (Svebak & Kerr, 1989) supported the idea that impulsivity (high non-planning, low serious-mindedness; low TDS scores for planning orientation in particular) related to preferences for so-called 'explosive' or 'paratelic' sports (baseball, cricket, touch football, surfing, windsurfing). In contrast, long-distance running was exclusively reported as a preferred sport among high planners, whereas rowing was exclusively preferred and performed by planners as well as by arousal avoiders.

Svebak and Kerr (1989) also concluded that extrinsic barriers due to sex-related social norms in Australian society might prevent some females from fulfilling their wish to perform 'paratelic' sports. In this study, they asked participants what kinds of sport they actually performed, as well as what kinds of sport that they would have preferred to perform if given a free choice. Their findings for males at this point indicated intrinsic barriers due to a lifestyle of high planning orientation and serious-mindedness, as well as low cognitive impulsivity, in males who did not fulfil their wish to perform a paratelic sport.

Kerr and Svebak (1989) also reported data on the relations between motivational lifestyles and preference for, as well as participation in, risk and safe sports. Classification of risk sports was based upon previous studies by Zuckerman (1983) and Rowland et al. (1986). These sports involved especially high levels of physical risk and included motor racing, downhill skiing, canoeing, caving, surfing, water skiing, and windsurfing. These sports were contrasted

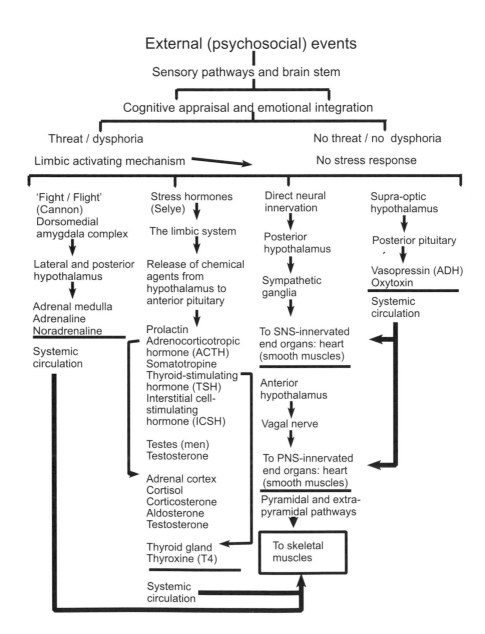

**Figure 6.3**   The four major activating control pathways from the brain to the regulation of metabolic activity in the skeletal muscles (modified from Everly, 1989, p. 42, figure 2.9)

with safe sports such as archery, bowling, frisbee, golf, snooker, and walking/ hiking. Findings supported the hypothesis that participants who opted for risk sports when given a free choice, as well as those who actually performed a risk sport, would score significantly lower on all three subscales of the TDS. This meant that preference for, and performance of a risk sport was associated with relative absence of serious-mindedness, planning orientation, and arousal avoidance.

The individual with a low biological threshold for activation would be at mismatch when opting for a risk sport and, conversely, the individual with a high biological arousal threshold would be at mismatch when becoming involved in endurance types of monotonous sports. These mismatch conditions might be boosted by a confounding factor of metamotivational state that is arousal avoiding in the former case and arousal seeking in the latter. In the former case, high levels of physiological arousal might be provoked beyond that strictly needed from the perspective of musculoskeletal task demands, thus resulting in failure to channel activation into coping well with the task, as well as in subsequent dysphoria in the form of anxiety. Conversely, in the latter case, a generalized state of dysphoria is also likely to develop due to failure to raise the necessary metabolic activity level for performing well and, on top of this, intense boredom, which is the emotional component of experiencing low arousal in the paratelic state, is likely to be experienced. The salience of the confounding metamotivational state must also be reflected in the biological substrate, which means that the more salient the state, the higher the physiological activation level of that substrate will be.

One approach to the study of mediating mechanisms would be to focus upon major activating pathways of the human body. They are described in Figure 6.3, which makes the distinction between the 'fight–flight' pathway, first described by Cannon some 70 years ago, and the stress hormone pathway (Selye, 1974), as well as the pyramidal and extrapyramidal innervation pathways to the skeletal muscles. The autonomic nervous system nerve stimulation of the heart and other smooth muscles via sympathetic and vagal pathways are also included, as well as the hormonal stimulation of smooth muscles that are activated when in a relaxed physical as well as calm mental state.

A talent for fight is an element in all competitive sport. This talent is more than just effortful active coping, because effort is always embedded within some constellation of metamotivational states. Proactive negativism is often instrumental. The Cannon pathway activates catecholamine production and thus boosts skeletal muscle metabolism, also indirectly by effects upon cardiovascular circulation. Combined with activation of the neural pathways to smooth and skeletal muscles, the psychobiological capacity for fight makes up the kind of good stress response, often termed *eustress*, which is a characteristic of successful coping. At a general conceptual level, therefore, the cate-cholamine axis and neuroelectric stimulation of muscles provide the candidate for a biological pattern of effortful activation in any combination of meta-motivational states which give rise to pleasant emotional experiences. In con-trast, *distress* (Selye, 1974) involves the pituitary–adrenocortical axis and appears to be more implicated in effortful failure to cope. Moreover, an ability to reverse from high to low levels of biological activation between competi-tions and strenuous practice may involve the fourth axis of smooth muscle hormonal stimulation that facilitates digestion and restoration, and it may be boosted by spending these periods mainly in the paratelic, conformist and sympathy metamotivational states.

These ideas are in concert with psychobiological research that was not founded upon reversal theory (e.g., the extensive psychobiological analysis of the process of learning to cope with parachuting; Ursin, Baade, & Levine, 1978). However, reversal theory has never claimed a need for a new psychobiology of man. Instead, reversal theory appears to offer a more sensitive psychological approach to the complex and often seemingly para-doxical processes of motivation and emotion that are involved in coping with stressors like those in sport.

# SPECIFIC PSYCHOPHYSIOLOGICAL APPROACHES TO MOTIVATION IN SPORT

A series of psychophysiological studies have been reported on biological substrates of the telic and paratelic metamotivational states. Most of these studies recruited participants according to measures of dominance rather than of state (see Apter & Svebak, 1992, for a review). Results from these studies, taken together, have documented systematic relations between particular types of motivational styles, sport preference and electro-myographic (EMG) activation patterns in skeletal muscles. Results have consistently demonstrated a trend for elevated EMG levels in muscles not strictly involved in perceptual-motor task performance among participants with a bias towards planning orientation and serious-mindedness, whereas such EMG background muscle tension was almost absent among individ-uals with an impulsive and playful lifestyle (e.g., Braathen & Svebak, 1990; Svebak, 1984; Svebak & Murgatroyd, 1985). The findings on sport prefer-ence, motivational style, and muscle response pattern provided a strong argument for a close look at muscle fibre composition, assessed from ana-lyses of biopsies from leg muscles.

One biopsy study has been performed so far to shed light upon the assumption of triangular relations proposed above (Figure 6.1). Results supported a genetically defined predominance of slow-twitch fibres among serious-minded and planning-oriented individuals, whereas a predominance of fast-twitch muscle fibres was seen among individuals with EMG responses associated with a playful and impulsive lifestyle (Svebak *et al.*, 1993). None of the participants in the biopsy study were active athletes.

All these studies, taken together, gave support to a triangular relationship between (1) motivational style, (2) biological predisposition, and (3) preference for, if not also excellence in, a particular type of sport (see Svebak, 1990).

# ELECTROMYOGRAPHIC FINDINGS FROM ELITE PERFORMERS OF DIFFERENT SPORTS

The examples of match/mismatch given above (Figure 6.2) may be of particular relevance to elite performance in sport. In one such study, Braathen and Svebak (1990) compared EMG recordings from elite athletes in 'explosive' sports, 'endurance' sports, and so-called 'mixed' sports when all performed a perceptual-motor task in the laboratory. All 26 participants in that study had won at least a bronze medal in a national contest over the preceding two years, and many had won medals in international competitions. The participants were recruited to the psychophysiological laboratory to form subgroups of endurance (cross-country skiing, long-distance running, etc.) and explosive (sprint, boxing, high jump, etc.) sports, balanced for gender, and the mean age was between 21 and 22 years. Results from the seemingly 'passive' (left) forearm, when the active (right) forearm was operating the joy-stick, are given in Figure 6.4.

The electromyographic changes seen in the group of endurance sport performers, included in Figure 6.4, present a pattern over the course of task performance that was termed a *physiological gradient* some 30 years ago (Malmo, 1965). The results supported the prediction that EMG gradients would be relatively high in elite performers of endurance sports. (One should keep in mind that such excellence is not possible without a predominance of slow-twitch muscle fibres.) The group of high-level explosive sport performers almost failed to respond with anything like electromyographic gradient activation during perceptual-motor task performance.

The EMG gradients reflect low, but systematic, build-up of muscle tension in muscles that are not strictly called upon by the extrinsic nature of the task. These gradient-related tension patterns are not typically perceptible by the participant. This means that the gradients are provoked by activation of motor neurons in the extrapyramidal pathways from the brain

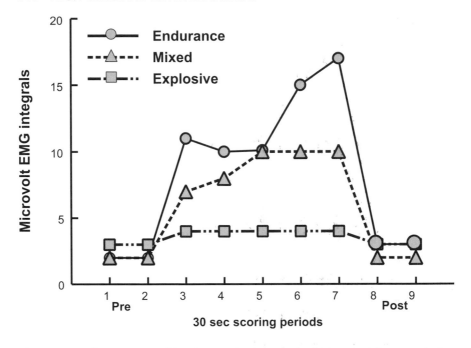

**Figure 6.4**   Electromyographic changes in the seemingly 'passive' forearm during the performance of a perceptual-motor task (video game) where the active forearm operated the joy-stick. Groups were recruited among elite performers of 'explosive', 'endurance', and 'mixed' types of sports (from Braathen & Svebak, 1990)

to these muscles. They may provide a functional platform of stabilizing muscle tension for instrumental planned movements channelled through the corticospinal pathways (pyramidal) that is the neural substrate for conscious motor control. Actions on impulse appear to depend less upon these enduring tension patterns and more upon a predominance of fast-twitch muscle fibres.

## PROSPECTIVE APPROACHES

Biological dispositions alone do not make a successful athlete. Biological talent has to be cultivated through time-consuming and effort-demanding practice. In this learning of sensory-motor skills, psychological characteristics are of extreme importance to the distinction between success and failure at high levels of athletic competition. For this reason, a long-term study of approximately 350 talented teenage performers of different sports in Norway was designed. Participants were aged 15 to 16 at the start, and the significance of electromyographic response patterns and a range of psychological characteristics as predictors of differences in level of excellence were investigated three years later.

Measures included sport-specific measures of goal-directed behavioural styles (Sport Orientation Questionnaire; Gill & Deeter, 1988 – subscales on competitiveness, win, and goal orientation), and scales developed within the framework of reversal theory (Telic Dominance Scale; Murgatroyd *et al.*, 1978 – subscales on serious-mindedness, planning orientation, arousal avoidance; Negativism Dominance Scale; McDermott & Apter, 1988 – subscales on reactive negativism, proactive negativism*).

The first psychophysiological study of talented teenage performers of endurance versus explosive sports included a subsample of 65 participants (Braathen & Svebak, 1994). At age 15, EMG findings were less consistent with motivational characteristics and sport preference than were EMG data from young adult elite sport performers. Moreover, results showed that goal and planning orientation, as well as high significance of physical competence, were characteristics of skilled endurance sport performers, whereas skilled performers of explosive sports scored relatively high on proactive negativism and sport-specific competitiveness. These relations in these types of sport failed to stand out among performers at the relatively moderate, although promising level.

Some motivational measures proved to be significant in their prediction of excellence over the three-year follow-up. Generally, skilled athletes at all age levels scored higher than promising athletes at the somewhat less skilful levels on measures of competitiveness. Those highly skilled at age 18 scored moderate on the significance of winning at age 15, thus indicating a reduced vulnerability to negative thinking in response to moderate achievements at the younger age levels (task-involvement rather than ego-involvement). The significance of physical competence was rated increasingly higher over the time period among athletes who later developed the highest levels of excellence. These motivational characteristics of the upper level athletes at age 18 may have facilitated neuromuscular and catecholamine pathway activation rather than pituitary–adrenocortical activation (see Figure 6.3). Obviously, as time goes by throughout adolescence, a selection takes place to bring out a pattern of triangular relationships that appear to become more consistent in the support of sport-specific excellence, as indicated above (Figure 6.4).

---

* The terms *reactive negativism* and *proactive negativism* have been proposed to distinguish between two forms of negativistic motivational states: reactive negativism is an emotional reaction to an interpersonal (extrinsic) disappointment or frustration, whereas proactive negativism is essentially hedonistic with intrinsic sources aiming at fun and excitement in its own right.

# THE USE OF PHYSICAL EXERCISE IN TREATMENT OF ALCOHOL ABUSE

High doses of enduring alcohol consumption affect all physiological systems of the body, including skeletal muscles and the heart (Urbano-Marquez *et al.*, 1989) as well as the brain. The detrimental processes of alcohol abuse damage cell membranes, nerve pathways, neurotransmitters, the intestines, the immune system, etc., resulting in symptoms such as cirrhosis of the liver, pancreatitis, bronchitis, thyroid problems, elevated blood pressure, diabetes, sleep disorders, and impotence (US Department of Health and Human Services, 1983). The overwhelming documentation of extensive degenerative bodily and social consequences of alcohol abuse calls for substantial preventive efforts in the population at large. This is not to downgrade the significance of positive effects of moderate social drinking. These effects include the anxiolytic and cheering consequences of a glass of wine in most individuals and reduced incidence of cardiovascular disease. Interestingly, an inverted U-shape relationship between reported alcohol consumption and mortality has been documented in general among social drinkers (Marmot, Rose, Shipley, & Thomas, 1981).

In the alcohol-abusing individual, the degenerative biological effects of alcohol present obstacles to psychobiological ambitions in rehabilitation. Psychotherapy and behaviour therapy may thus be counteracted by extensive biological malfunction. For this reason, effects of physical exercise in treatment of alcohol-abusing patients may turn out to be important in themselves and also, in a more indirect way, in supporting long-term effects of more traditional therapeutic interventions.

In concert with the triangular relations outlined in Figures 6.1 and 6.2 above, the use of exercise in rehabilitation of alcohol-abusing males was tested in a project at an inpatient clinic in Western Norway (see Svebak, 1996). All patients were males, and they stayed at the clinic for five weeks. They were admitted after being at least two weeks free from alcohol consumption. The control group was offered the usual treatment, where it was left to the patient to spend or not to spend time on some kind of physical exercise. Most patients spent little, if any, time on such exercise when not encouraged by staff. In the 'treatment' groups, in contrast, patients had to commit themselves to taking part in regular training sessions three days per week. One treatment group performed 'basic training' (mixture of aerobic and strength promotion). The other treatment group was given the opportunity to practise a sport that they labelled as 'most preferable', while also taking part in basic training sessions.

The exercise component of rehabilitation represented a marked change from traditional treatment programmes at alcohol-abuse intervention clinics in Norway. Emphasis has been on the importance of psychotherapy and group therapy in conjunction with occupational therapy and medication. For much of the time, patients sit in small groups chatting with each other, smoking cigarettes, or just waiting for the next meal. A passive lifestyle of this kind can be expected to cause poor aerobic capacity in everyone, independent of habitual drinking patterns. This type of traditional intervention pays no attention to the fact that alcohol abuse is a psychobiological condition which has detrimental effects upon the skeletal muscles.

It was predicted that, with a reduced likelihood of triangular mismatch between biological composition, motivational style, and exercise activity, the treatment group with a substantial time spent on exercise based upon preferred activity, rather than a standard exercise programme, would be the more likely to adopt a healthy lifestyle in the 12-month period after leaving the clinic, compared with the standard exercise and usual treatment groups.

Sixty-two males were recruited for the project (age range 20–55 years). They all met DSM-III-R criteria for alcohol abuse and dependence and underwent a routine physical examination. Patients with signs of physical diseases that involved risk of physical hazard when involved in exercise (cardiovascular dysfunction, etc.), and patients using beta-adrenergic blocking agents, were excluded. Four of the five weeks at the clinic were available for active treatment.

The usual treatment (control) group numbered 16 males who did not take part in any organized physical training programme. Instead, comparable time was spent on non-sport activities according to preferences and resources in the actual group (e.g., playing cards, cooking, painting, sewing). Time spent on organized non-sport activities in the control group was three sessions per week, and the same amount of time was spent on physical training in the two other treatment groups.

The basic training group comprised 24 males who performed a standard endurance and strength-promoting exercise programme. They spent one hour per day, three days per week, on jogging, swimming, and trail walking, as well as on activities such as weightlifting, sit-ups, and arm push-ups.

In the second treatment group, the two first weeks were spent on endurance and strength-oriented training, while the two last weeks were spent on sports that were perceived by each patient as among the most enjoyable kinds of exercise activities. Approximately 60% of the patients in this group preferred explosive sports like volleyball and tennis, and about 40% preferred aerobic (endurance) activities like swimming and trail walking. The patients in the group with free choice of activities spent the same amount of time per day on organized exercise as did patients in the group with standard training activities.

Analyses of variance confirmed that there was an overall highly significant interaction of the group and time factors due to change from pre- to post-treatment in VO$_2$max. A particularly marked *increase* occurred among patients in the standard training group, whereas a moderate *reduction* of aerobic capacity was computed for the control patients over the internship period.

The typical relapse ratio in Norway over the first year after treatment at a clinic for alcohol-abuse intervention has been around 80%. The highest relapse ratio in the present study was computed for patients in the control group, with those in the standard training condition scoring almost as high as the controls (around 80%). Interestingly, the patients with an element of free choice of physical activities showed a relapse ratio of 50%, and the overall difference between groups was significant at the 5% level (see Svebak, 1996, for more details).

The long-term evaluation of relapse ratio should be viewed as tentative in light of the risk that subjective reports may fail to present the true status of the patient. However, most patients within the 'free choice' group confirmed that they were still active in physical training, whereas most of those in the standard training condition reported having stopped exercising on a regular basis. This tentative information is in concert with the assumption that adherence to a health-promoting lifestyle of physical exercise is strongly dependent upon coordination of the biological composition with motivational characteristics. Moreover, this coordination is of little value unless combined in a triangular relationship that also involves a sport that acts as the ideal behavioural expression of these psychological and biological characteristics. A mismatch is likely to inherently provoke some kind of frustration or lack of enjoyment, whereas coordination fosters enjoyment and may even result in athletic excellence.

# ACKNOWLEDGEMENTS

Most of the author's own research, reviewed in this presentation, was supported by grants from the Norwegian Research Council and funds from the University of Bergen.

# REFERENCES

Apter, M. J. (1982). *The experience of motivation: The theory of psychological reversals*. London: Academic Press.

Apter, M. J. (1989). *Reversal theory: Motivation, emotion and personality*. London: Routledge.

Apter, M. J. & Smith, K. C. P. (1985). Experiencing personal relationships. In M. J. Apter, D. Fontana & S. Murgatroyd (Eds.), *Reversal theory: Applications and developments* (pp. 161–178). Cardiff: University College Cardiff Press.

Apter, M. J. & Svebak, S. (1992). Reversal theory as a biological approach to individual differences. In A. Gale & M. W. Eysenck (Eds.), *Handbook of individual differences: Biological perspectives* (pp. 323–353). Chichester: Wiley.

Barratt, E. S. (1985). Impulsiveness substraits: Arousal and information processing. In J. T. Spence & C. E. Izard (Eds.), *Motivation, emotion and personality*. Amsterdam: Elsevier.

Braathen, E. T. & Svebak, S. (1990). Task-induced tonic and phasic EMG response patterns and psychological predictors in elite performers of endurance and explosive sports. *International Journal of Psychophysiology*, **9**, 21–30.

Braathen, E. T. & Svebak, S. (1994). EMG response patterns and motivational styles as predictors of performance and discontinuation in explosive and endurance sports among talented teenage athletes. *Personality and Individual Differences*, **17**, 545–556.

Callen, K. (1983). Mental and emotional aspects of long-distance running. *Psychosomatics*, **24**, 133–151.

Dale, E., Gerlach, D. H. & Wilhite, A. L. (1979). Menstrual dysfunction in distance runners. *Obstetric Gynecology*, **54**, 47–53.

Duda, J. L. (1993). Goals: A social cognitive approach into the study of achievement motivation in sport. In R. N. Singer, M. Murphy & L. K. Tennant (Eds.), *Handbook of research on sport psychology* (pp. 421–437). New York: Macmillan.

Duda, J. L. & White, S. A. (1992). Goal orientations and beliefs about the causes of sport success among elite skiers. *The Sport Psychologist*, **6**, 334–343.

Everly, G. S. (1989). *A clinical guide to the treatment of the human stress response*. New York: Plenum Press.

Fox, E. L. (1984). *Sport physiology* (2nd edn.). Tokyo: Holt-Saunders.

Fox, E. L. & Mathews, D. K. (1974). *Interval training: Conditioning for sports and general fitness*. Philadelphia: W. B. Saunders.

Gavin, J. (1988). *Body moves: The psychology of exercise*. New York: Stackpole Books.

Gill, D. L. & Deeter, T. E. (1988). Development of the Sport Orientation Questionnaire. *Research Quarterly for Exercise and Sport*, **59**, 191–202.

Harlow, R. G. (1951). Masculine inadequacy and compensatory development of physique. *Journal of Personality*, **19**, 312–323.

Henry, F. M. (1941). Personality differences in athletes, physical education and aviation students. *Psychological Bulletin*, **38**, 745.

Kaplan, H. I., Sadock, B. J. & Grebb, J. A. (1994). *Kaplan and Sadock's synopsis of psychiatry: Behavioral sciences, clinical psychiatry*. Baltimore: Williams & Wilkins.

Kerr, J. H. (1997). *Motivation and emotion in sport: Reversal theory*. London: Psychology Press.

Kerr, J. H. & Svebak, S. (1989). Motivational aspects of preference for, and participation in, 'risk' and 'safe' sports. *Personality and Individual Differences*, **10**, 797–800.

Malmo, R. B. (1965). Physiological gradients and behavior. *Psychological Bulletin*, **64**, 25–234.

Marmot, M. G., Rose, G., Shipley, M. J. & Thomas, J. B. (1981). Alcohol and mortality: A U-shaped curve. *Lancet*, **1**, 580–583.

McDermott, M. R. & Apter, M. J. (1988). The Negativism Dominance Scale (NDS). In M. J. Apter, J. H. Kerr & M. P. Cowles (Eds.), *Progress in reversal theory* (pp. 373–376). Amsterdam: North-Holland/Elsevier.

Morgan, W. P. (1980). The trait psychology controversy, *Research Quarterly for Exercise and Sport*, **51**, 59–76.

Murgatroyd, S., Rushton, C., Apter, M. J. & Ray, C. (1978). The development of the Telic Dominance Scale. *Journal of Personality Assessment*, **42**, 519–528.

Nicholls, J. G. (1989). *The competitive ethos and democratic education*. Cambridge, MA: Harvard University Press.

Pargman, D. (1986). *Stress and motor performance: Understanding and coping*. New York: Mouvement Publications.

Reilly, T., Secher, N. Snell, P. & Williams, C. (Eds.) (1990). *Physiology of sports*. London: E & FN Spon.

Roberts, G. C. & Ommundsen, Y. (1996). Effects of goal orientations on achievement beliefs, cognition and strategies in team sports. *Scandinavian Journal of Medicine and Science in Sports*, **6**, 46–56.

Rowland, G. L., Franken, R. E. & Harrison, K. (1986). Sensation seeking and participation in sporting activities. *Journal of Sport Psychology*, **8**, 212–220.

Selye, H. (1974). *Stress without distress*. Philadelphia: Lippincott.

Steinberg, H. & Sykes, E. A. (1985). Introduction to symposium on endorphins and behavioural processes: Review of literature on endorphins and exercise. *Pharmacology, Biochemistry and Behavior*, **23**, 857–862.

Schurr, K. T., Ashley, M. A. & Joy, K. L. (1977). A multivariate analysis of male athlete characteristics: Sport type and success. *Multivariate Experimental Clinical Research*, **3**, 53–68.

Svebak, S. (1984). Active and passive forearm flexor tension patterns in the continuous perceptual-motor task paradigm: The significance of motivation. *International Journal of Psychophysiology*, **2**, 167–176.

Svebak, S. (1990). Personality and sports participation. In G. P. H. Hermans & W. L. Mosterd (Eds.), *Sports, medicine and health* (pp. 87–96). Amsterdam: Elsevier Science Publishers (Biomedical Division).

Svebak, S. (1996). Alcohol abuse, physical fitness and the prevention of relapse. In J. H. Kerr, A. Griffiths & T. Cox (Eds.), *Workplace health, employee fitness and exercise* (pp. 145–157). London: Taylor & Francis.

Svebak, S., Braathen, E. T., Sejerstad, O. M., Bowim, B., Fauske, S. & Laberg, J. C. (1993). Electromyographic activation and proportion of fast versus slow twitch muscle fibers: A genetic disposition for psychogenic muscle tension. *International Journal of Psychophysiology*, **15**, 43–49.

Svebak, S. & Kerr, J. H. (1989). The role of impulsivity in preference for sports. *Personality and Individual Differences*, **10**, 51–58.

Svebak, S. & Murgatroyd, S. (1985). Metamotivational dominance: A multimethod validation of reversal theory constructs. *Journal of Personality and Social Psychology*, **48**, 107–116.

Svebak, S. & Stoyva, J. (1980). High arousal can be pleasant and exciting: The theory of psychological reversals. *Journal of Biofeedback and Self-Regulation*, **5**, 439–444.

Taylor, C. B., Sallis, F. J. & Needle, R. (1985). The relation of physical activity and exercise to mental health. *Public Health Reports*, **100**, 195–201.

Thirer, J. & Greer, D. L. (1981). Personality characteristics associated with beginning, intermediate and competitive body builders. *Journal of Sport Behavior*, **4**, 3–11.

Urbano-Marquez, A., Estruch, R., Navarro-Lopez, F., Grau, J. M., Mont, L. & Rubin, E. (1989). The effect of alcoholism on skeletal and cardiac muscle. *The New England Journal of Medicine*, **320**, 409–415.

Ursin, H., Baade, E. & Levine, S. (Eds.) (1978). *Psychobiology of stress: A study of coping men*. New York: Academic Press.

US Department of Health and Human Services (1983). *Alcohol and health (Fifth special report to the U.S. Congress)*. Rockvill, MD: Author.

Zuckerman, M. (1983). Sensation seeking and sports. *Personality and Individual Differences*, **4**, 285–293.

# SECTION III

# RECREATIONAL PARTICIPANTS

# 7

# The Experience of Risk Sport: Dominance, States, and Injuries

**Nicola A. Cogan** and **R. Iain F. Brown**

*University of Glasgow, Scotland*

## INTRODUCTION

In recent years there has been a dramatic increase in the number of participants engaging in high-risk leisure activities such as mountain climbing, sky diving, parachute jumping, extreme skiing, and snowboarding. Risk sports are characterized by physical and psychological challenges encountered by participants as they confront elements of the environment. In these sports there may be inherent risks in terms of natural and unpredictable danger and the quality of instruction and equipment may be of critical importance to the participant's safety (Hargarten, 1996).

Not only are more people participating in these activities, but their demographics include a widening range and a growing number of female participants (Celsi, 1992). Further, through increased media coverage these activities have been used in advertising to promote various soft drinks, alcohol, and even holidays. For instance, recall recent TV advertisements,

*Experiencing Sport: Reversal Theory.* Edited by J. H. Kerr.
© 1999 John Wiley & Sons Ltd.

including a skydiver on a surfboard freefalling for a Coca Cola, or the parachutist on a slalom ski, skimming over the top of a body of water with the voice-over 'Life is short, play hard!'. These scenes are breathtaking as each image captures and reflects a growing fascination with the excitement of high-risk sports.

Beyond experimentation and thrill, what is it about playing the edge that attracts and sustains the interest of those few who continue and become veterans of these sports? What motivates people to seek out dangerous sport activities where there is a high degree of risk in terms of physical injury, and even death? Are certain types of people more prone to seek out these activities than others?

From a research perspective, these questions continue to be interesting and challenging areas for investigation.

## MOTIVATION AND RISK SPORTS

Participation in dangerous sports constitutes one of the intriguing problems in motivation theory. If confrontation with danger is related to fear and fear is considered to be the motivation for avoidance behaviour (Heimer, 1988; Piet, 1987), the question remains why certain people seek risk recreational sports. One example of research examining the motivation of individuals who pursue dangerous sport activities in which there is a high risk of physical injury was a study of surfers by Farmer (1992). Fifty surfers responded to questionnaires distributed at surf shops in 12 US cities. The questionnaire contained a modified version of Kenyon's (1968) Physical Activity Attitudinal Scale. The instrument used to measure participants' motivation for surfing contained six categories (vertigo, catharsis, aesthetic, social, health and fitness, competition) which were ranked in order of importance. The study's findings revealed that vertigo, catharsis, and aesthetic rewards were important for surfers, while competition and health and fitness were not. The most important motive for surfing was the pursuit of vertigo. Vertigo activities are usually sought after for their own sake, purely for pleasure as a form of excitement seeking.

Similar findings were obtained by Bakker (1993) in a study examining the motivation of young elite speed skaters. Thirty-two skaters were interviewed to determine the reasons why they were prepared to invest a lot of time in speed skating. Results showed that the participants were primarily motivated by the act of skating itself, which was identified as the sensations, perceptions and self-expressiveness associated with the sport. Fun and enjoyment also appeared to be a key motivation factor for participation.

Based on the results of studies such as Farmer's (1992) and Bakker's (1993), it can be argued that dangerous events are sought when the rewards outweigh the punishments of danger. It could be argued that risk sport activities provide intrinsically rewarding experiences that are unique to this form of sport activity. Since presumably not everyone is willing to take the same risks for the same rewards, personality variables must complement this point of view. The next section outlines personality research which has focused on individual differences in risk sport participation.

## SENSATION SEEKING

The most widely publicized and well-established theory used to explain the personality profile of individuals engaged in high-risk sports was proposed by Zuckerman (1979). He suggested that sensation seekers are attracted to risk behaviour which could be classified by its consequence of physical harm or injury. *Sensation seeking* was referred to as a common underlying and stable trait, and was defined as 'the need for varied, novel and complex sensations and experiences and the willingness to take physical and social risks for the sake of such an experience' (Zuckerman, 1979).

A study conducted by Goma (1991) compared scores on the Sensation Seeking Scale (SSS) (Zuckerman, 1979) of sport participants who engaged in different risky sports (alpinists, mountaineers, and a miscellaneous group of risk sport participants) and those who did not engage in any kind of risky sport activities. Results showed that those who engaged in risky activities differed significantly from the control group, demonstrating high scores on sensation seeking. These results were much in line with those found in a group of skiers by Connelly (1981) and in a group of mountaineers by Fowler, Knorring, and Oreland (1980).

## REVERSAL THEORY, PARADOXICAL BEHAVIOUR, AND DOMINANCE RESEARCH ON RISK SPORT

Reversal theory (Apter, 1982) differs from most other theories of personality since, on the whole, these tend to emphasize consistency and stability in human behaviour. This is not to deny that there may be important types of personality stability. Indeed, reversal theory is also concerned with consistent biases and predispositions which underlie inconsistencies in behaviour and experience (Apter, 1989).

Human beings engage in a whole range of activities that are counterproductive to the maintenance of their health and welfare. For example, risk-sport participants can be distinguished from other athletes by their deliberate seeking out of situations in which there is a high risk of injury or death. This type of behaviour has been termed *paradoxical behaviour* (Apter, 1982). Such behaviour is opposite to that which might be expected if the maintenance of good health and survival of the individual is considered to be of paramount importance. Reversal theory has proved useful in providing a psychological framework for understanding why people engage in potentially harmful sport activities (Apter, 1992). It introduces a new level of analysis into psychological discourse – the metamotivational level.

## Telic Dominance

The first study of risk and safe sport participants' dominance characteristics was carried out using the Telic Dominance Scale (TDS) (Murgatroyd, Rushton, Apter, & Ray, 1978). Kerr and Svebak (1989) examined preference for and participation in risk sports within a student population. Participants were asked to list their first three preferences for summer and winter sports and also up to three summer and winter sports in which they actually participated. Sports classified as high in physical risk of injury, even death, to the participants included downhill skiing, motor racing, surfing, and sailboarding. So-called safe sports with somewhat lower levels of physical risk included archery, bowling, frisbee, golf, and yoga.

In the study's first analysis, a strong significant difference was found on TDS arousal avoidance subscale scores between those who (given a free choice) opted for risk and those who opted for safe sports. Those who opted for risk sports had significantly lower arousal avoidance scores. Group mean differences on TDS serious-mindedness and planning orientation subscale scores also approached significance. Secondly, those who participated in these sports during the summer and winter were compared. It was found that risk sport participants scored significantly lower on the TDS arousal avoidance subscale. For winter sport participants, a significant difference was also found between serious-mindedness subscale scores. Safe winter sport participants scored higher and were therefore more serious than risk winter sport participants. The authors postulated that these results indicate that a preference for and participation in risk sports is strongly associated with a generally paratelic lifestyle.

The study carried out by Kerr and Svebak (1989) concentrated on a general student population. In contrast, Kerr (1991) examined the telic dominance characteristics of more experienced risk and safe sport performers. Regular and in some cases high-level performers of risk sports were actively sought out and recruited as participants. Australian male surfers and sailboarders, both considered to be risk sport participants, were compared with weight trainers, by comparison relatively safe sport performers. The results generally supported reversal theory predictions that risk sport participants would be more paratelic dominant than safe sport participants, as they scored significantly lower on all three subscales of the TDS as well as on total scores. The results of Kerr's study further support the idea that paratelic dominant individuals enjoy high arousal and some actively seek out risk sport where pleasant feelings can be induced.

## Negativism Dominance

Studies examining negativism dominance in the sport context have been relatively few, and have produced mixed findings. Vlaswinkel and Kerr (1990), using a Dutch version of the Negativism Dominance Scale (NDS) (McDermott & Apter, 1988), compared a student group of risk sport participants with a student group of safe sport participants. Results showed that individuals who engaged in the risk sports scored significantly higher on the reactive negativism subscale than participants in safe sports. In an attempt to examine an elite level of performance, Vlaswinkel and Kerr (1990) also examined responses from elite level groups of motor cycle racers (risky), Olympic sailors (less risky) and long-distance runners (safe). Statistical analysis of the NDS scores revealed no significant differences between groups on NDS subscales or on total score.

Chirivella and Martinez (1994) examined the NDS scores of athletes who participated in various sports of progressively different levels of risk (low risk: tennis; intermediate risk: karate; high risk: parasailing). They found that tennis players (low risk) scored significantly higher on both the NDS reactive negativism subscale and total negativism dominance. These results tend to suggest that risk sport participants may be rather conformist and support Goma's (1991) findings that individuals who engage in high physical risk sports generally conformed to social norms.

Research has shown that gender differences have also been identified in this area of investigation. For example, Braathen and Svebak (1992) found that talented teenage male athletes in risk sports scored significantly higher on reactive negativism subscales than female risk sport athletes. McDermott (1988) suggested that, for males, proactive rebelliousness was associated with arousal seeking, while in females it was related to individualism. Similarly, reactive rebelliousness in females was related to high irritability, while in males it was associated with high individualism. Braathen and Svebak's (1992) findings suggest that personality interacts with gender to produce differences in NDS scores, but they do not explain why an individual's subjective experience of risky and dangerous situations can influence risk sport participation.

## RISK PERCEPTION

Analyses of how people perceive risk of harm and how they make decisions based on those perceptions have proved fruitful in the area of dangerous sport behaviour (Greenberg & Schneider, 1995). Risk is partly a function of the objective situation and partly a function of the individual's appraisal of the situation (Rossi & Cereatti, 1993; Zuckerman, 1982). Appraisal of a situation may depend on past exposures to the same or similar risky situations, and on the personality of the individual.

If, as Wilde (1982) suggested, participants are aware of the risks, they must be either purposely seeking them out or prevented from perceiving their severity by what Elkind (1974) described as a 'personal fable', that is, belief in one's immunity from negative consequences. Zuckerman (1979) argued that risk sport participants are high sensation seekers and have a pronounced tendency to underestimate risk in relation to low sensation seekers. These individuals were said to display a sense of indestructibility, a seeming lack of awareness of negative consequences, and bravado or a grandiose show of courage. In contrast, Gonzalez (1994) found that individuals who engage in risk sports were most likely to acknowledge the dangers associated with their activities. Teigen, Brun, and Slovic (1988) analysed what constitutes risk and how people take risks. They concluded that, among successful risk takers, risk taking can be regarded as a form of decision making under uncertainty, where at least one option involves the possibility of loss, harm, or damage.

In relation to risk sport participation, a recent interview with Tom Burt, an American professional snowboarder describing snowboarding in Alaska, illustrates this point:

> Being scared as you imagine your descent on a peak, and knowing it could be your last ever. There are no guarantees. Even with a guide, there is still nothing quite like landing on top of a mountain you know has never seen human foot prints – our turns will be the first. All senses are heightened as we drop – unaware if the first turn will set the whole mountain in motion.
> (*Transworld Snowboarding*, 1997)

Burt is like many risk sport participants who report their experiences of risk as having a kind of duality. Individuals who regularly experience what Apter (1992) has called the 'dangerous edge' describe being scared and afraid, yet at the same time experiencing pleasant excitement. This experience may be a reflection of the emotions associated with rapid reversals between the telic and paratelic states.

# SPORT INJURIES

Dangerous sports can be defined by their high degree of physical risk. Even the most experienced and skilled participants may suffer from painful injuries. For example, in a study examining injuries associated with in-line skating, Ellis and Kierulf (1995) reported that the US Consumer Product Safety Commission estimated that approximately 30,000 injuries were sustained by in-line skaters of all ages and of all levels of experience in 1992. Bladin and McCrory (1995), in an overview of winter sport activities, found that an experienced group of snowboarders had an injury rate two to three times that of other groups.

Recent reports of injuries experienced by professional snowboarders demonstrate the physical dangers associated with this sport. For example, Simon Smith, British snowboard champion, broke his back while riding, and required titanium rods to be inserted to support his spine. He has since bent these rods, but continues to ride despite the pain. Two years ago while riding in Alaska, Matt Goodwill, an American professional snowboarder, fell 50 feet into a crevasse and barely clawed his way up and out. He continues to ride in the extreme Alaskan wilderness.

In a review of research examining injuries associated with skateboarding, in-line skating, snowboarding, and motorcycling, Hargarten (1996) pointed out that the word 'accidents' should not appear in scientific manuscripts describing such injury events. He argued that an accident is an unexpected and undesirable event, something that occurs unexpectedly or unintentionally. He pointed out that these incidents are not unexpected, that there is a pattern to these injury events and that they are therefore predictable.

If serious injuries can be expected as 'part and parcel' of participation in risk sports, then what motivates people to continue to pursue such dangerous activities? The investigation of psychological factors associated with injuries has provided some insight into this seemingly paradoxical behaviour. For example, Connelly (1981) compared skiers, including ski instructors, who reported skiing injuries in the past and skiers who did not report any injuries. He found that skiers who had accidents scored higher on the SSS (Zuckerman, 1979). These results suggest the skiers who suffered injuries took more risks, rather than that they were simply less competent (since the ski instructors were undoubtedly more competent than most skiers) and that there is a relationship between personality characteristics (in this case sensation seeking) and risk of physical injury.

Evidence linking SSS subscales to TDS subscales has suggested that risk sport participants who score high on sensation seeking also score high on arousal seeking (Chirivella & Martinez, 1994). It therefore seemed worthwhile to investigate whether risk sport participants who score high on arousal seeking have experienced a greater number of physical injuries than safe sport participants. It also seemed that a comparison of subjective risk (perception of risk) and objective risk (injuries experienced) might provide greater insight into risk sport participants' motivation for pursing their chosen sport activity.

# A NEW STUDY ON RISK/SAFE SPORTS

Using the underlying framework of reversal theory, Cogan and Brown (1998) examined the relationship between telic and negativism dominance and participation in risk and safe sports using the TDS and the NDS. Since previous studies examining the relationship between negativism dominance and sport participation (Braathen & Svebak, 1992; Vlaswinkel & Kerr, 1990) have produced mixed findings, this appeared to be an especially useful area for investigation.

Previous research has shown that reversal theory presents special problems for the design of research studies (Svebak & Apter, 1987). Although dominance can be measured by using a psychometric measure, such a task may induce the telic state in participants. For this reason, the Telic/Paratelic State Instrument (T/PSI) (Calhoun, 1995; Calhoun & O'Connell, 1995) was used to check that participants would remain in their dominant state (telic or paratelic) throughout the completion of the questionnaire package so that their responses would truly reflect their dominance characteristics.

Using an Injury Behaviour Checklist, the study also examined the pattern of injuries associated with risk sport participation from a psychological perspective. The purpose of this part of the investigation was to demonstrate that risk sports do in fact present undoubted risk of physical injury. Further, a comparison between the participants' perception of risk and their physical risk-taking behaviour was also made (measured by examining injuries sustained by risk and safe sport participants). It was felt that this would aid verification of the relationship between objective physical risk and TDS scores. It was expected that participants scoring high on the TDS would sustain fewer physical injuries. Similarly, an attempt to investigate the relationship between NDS scores and injuries sustained was made in order to determine whether negativism dominance and physical risk taking bear any kind of relationship.

Cogan and Brown (1998) used two groups of sport participants who engaged in one of two different sports as a regular leisure activity. The first group consisted of 36 snowboarders (mean age = 22.22; $SD$ = 1.92). The second group was composed of 26 badminton players (mean age = 21.57; $SD$ = 3.94). Snowboarding was selected as a risk sport and badminton was thought to be, by comparison, a good deal less risky. The two groups were matched for age, sex, education, and ethnicity.

Participants were asked to complete a demographic questionnaire, the TDS, the NDS, the T/PSI, and an Injury Behaviour Checklist which asked participants to indicate whether and how often they had incurred broken bones, muscle strains, serious cuts, experienced shock, or incurred other injuries, both while participating in the target sport (i.e., either badminton or snowboarding) and again in any other sporting activities in which they regularly participated.

The use of the TDS and NDS are well documented in reversal theory research, but the T/PSI is a relatively new instrument. The T/PSI is a 12-item scale with two subscales: serious-minded/playful (7 items) and arousal-avoidant/arousal-seeking (5 items). Scores for each item are totalled to provide a score for each subscale and the total of the two subscales provides an overall T/PSI score (Calhoun, 1995; Calhoun & O'Connell, 1995; see also Appendix B).

The two groups of participants were contacted in different ways. High-risk sport participants were recruited during the 1996–1997 Scottish ski season at the Glencoe Ski Resort. The first step consisted of an on-site interview in order to obtain names and addresses of individuals who were actively involved with the Scottish snowboarding scene. The questionnaires were mailed to the addresses of individuals who agreed to participate further in the study. The mailing included a consent form, a covering letter explaining the purpose of the study (though participants remained unaware of the experimental hypotheses) and a stamped, pre-addressed return envelope. The questionnaires had a key number so that participants could, if they wished, answer them anonymously. Two weeks after the initial mailing, a reminder postcard was sent to all non-respondents. The return rate was 90% for the group of snowboarders. The participants in the control group were badminton players who were contacted at several sport centres in the Glasgow area. If they agreed to participate, they received a questionnaire package in the same way as the other group. The return rate was 60% for the group of safe sport participants.

Independent $t$-tests were used in the treatment of the data, except for the Injury Behaviour Checklist data which was analysed using the Mann–Whitney $U$-test.

# SUMMARY OF RESULTS

Analysis of the demographic data revealed no significant differences between the two groups in age, educational level, employment, ethnicity, or enthusiasm for their chosen sport activities. The only significant differences between risk and safe sport participants were in perceived level of risk ($t = -15.13$, $p < 0.000$) in the sport they pursued and in the length of time involved in their chosen sport activity ($t = 2.3$, $p < 0.025$).

## Reversal Theory Measures

Table 7.1 shows the mean scores and standard deviations for the risk and safe sport participants for total score and each subscale of the reversal theory measures (TDS, NDS, T/PSI), as well as the level of significance.

For the TDS, overall scores showed that safe sport participants were significantly more telic dominant than risk sport participants. They also scored significantly higher on the serious-mindedness and arousal-avoidance subscales. No significant differences between groups were found on the planning-orientation subscale.

NDS results showed that risk sport performers scored significantly higher than safe sport performers on total NDS scores and on proactive

**Table 7.1**  Means and standard deviations for risk and safe sport participants for Telic Dominance Scale (TDS), Negativism Dominance Scale (NDS), and Telic/Paratelic State Instrument (T/PSI) scores (from Cogan & Brown, 1998)

| Variable | Risk | | Safe | | |
| --- | --- | --- | --- | --- | --- |
| | Mean | SD | Mean | SD | p-level |
| **TDS** | | | | | |
| Arousal avoidance | 5.21 | 1.78 | 7.87 | 1.80 | 0.0001 |
| Planning orientation | 5.93 | 1.91 | 6.21 | 1.08 | 0.466 |
| Serious-mindedness | 4.04 | 1.89 | 5.00 | 1.55 | 0.038 |
| Total TDS | 15.18 | 3.37 | 18.98 | 3.21 | 0.0001 |
| **NDS** | | | | | |
| Proactive negativism | 6.47 | 2.86 | 3.96 | 2.51 | 0.001 |
| Reactive negativism | 4.89 | 2.16 | 4.15 | 2.41 | 0.213 |
| Total NDS | 11.36 | 3.83 | 8.12 | 2.63 | 0.000 |
| **T/PSI** | | | | | |
| Serious-minded/Playful | 23.69 | 3.75 | 21.19 | 3.88 | 0.013 |
| Arousal-avoidant/Arousal-seeking | 19.05 | 3.16 | 16.88 | 2.98 | 0.008 |
| Total T/PSI | 42.75 | 5.84 | 38.08 | 4.11 | 0.001 |

negativism, but no significant difference was found between the two groups on the reactive negativism subscale.

Scores on total T/PSI, the serious-minded/playful subscale and the arousal-avoidant/arousal-seeking subscale were significantly different for the two groups. These results confirmed that participants remained in their dominant state throughout the completion of the questionnaire package.

## Injury Behaviour Checklist

Risk sport participants were found to have experienced significantly more injuries across all categories (broken bones, muscle strains, serious cuts, concussion, shock, other) than safe sport participants (see Table 7.2). The most significant finding was for the 'broken bones' item, suggesting that risk sport participants also experienced more severe injuries through sport participation.

A similar analysis of participants' scores on injury items for additional sport activities (see Table 7.2) revealed that risk sport participants experienced significantly more broken bones, muscle strains, and serious cuts than safe sport participants.

The analysis of injuries sustained by risk and safe sport participants indicated that individuals who engage in dangerous sport activities are undoubtedly at greater risk of receiving serious physical injuries than are safe sport participants. Further analysis examined whether there was a relationship between participants' scores on reversal theory measures and injuries experienced for both groups.

A biserial correlation was used to determine the relationship between injuries experienced by risk and safe sport participants and scores on the TDS and the NDS. This test seemed appropriate, as one variable is quantitative and measured on an interval scale (TDS) and the other is

**Table 7.2** Mann–Whitney $U$-tests comparing risk and safe sports participants' scores for injuries incurred through participation in sport of choice (snowboarding or badminton) and additional sport activities (from Cogan & Brown, 1998).

| Variable | Sport of choice | | | Additional sport activities | | |
|---|---|---|---|---|---|---|
| | $U$ | $Z$ | $p$-level | $U$ | $Z$ | $p$-level |
| Broken bones | 226 | −4.2109 | 0.0000 | 299 | −3.4188 | 0.0006 |
| Muscle strains | 245 | −3.8803 | 0.0001 | 189 | −4.5951 | 0.0000 |
| Serious cuts | 231 | −4.0403 | 0.0001 | 173 | −4.9523 | 0.0000 |
| Concussion | 382 | −2.0105 | 0.0444 | 426 | −1.0310 | 0.3022 |
| Shock | 260 | −3.9145 | 0.0001 | 408 | −1.5613 | 0.1185 |
| Other | 403 | −1.9658 | 0.0493 | 439 | −0.7546 | 0.4505 |

dichotomous but with underlying continuity (see Cogan & Brown, 1998, for full details).

In participants' first choice of sport (i.e., snowboarding or badminton), significant correlations were found between the total TDS scores and serious cuts and shock. Some significant correlations were also found for the TDS subscales: serious-mindedness was significantly correlated with other injuries, planning orientation was significantly correlated with shock, and arousal avoidance was significantly correlated with broken bones, serious cuts, and shock.

In additional sport activities, overall telic dominance was significantly correlated with broken bones and serious cuts. Significant correlations were also found between serious-mindedness and serious cuts, and between arousal avoidance and broken bones, muscle strains, and serious cuts. These results support the pre-experimental expectation that a relationship would exist between the TDS and sport injuries experienced.

Significant correlations were also found between the NDS proactive subscale and muscle strains and concussion experienced as a result of participation in additional sport activities, suggesting a possible link between NDS proactive negativism and injuries incurred.

## DISCUSSION

This chapter documents the use of reversal theory measures in an examination of motivational aspects and personality profiles of participants engaged in risk and safe sports. The application of psychological measures, in combination with an Injury Behaviour Checklist, revealed links between motivation, incidence of injuries and participation in safe and risk sports.

The results of Cogan and Brown's (1998) study replicate the demonstrated relationship between arousal avoidance and its opposite, arousal seeking (as measured by the TDS) and participation in risk and safe sports. Those who participated in a risk sport (snowboarding) scored significantly lower on the arousal avoidance subscale than those who took part in a safe sport activity (badminton) This finding supports past research (e.g., Chirivella & Martinez, 1994; Kerr, 1991; Kerr & Svebak, 1989) suggesting that safe sport participants tend to avoid situations which generate high arousal. Since some high-arousal seekers find more pleasure in dangerous environments than low-arousal seekers, it seems probable that they will search out more dangerous recreational experiences.

In this study, the risk sport participants participated in a mountain environment far removed from quick evacuation or medical aid. Weather is a constant concern, with high winds, low temperature and poor visibility often the norm. There are threats of avalanches or rock falls and high altitude related illnesses which often occur above 8,000 feet. Snowboarding represents an extreme form of recreation, both in terms of the environment and behaviour.

Clearly, activities such as snowboarding can offer opportunities where the outcomes are fateful, challenging and dependent on the actions of the participant. The snowboarders may be seeking arousing experiences in an environment that demands a full measure of personal commitment and decision making and is characterized by uncertainty of outcome and intrinsically important rewards such as the pursuit of vertigo (Farmer, 1992). Considering the present research findings and previous work in human attraction to situations involving complexity and novelty (Zuckerman, 1979), it is not surprising that participants scoring low on the arousal-avoiding subscale tended to seek out environments that are considered dangerous.

A parallel trend on the TDS serious-mindedness subscale was apparent, with risk sport participants scoring significantly lower than the safe sport participants. Again this finding replicates previous research (Kerr, 1988, 1991) suggesting that individuals who engage in safe sport activities tend to be oriented towards goals which are seen as being important, rather than merely acting as endpoints for ongoing activities, enjoyed in themselves.

No significant difference was found between participants' scores on the TDS planning-orientation subscale, suggesting that the risk and safe sport participants in the study plan equally well. Both groups can be characterized as individuals who plan ahead and organize their activities rather than take things as they come. This may be important in the light of safety considerations in risk sports, which often require participants to plan their activities carefully. Failure to do so can result in tragedy, therefore attention is paid to every aspect of preparation (Man, 1996). This finding supports previous research suggesting that dangerous recreations involve a deliberate process in which an individual's skills and abilities are weighed against projected requirements and possible negative outcomes (Timmermans, 1996). By virtue of their skills and planned behaviour, participants display a substantial amount of control and influence over outcomes.

Participants' self-assessment of risks in Cogan and Brown (1998) also showed they were reasonably realistic in both their self-expectations and their assessment of risk presented by their sport activities. In past research examining sensation seekers in sport activities (Ewert, 1985; Schroth, 1994), individual high-risk sport participants were not shown to have a different outlook in terms of their perception of risk compared to safe sport athletes. As a consequence, the risk sport participants in the Cogan and Brown (1998) study may be seen as running risks in a relatively calculated fashion, rather than taking them spontaneously (Teigen, Brun, & Slovic, 1988). Research conducted by Gridley (1990) adds further support for the present research findings that risk sport participants plan their activities. Following interviews with rock climbers and high-speed motorcyclists, he demonstrated that risk sport enthusiasts exert considerable impulse control over their sporting behaviour through planning and considering how to minimize risk.

Impulsiveness is related to non-planning and spontaneous behaviour. It is well known that impulsive individuals act without thinking and do not plan ahead for the consequences of their behaviour. The characteristics of the impulsive person would probably affect the individual's appraisal of the situation, resulting in an inaccurate perception of the potential risk (Gridley, 1990). Consequently, risk sport participants who are impulsive might be at greater physical risk than those who obtain low scores on the arousal-avoidance subscale but plan well.

The results of Cogan and Brown's (1998) study demonstrate the utility of the TDS in identifying characteristics that are specific to people who are attracted to different kinds of sport activities. Risk takers do seem to have a personality profile that is distinct from that of individuals who participate in safe sports. Overall, risk sport participants were shown to be significantly more paratelic dominant than safe sport participants. Even during the completion of the questionnaires – a task which might have been expected to induce reversal to a telic state – results from the T/PSI demonstrated that paratelic dominant participants remained in their dominant state throughout, providing validating support for the results using the TDS.

Risk sport participants also scored significantly higher than safe sport participants on total NDS scores, largely as a result of strongly significant differences between groups on the proactive negativism subscale. This finding supports McDermott's (1988) suggestion that proactive negativism represents a rebellious form of excitement seeking where fun and enjoyment are sought for their own sake. Some past research has contradicted this viewpoint (Goma, 1991; Vlaswinkel & Kerr, 1990).

## Links between Snowboarding and Surfing

Snowboarding is a sport that originally appealed to surfers looking for something to do in the winter months because of the similarity between riding the waves and riding the snow (*Transworld Snowboarding*, 1997). Both forms of sport activity share similar characteristics and therefore attract similar sport participants. Cogan and Brown (1998) found that snowboarders tended to be additionally involved in the risk sports of surfing, skateboarding, and BMX riding.

Farmer (1992) found that surfing could be described as an expressive leisure activity, defined as a vertigo sport. Competition against other individuals was not valued and there were no leadership hierarchy or formal rules or regulations, and little organization within the surfing culture. He also found that surfers especially valued escape from society and flirting with danger. It might be argued that the motivation and values of snowboarders are different from those held by athletes in other types of risk sport, such as motorcycle racers and Olympic sailors. In contrast to safe sport performance, participation in dangerous sport activities may be a means for surfers and snowboarders to dissociate from the mainstream of society and to associate with particular subcultures. It might be fruitful to conduct a study of risk seekers not only as individuals but also as members of a subculture where risk taking prevails as a social value, even as a shared norm.

## Psychopathic and Non-psychopathic Excitement Seekers

De Marco and Pierangela (1988) argued that individuals who participate in high-risk sports are not reckless or psychopathic and do not suffer from an inferiority complex. On the contrary, they argued that athletes practising dangerous sports have above-average intelligence and show cool-headedness, caution, and psychological maturity in their pursuit of danger. Motivation to pursue such activities was said to derive from the excitement, stimulation, and arousal induced by the experience. These findings support Cogan and Brown's (1998) findings, suggesting that risk sport participants are non-psychopathic excitement seekers. In other words, a distinction should be made between psychopathic and non-psychopathic excitement seekers (Gridley, 1990). Professional autosport racers, for example, might be distinguished from psychopathic joyriders by the amount of time spent planning how to minimize risk to themselves and others (Heino, Molen, & Wilde, 1996).

## The Escape to Nature

It has been suggested that humans function optimally in environments that possess attributes of the natural setting in which they evolved (Dubos, 1968). The natural environment is said to offer escape from overly complex, chaotic stimulation in everyday life and to be valued because it heightens the individual's sense of control, competency, and esteem (Knopf, 1983; Ladd, 1978).

Therefore, the motives people have for pursuing risk sports may not only stem primarily from the extreme arousal induced by the experience of risk itself, but also from an athlete's mastery over the situation or environment. McDermott (1988) suggested that maintaining control over one's immediate environment may be a by-product of the proactive, excitement-seeking form of negativistic activity. As has been illustrated, snowboarding takes place in a mountain environment, where nature itself presents its own risks to those who venture into this unpredictable habitat. Gullies, rock crevices, cliff drops, and avalanche risks are the norm for this extreme sport activity. However, these obstacles of danger become obstacles presenting challenges to be overcome to those who dare to ride the terrain of the mountain. This natural environment becomes a play area for those who have been referred to as 'free riders' looking for the narrowest gully to ride through and the steepest cliff drops to jump from.

Motivational research in outdoor recreation has found that the escape motive remained the dominant motive for risk sport participants, providing strong evidence that a large share of recreational behaviour is in fact coping behaviour designed to offset the demands of modern living (Crandall, 1980).

## Risk Sport Participation and Injury

Snowboarders were shown to have sustained significantly more broken bones, muscle strains, serious cuts, concussion, shock and other (miscellaneous) injuries than badminton players. Furthermore, the most significant difference found between the two groups was on the broken bones injury item, which suggests that participants in risk sports also sustained injuries of a more serious nature. Consistent with previous findings (Chirivella & Martinez, 1994), those who took part in snowboarding also tended to take part in additional risk sports (e.g., surfing, BMX riding, and skateboarding) while those who took part in badminton pursued additional safe sports (e.g., swimming, jogging, and tennis). A recognizably similar, although less sharp, difference in the pattern of injuries incurred in additional sports was found between risk and safe sport participants.

Significant correlations were obtained between total TDS scores and serious cuts and shock incurred in the participants' preferred sport, and broken bones and serious cuts incurred in additional sports. Participants who scored low on the TDS tended to have experienced more of these injury types. There were several other significant correlations between types of injury and TDS subscales, but there was no clear pattern. For the NDS, participants who scored high on proactive negativism were more likely to have suffered muscle strain and concussion in additional sports.

Overall these results supported the prediction that there would be a relationship between participants' scores on the TDS, the NDS proactive-negativism subscale, and injuries incurred. They also supported results obtained elsewhere using sensation-seeking measures and participants' sport injury history for analysis, which indicated that individuals high in excitement seeking take more physical risks and therefore experience more physical injuries (Connelly, 1981).

# FUTURE RESEARCH

An interesting area for future reversal theory sport research might be to examine arousal seeking in risk sports and its relationship with addiction. Some evidence suggesting that participation in high-risk sports has an addictive quality and that the personality profiles of individuals who pursue such activities have similarities to the profiles of known addictive personalities has also been produced (Geifman, 1992).

Of related interest is research examining addiction to exercise which has found that individuals involved in sport activities can become addicted to the almost blissful, trance-like state induced by physical exercise. This has been linked to the release of endorphins, the brain's pain dulling, opiate-like drugs. Increases in endorphin levels through sport activities and the accompanying euphoric effects have been suggested as part of a possible psychophysiological mechanism underlying the addiction to exercise (Steinberg, Sykes, & Le Boutillier, 1995). This might also be true of participation in risk sport.

Reversal theory researchers could attempt to establish whether there is an addictive element to risk sports which is similar to other addictions (Brown, 1997) and indeed whether certain people are more prone to become addicted to dangerous sport activities than others.

# CONCLUDING COMMENTS

This chapter has aimed to provide some insight into the apparent paradox of human participation in dangerous or risk sport. Snowboarders attempt to get close to 'the dangerous edge' (Apter, 1992) because that is where their levels of felt arousal are likely to be highest. The paradox is that in order to experience high arousal by approaching danger, they must feel confident and capable of handling that danger within what Apter (1992) has called a 'protective frame'. That is to say, snowboarders take risks while at the same time feeling safe.

It is clear from the results of Cogan and Brown's (1998) study that risk sport participants can be distinguished from those who participate in safe sports in terms of personality and motivation, and that the rewards accruing from their contrasting leisure pursuits are different. The experience of high levels of excitement in the face of danger valued by risk sport participants is unattractive, unrewarding, and something to be avoided by safe sport participants. They achieve their own brand of satisfaction and pleasure of a fundamentally different kind from their own safe sport participation.

# REFERENCES

Apter, M. J. (1982). *The experience of motivation*. London: Academic Press.

Apter, M. J. (1989). *Reversal theory: Motivation, emotion and personality*. London: Routledge.

Apter, M. J. (1992). *The dangerous edge: The psychology of excitement*. New York: The Free Press.

Bakker, F. C. (1993). Motivation of young elite speed skaters. *International Journal of Sport Psychology*, **24**, 432–442.

Bladin, C. & McCrory, P. (1995). Snowboarding injuries: An overview. *Sports Medicine*, **19**, 358–364.

Braathen, E. T. & Svebak, S. (1992). Motivational differences among talented teenage athletes: The significance of gender, type of sport and level of excellence. *Scandinavian Journal of Medicine and Science in Sports*, **2**, 153–159.

Brown, R. I. F. (1997). A theoretical model of the behavioural addictions – applied to criminal offending. In J. E. Hodge, M. MacMurran & C. R. Hollins (Eds.), *Addicted to Crime?*. Chichester and New York: Wiley.

Calhoun, J. E. (1995). *Construct validity of the Telic/Paratelic State Instrument: A measure of reversal theory constructs*. Unpublished doctoral dissertation, University of Kansas School of Nursing.

Calhoun J. E. & O'Connell, K. A. (1995, July). *Construct validity of the Telic/Paratelic State Instrument: A measure of reversal theory constructs*. Paper presented at the 7th International Conference on Reversal Theory, Melbourne, Australia.

Celsi, R. L. (1992). Transcendent benefits of high risk sports. *Advances in Consumer Psychology*, **19**, 636–641.

Chirivella, E. C. & Martinez, L. M. (1994). The sensation of risk and motivational tendencies in sports: An empirical study. *Personality and Individual Differences*, **16**, 777–786.

Cogan, N. A. & Brown, R. I. F. (1998). Metamotivational dominance, states and injuries in risk and safe sports. *Personality and Individual Differences*.

Connelly, P. M. (1981). *An exploratory study of adults engaging in high risk sport of skiing*. Unpublished Masters Thesis, Rutgers University.

Crandall, R. (1980). Motivations for leisure. *Journal of Leisure Research*, **12**, 45–54.

De Marco, P. & Pierangela, M. (1988). Why high risk sports? *Movimento*, **4**, 18–20.

Dubos, K. (1968). *So human an animal*. New York: Charles Scribner's Sons.

Elkind, D. (1974). *Children and adolescence: Interpretive essays on Jean Piaget*. New York: Oxford University Press.

Ellis, J. A. & Kierulf, J. C. (1995). Injuries associated with in-line skating from the Canadian hospitals injury reporting and prevention program database. *Canadian Journal of Public Health*, **86**, 133–136.

Ewert, A. W. (1985). Why people climb: The relationship of participant motives and experience level to mountaineering. *Journal of Leisure Research*, **17**, 241–250.

Farmer, R. J. (1992). Surfing: Motivation, values and culture. *Journal of Sport Behaviour*, **15**, 241–257.

Fowler, C. J., Knorring, J. & Oreland, L. (1980). Platelet monoamine oxidase activity in sensation seeking. *Psychiatric Research*, **3**, 273–279.

Geifman, S. E. (1992). Participation in high risk sports and addiction. *International Journal of Psychology*, **3/4**, 362.

Goma, M. (1991). Personality profile of subjects engaged in high physical risk sports. *Personality and Individual Differences*, **12**, 1087–1093.

Gonzalez, J. (1994). Adolescents' perceptions of their risk taking behaviour. *Adolescents*, **29**, 701–709.

Greenberg, M. R. & Schneider, D. F. (1995). Gender differences in risk perception: Effects differ in stressed vs. non-stressed environments. *Risk Analysis*, **55**, 503–511.

Gridley, M. C. (1990). Psychopathic vs. nonpsychopathic thrill seeking. *Psychology, A Journal of Human Behaviour*, **27**, 18–20.

Hargarten, S. W. (1996). So, just do it: Go upstream. *Academic Emergency Medicine*, **3**, 293–294.

Heimer, C. (1988). Social structure, psychology and the estimate of risk. *Annual Review of Sociology*, **14**, 491–519.

Heino, A., Molen, H. & Wilde, G. S. (1996). Risk perception, risk taking, accident involvement and the need for stimulation. *Safety Science*, **22**, 35–48.

Kenyon, G. S. (1968). Six scales for assessing attitudes toward physical activity. *Research Quarterly*, **39**, 96–105.

Kerr, J. H. (1988). Speed sports. The search for high arousal experiences. *Sportswissenschaft*, **2**, 185–190.

Kerr, J. H. (1991). Arousal seeking in risk sport participants. *Personality and Individual Differences*, **12**, 613–616.

Kerr, J. H. & Svebak, S. (1989). Motivational aspects of preference for and participation in risk and safe sports. *Personality and Individual Differences*, **10**, 797–800.

Knopf, R. C. (1983). Recreational needs and behaviour in natural settings. In I. Altman & J. Wohlwill (Eds.), *Behaviour and the Natural Environment*. New York: Plenum.

Ladd, F. C. (1978). City kids in the absence of legitimate adventure. In S. Kaplan (Ed.), *Humanscope environments for people* (pp. 443–447). North Seituate, MA: Duxbury Press.

Man, N. C. (1996). Injury prevention: Who me? *Academic Emergency Medicine*, **3**, 291–292.

McDermott, M. R. (1988). Measuring rebelliousness: The development of the Negativism Dominance Scale (NDS). In M. J. Apter, J. H. Kerr & M. P. Cowles (Eds.), *Progress in reversal theory* (pp. 297–312). Amsterdam: North-Holland/Elsevier.

McDermott, M. R., & Apter, M. J. (1988). The Negativism Dominance Scale (NDS). In M. J. Apter, J. H. Kerr & M. P. Cowles (Eds.), *Progress in reversal theory* (pp. 373–376). Advances in Psychology series, 51. Amsterdam: North-Holland/Elsevier.

Murgatroyd, S., Rushton, C., Apter, M. J. & Ray, C. (1978). The development of the Telic Dominance Scale. *Journal of Personality Assessment*, **42**, 519–528.

Piët, S. (1987). What motivates stuntmen? *Motivation and Emotion*, **11**, 195–213.

Rossi, B. & Cereatti, L. (1993). The sensation seeking in mountain athletes as assessed by Zuckerman's sensation seeking scale. *International Journal of Sport Psychology*, **24**, 417–431.

Schroth, M. L. (1994). A comparison of sensation seeking among different groups of athletes and nonathletes. *Personality and Individual Differences*, **18**, 219–222.

Steinberg, H., Sykes, E. A. & Le Boutillier, N. (1995). Exercise addiction: Indirect measures of endorphins? *Motivation for Participation in Sport and Exercise*, 6–14.

Svebak, S. & Apter, M. J. (1987). Laughter: An empirical test of some reversal theory hypotheses. *Scandinavian Journal of Psychology*, **28**, 189–198.

Teigen, K. H., Brun, W. & Slovic, P. (1988). Societal risks as seen by a Norwegian public. *Journal of Behavioural Decision Making*, **1**, 111–130.

Timmermans, D. (1996). Risk and uncertainty. *Journal of Decision Making*, **9**, 71–76.

*Transworld Snowboarding* (1997). *The Interview Edition*, **10** (6), 94–102.

Vlaswinkel, E. H. & Kerr, J. H. (1990). Negativism dominance in risk and team sports. *Perceptual and Motor Skills*, **70**, 289–290.

Wilde, G. J. S. (1982). The theory of risk homeostasis: Implications for safety and health. *Risk Analysis*, **2**, 209–225.

Zuckerman, M. (1979). *Sensation seeking: Beyond the optimal level of arousal*. Hillsdale, NJ: Erlbaum.

Zuckerman, M. (1982). *Behavioral expressions and biosocial bases of sensation seeking*. Cambridge: Cambridge University Press.

# 8
# Metamotivational States in Sport Locations and Activities

**Paul Tacon**

*York University, Canada*

**John H. Kerr**

*University of Tsukuba, Japan*

## INTRODUCTION

Whether it was the school gymnasium and sport fields or international stadia or arenas, for many people who no longer take part, there remains something special about the locations in which they participated in sport. For those who are still participating or spectating, the swimming pool, the tennis court, the golf course, or other facility are places in which they are likely to feel at ease and comfortable, having a feeling of familiarity with the place and of being at home.

Bale (1994, p. 13) has described the special feeling associated with what he terms sports landscapes as 'a sense of place'. He claims that these

*Experiencing Sport: Reversal Theory.* Edited by J. H. Kerr.
© 1999 John Wiley & Sons Ltd.

particular localities possess nuances and unique flavours which affect the perception and interpretation of our experience of sport in many different ways. Much of this sense of place is concerned with the sensory pleasures which sport locations provide for those who willingly occupy them. He states:

> People may be attracted to particular sports because of their own psychological make up; others because they feel that the landscapes of sports symbolise deeply held needs, and other [sic] because such places generate affection through sentiment. . . . As with other landscapes of spectacle (Ley & Olds, 1988) it is possible to 'engage with' the sport place, using it to nurture friendships, and to 'commune' with landscape and nature. This is not to say that the very landscapes which create topophilia in some create topophobia in others, nor that landscape, affection and nostalgia are untutored by myth.
>
> (Bale, 1994, p. 146)

Reversal theory (Apter, 1989) is a psychological theory which takes a similar view of the manner in which environments or locations can influence people's experiences. For example, within reversal theory it has been hypothesized that, in one's environment, physical surroundings can determine metamotivational state. Entering a football stadium to watch a game or going to the theatre will likely induce the paratelic state. Alternatively, going to work would probably induce the telic state. According to Apter (1989, p. 49):

> Law courts, police stations, hospitals, dentists' waiting rooms . . . may all induce the telic mode in most people. Fairgrounds, casinos, public houses and bars . . . will strongly tend to induce the paratelic mode.

In such situations, the individual may indirectly control reversals by bringing about changes in the immediate environment which would prompt a reversal between states. Such reversals are referred to as *contingent* reversals, inasmuch as the reversal between states is contingent upon an environmental event taking place. Unless compelled to do otherwise, it is to be expected that the person's *bias* for a particular state (metamotivational dominance) will, over the long run, determine a person's probability of being in a telic-oriented or paratelic-oriented environment. More immediately, such factors as availability, satiation, or fatigue would also have an impact upon choice of environmental setting.

As the quote from Bale (1994) also points out, it is important to remember that not all people will interpret a particular objective environment in the same manner. Thus, the same objective event may be telic for one person and paratelic for another. For example, while one's workplace will be considered by many to be a generally telic situation, a few will perceive it as primarily paratelic, a place where they can relax, have fun and socialize with others, a place where telic behaviour is of secondary importance.

Likewise, for the theatre critic, going to the theatre would probably induce the telic state, rather than the paratelic state likely to be operative in
other theatre-goers. Similarly, participation in sport may be paratelic for
most people, but for the professional athlete it is more likely to be a telic
event.

It is also important to remember the body of research by Schachter (e.g.,
Schachter & Singer, 1962) and others (see Reisenstein, 1983; Sinclair, Hoffman, Mark, Martin, & Pickering, 1994). Schachter's two-factor theory of
emotion stresses the importance of cognitive factors (in particular the label
we place on an event in which we are physiologically aroused) in the
interpretation of our arousal in terms of the emotion we are experiencing.
While not all agree with Schachter's theory, most psychologists today do
believe that cognitive factors are essential ingredients of emotion and
motivation.

Korpela and Hartig's (1996) results not only support reversal theory's
contention that physical surroundings may affect mental state, but they
also reinforce Schachter's two-factor theory. The authors studied students'
stated favourite and unpleasant places in a city along with a 'neutral' central square. Significant differences were found in the students' emotional
states at these three locations. Thus, participants associated significantly
higher positive affect and significantly lower anger/aggression and fear
arousal with their favourite place compared to the central square. The
authors argued that these results are consistent with theories on the self-
regulation of emotions. Others (most recently Knez, 1995) have reported
that quite specific aspects of particular locations, such as indoor lighting,
the playing of different kinds of music, and even the colour of painted walls
and ceilings affect mood and cognition.

To date, reversal theory has not paid much attention to the degree to
which individuals are consciously aware of their operative metamotivational state. However, it would follow from what Apter (1989) has said
about individuals inducing selected metamotivational states by entering
appropriate settings, that people are aware of their operative metamotivational state and of that state's appropriateness for a particular setting. Also,
people are generally aware of their levels of arousal and make use of
techniques that have worked in the past to enhance or decrease arousal
level according to what is desired (Thayer, 1989). Some are quite consciously employed, but Thayer suggests that, more frequently, there is only
a very low awareness of what is occurring.

Reversal theory distinguishes between *felt* arousal and *preferred* arousal.
The former is the extent to which people feel themselves to be 'worked up'
at any particular time. The latter, as the name implies, refers to the level of
arousal that the individual would have preferred (or, perhaps, the level that
the person deemed to be ideally appropriate) rather than the one that was

experienced. It has also been suggested (Apter & Svebak, 1989) that differences between these two levels of arousal will lead to *tension stress*, which in turn is likely to be accompanied by negative emotions in the form of unpleasant negative hedonic tone (Cox & Kerr, 1989). If indeed these differences do commonly occur, it suggests that the techniques mentioned by Thayer (1989) above for moderating arousal level may be less than perfect.

Below we present two examples of studies involving recreational sport situations which are concerned with how environmental factors influence metamotivational states and arousal (Kerr & Tacon, 1999).

# METAMOTIVATIONAL STATES ON ENTERING A SPORT CENTRE AND OTHER LOCATIONS

The initial study described here was designed to test reversal theory assertions that particular settings induce particular metamotivational states (Apter, 1989). Specifically, participants were tested as to whether their operative metamotivational state was telic or paratelic immediately prior to entering one of four locations. Two of these locations were chosen because they were thought likely to induce a telic state, two as likely to induce a paratelic state.

Participants in this first study were four groups, each of 100 Dutch students ($N = 400$). Mean ages and standard deviations were: group 1, $M = 20.4$, $SD = 1.59$; group 2, $M = 19.3$, $SD = 1.36$; group 3, $M = 20.2$, $SD = 1.02$; group 4, $M = 19.9$, $SD = 1.36$. Groups were divided equally in terms of gender. The Dutch version of the Telic State Measure, used by Kerr and Vlaswinkel (1993), was employed in this study. It, like the version employed in the second study, consisted of five response dimensions including, serious–playful, planning–spontaneous, felt arousal (low–high), preferred arousal (low–high), and investment of effort in the task (low–high). Each dimension has a 6-point scale with defining adjectives at either end. If desired, a sixth item, arousal discrepancy, is calculated by subtracting the score on the felt arousal dimension from that on the preferred arousal dimension.

Individuals entering one of four different locations were approached immediately upon entering the location and were asked to complete the Telic State Measure (TSM). Care was taken to ensure that no participant appeared in more than one group. This procedure was continued until complete data on 50 males and 50 females had been collected at each site. The two *telic* locations were the university library (group 1) and a lecture theatre just prior to a lecture on statistics (group 2). The two *paratelic*

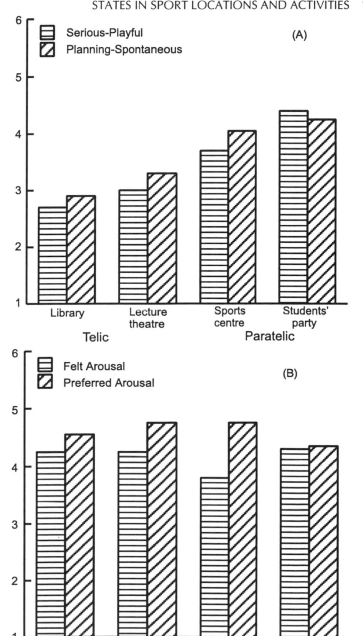

**Figure 8.1**   Mean TSM item scores for the four locations: (A) serious–playful, planning–spontaneous; (B) felt arousal, preferred arousal (from Kerr & Tacon, 1999).

locations were the university sport centre (group 3) and a party at the students' union building (group 4).

Group mean differences were examined using analysis of variance procedures. Age differences across groups and sex differences within groups were not significant. Highly significant differences between group mean scores existed on the TSM serious–playful and planning–spontaneous dimensions (Figure 8.1a). Both were at the $p = 0.001$ level of confidence. Students were found to be less serious and less planning oriented upon entering a paratelic location (sport centre or party) than when entering a telic location (the library or lecture theatre). These results were as predicted.

Somewhat puzzling, however, was the lack of significant differences in felt arousal (Figure 8.1b), since one might have expected higher scores than were found at the paratelic venues. In fact, taken together, scores for paratelic situations were very slightly lower than those for telic situations. It is probable in this recreational situation that felt arousal increased as the paratelic event progressed, such that the individual needed to feel a part of the event before felt arousal increased. Awareness of the arousal levels of others in the setting might also have been important in determining felt arousal level. Preferred arousal scores (Figure 8.1b) revealed no significant differences between groups. Analysis of effort scores was not undertaken as students were not actually involved in a meaningful task at the time of measurement.

Figure 8.1b reveals that arousal scores, and especially preferred arousal scores, are quite high for all groups. Indeed, in all four locations, the mean scores on the preferred arousal dimension were higher than for felt arousal. When taken together, this resulted in significant differences ($p < 0.04$) between groups in arousal discrepancy. The largest discrepancies were for the sport centre (paratelic) and lecture theatre (telic) groups. While not as great as those found for the serious–playful and the planning–spontaneous dimensions, these results do suggest that both telic and paratelic events participants, dissatisfied with their current levels of arousal, were experiencing some tension stress and felt that a greater level of arousal would have been more appropriate. It may be that what occurred here with regard to arousal is related to the overall environment in which all these events took place (i.e., the university campus). More satisfying levels of arousal might be obtained in other, non-university locations.

# EXPERIENCE AND AWARENESS OF STATES AND AROUSAL IN RECREATIONAL SPORT

The second study was designed to test whether a particular sport setting can evoke a particular metamotivational state (i.e., the paratelic state) and felt arousal level and how aware participants were of their operative state and arousal level. The recreational sport activity of playing badminton was used in this study. The research methodology required participants to project what their actual and ideal metamotivational state characteristics would be prior to performing, as well as report their metamotivational characteristics pre- and post-playing a real game of badminton. In the original Kerr and Tacon (1999) study, similar measurements were also taken in a 'telic' situation involving a mid-term examination, mirroring the methodology used in the badminton situation. The results for the telic situation are not reported here, but can be found in Kerr and Tacon (1999).

Participants in this second study were 44 female and 32 male first-year students enrolled in a recreational badminton class at Nijenrode University in the Netherlands. As with Study 1, the Telic State Measure (TSM) for Dutch-speaking populations (Kerr & Vlaswinkel, 1993) was employed, this time in a repeated measures design. There were four administrations of the TSM, presented in pairs with an interval of approximately four weeks between the paired administrations. As this was a repeated measures design, only those students who had fully completed all four TSM paired presentations were included in the study.

For the first test, participants were instructed to:

*Imagine you are about to play a game of recreational badminton. Please indicate on the scales how you think you would feel immediately before playing badminton.*

Once this was done, all participants were asked to again complete the TSM but according to the following instructions:

*Imagine you are about to play a game of recreational badminton. Please indicate on the scales what you think would be the* optimal *feelings to have immediately before playing badminton.*

After a four week interval the paratelic event (playing recreational badminton) took place. Immediately prior to this event, all students were given the TSM with the instructions to 'rate your feelings at this moment'. Similarly, once the badminton class was over, students completed the fourth administration of the TSM questionnaire which came with the same instructions as for the third presentation – that is, to 'rate your feelings at this moment'.

No evaluation data on performance was collected during the recreational badminton game as it was considered inappropriate since it might have altered the event from a purely paratelic one that was played for fun, to one with a telic component.

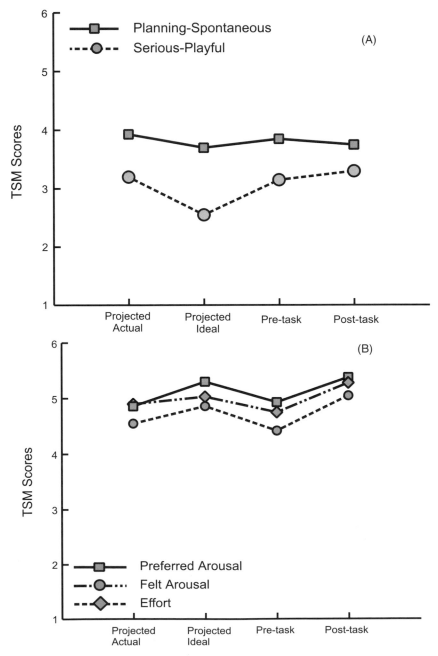

**Figure 8.2** Mean TSM item scores for the recreational sport activity setting: (A) serious–playful, planning–spontaneous; (B) felt arousal, preferred arousal, effort invested in the task (from Kerr & Tacon, 1999).

Results across the four sessions for the serious–playful continuum (Figure 8.2a) showed significant differences ($F(3, 225) = 3.94, p = 0.001$). Comparisons between presentations 1 and 2, 2 and 3, and 2 and 4 all yielded an alpha of 0.05 or better. Mean scores were consistent across three of the four presentations, and were all in the low end of the paratelic range. For presentation 2, however, the mean score was significantly more telic. Why this was the case is difficult to say. Possibly, when asked about ideal states for playing badminton in a physical education context, students' expectations were that they should give the impression that they were very serious about sport – even recreational sport. Also, the badminton was taking place as part of a course in a university setting, which may have provided a telic overtone to the projected event. In any event, the mean score on presentation 2 was in the telic range of the scale.

Figure 8.2a also reveals consistent scores across all four presentations for planning–spontaneous, well within the paratelic range. These students were not very planning oriented in this situation, which is what would be expected for persons operating in the paratelic state.

For felt arousal (Figure 8.2b), significant differences existed between presentations ($F(3, 225) = 4.93, p = 0.0037$). Also, significant differences were revealed between presentations 1 and 4, and 3 and 4 at the 0.05 level of confidence or better. Note that the projected actual (presentation 1) and pre-task (presentation 3) felt arousal means were very similar. The ideal arousal mean was somewhat higher (presentation 3), with the highest arousal level being for the post-task presentation. This data resembles other pre-post findings such as those by Kerr and van Schaik (1995) in rugby and Kerr and Vlaswinkel (1993) in recreational running.

For preferred arousal, significant differences were obtained across TSM administrations ($F(3, 225) = 3.90, p = 0.0001$). Significant differences at the 0.05 level of confidence or better existed between presentations 1 and 2, 1 and 4, 2 and 3, and 2 and 4 (Figure 8.2b). Note that these preferred arousal scores were somewhat higher than the felt arousal scores across all four presentations. Thus, in each instance, participants would have liked to have had higher arousal than they actually experienced. Note also that the profiles for the questions on felt arousal and preferred arousal were remarkably similar across presentations, suggesting some constancy in the differences between *actual* and *preferred* under all conditions.

With regard to the amount of effort expended (Figure 8.2b), significant differences were again found across the TSM presentations ($F(3, 225) = 4.85, p = 0.0034$). Also, significant differences at the 0.05 level of confidence or better were observed between presentations 1 and 4, and 3 and 4. While no differences between scores for the first three TSM presentations were noted, it is not surprising to find that there were presentation differences (between 1 and 4, and 3 and 4) with post-task scores. One would expect post-task scores to be much higher after vigorous activity.

# DISCUSSION AND SUGGESTIONS FOR FUTURE RESEARCH

Perhaps the most important conclusion is that the results from both studies confirmed previous research findings by others on the influence of physical surroundings on mental state (e.g., Korpela & Hartig, 1996; Knez, 1995). Reversal theory has proved to be a useful theoretical base from which empirical investigations in this area of study may be carried out.

The present two studies taken together show that people's moods are affected by particular physical settings and locations and in a manner that is predicted by reversal theory. Participants were found to be significantly more paratelic when entering a sport centre or student union party and significantly more telic on entering a university library or lecture theatre. This result is hardly surprising, as it confirms what we know from everyday experience. It may be that the moods induced by particular locations are linked to the individual's experiences of previous activities in such locations. For those who enjoy participating in sport, sport locations like the sport centre may elicit similar pleasant psychological responses as students' 'favourite places', identified in Korpela and Hartig's (1996) study. Bale (1994, p. 121), in talking about the characteristics of sports landscapes which people find attractive, create fond memories, or provide a sense of place, stated:

> Such sources of topophilia, resulting from sensory pleasures, might intuitively be thought to be solely visual but the other senses – aural, olfactory and tactile – also create topophilic sentiments linking sport and place. Nostalgia and myth further foster and evoke such feeling.

It may also be true that current mood (along with other internal factors such as dominance) affects the kind of location that people seek out. For example, when in a paratelic state, are people not more likely to seek activities and locations that are paratelic in nature? It seems likely that a two-way process may operate. People may seek out certain locations or environments to induce particular metamotivational states and/or when people have certain metamotivational states operative they will look for locations and situations which allow that state to be maintained. This would seem to be especially true for people in the paratelic state, who generally want to prolong, for as long as possible, activities which provide the immediate sensation of having fun and experiencing thrills. This would be consistent with the arguments of theories on the self-regulation of emotions (e.g., Thayer, 1989), as well as reversal theory.

However, the relationship between environment and activity is perhaps more complicated than the simple relationship described above. There are likely to be a number of factors which mutually influence the activity pattern in a particular space or location. For example, as a study by Bloch and Laursen (1996) showed, attempts by planners to create spaces for particular purposes are not always successful. In their study of a sport playground, they showed that the planners' vision of the playground as a meeting place where children and adults could play and take part in physical activities (paratelic activities) was not realized. It seems that the planners assumed that a new physical environment would by itself provoke new patterns of activity, but in this case adequate provision for local play already existed and, hence, children and parents never developed an affiliation with the playground and did not use it in the way that was intended.

The second study revealed that participants were not only aware of, but were quite accurate in estimating, the appropriate metamotivational state and arousal level for participating in their usual recreational sport setting. Previous research (e.g., Morris & Reilly, 1987; Thayer, 1989) indicated that people were capable of self-regulating their mental state. However, Thayer's (1989) argument that people would only have a very low awareness of what was occurring does not seem to hold up in this case. Students' projected scores for actual and ideal states were similar to their scores recorded just before playing badminton.

Evidence from previous sport research (Kerr & van Schaik, 1995; Males & Kerr, 1996) has shown that high-level performers were aware of, and proficient at achieving, the mental states and arousal levels that they desired for performance in sport. Indeed, successful athletes were consistently better at achieving and maintaining stable emotional patterns than less successful athletes (Kerr, 1997). However, it comes as something of a surprise that students involved in recreational sport were also sensitive to the motivational states and arousal levels required.

That felt arousal levels were significantly higher after playing badminton was not surprising and was in accord with previous studies by Kerr and Vlaswinkel (1993) and, more recently, by Kerr and van Schaik (1995). As mentioned above, high felt arousal is a recognized feature of activity in the paratelic state, where it is actively sought after and enjoyed.

It would be interesting to speculate as to how participants engaged in non-recreational sports would score in comparison to the recreational group in the second study. Research into when, and under what conditions, sport changes from a paratelic to a telic activity would seem important. Can one assume that competitive amateur sport (such as playing at university for a varsity team), where winning may be more important, would be a telic experience and, if so, might one expect a different TSM profile? Would the same results hold true for professional sport (which is a vocation) where the elite athlete devotes inordinate amounts of time to the sport? (Kerr, 1987, for example, found that professional sport performers were significantly more telic dominant than serious amateurs and recreational performers.) One way of answering these questions might be to compare results for those representing their university with those who are enrolled in a recreational course and, further, to compare these two groups with professional players.

In similar vein, what are the structures that a university setting imposes on any recreational event or activity? Certainly the formal organized nature of such sports (and perhaps the notion that a university represents a respected place for higher learning where people are expected to be serious) may influence participants' operative metamotivational states. Thus, can it be assumed, for example, that playing baseball in a recreational course is akin to a pick-up game at the local sandlot? Would these factors alter the telic and paratelic components of the situation or is a recreational game a recreational game, regardless of setting?

Finally, in the badminton study, no attempt was made to measure performance because it was feared that to do so might affect the predominantly paratelic nature of the event. Perhaps a future study could circumvent this problem in one of three ways: asking each participant 'How did you do?' just after the post-task TSM administration; by having trained observers posing as bystanders secretly note the participant's performance in some quantifiable manner; or by videotaping the performance and applying performance evaluation measures afterwards. These approaches are not without ethical considerations that would need to be resolved. Measuring performance would bring future TSM research of recreational sports activities into line with previous research on competitive sport where measurement of performance has been a central concern (e.g., see Kerr, 1997, for a review).

# REFERENCES

Apter, M. J. (1989). *Reversal theory: Motivation emotion and personality.* London: Routledge.

Apter, M. J. & Svebak, S. (1989). Stress from the reversal theory perspective. In C. D. Spielberger, I. G. Sarason & J. Strelau (Eds.), *Stress and anxiety* (Vol. 12, pp. 39–52). New York: Hemisphere.

Bale, J. (1994). *Landscapes of modern sport.* London: Leicester University Press.

Bloch, C. & Laursen, P. F., (1996). Play, sports and environment. *International Review for the Sociology of Sport*, **31**, 205–215.

Cox, T. & Kerr, J. H. (1989). Arousal effects during tournament play in squash. *Perceptual and Motor Skills*, **69**, 1275–1280.

Kerr, J. H. (1987). Differences in the motivational characteristics of 'professional', 'serious amateur' and 'recreational' sports performers. *Perceptual and Motor Skills*, **64**, 379–382.

Kerr, J. H. (1997). *Motivation and emotion in sport: Reversal theory*. Hove, UK: Psychology Press.

Kerr, J. H. & Tacon, P. (1999). Psychological responses to different types of locations and activities. *Journal of Environmental Psychology*, **27**(1) (in press).

Kerr, J. H. & van Schaik, P. (1995). Effects of game outcome on psychological mood states in rugby. *Personality and Individual Differences*, **19**, 407–410.

Kerr, J. H. & Vlaswinkel, E. H. (1993). Self-reported mood and running under natural conditions. *Work and Stress*, **7**, 161–177.

Knez, I. (1995). Effects of indoor lighting on mood and cognition. *Journal of Environmental Psychology*, **15**, 39–51.

Korpela, K. & Hartig, T. (1996). Restorative qualities of favorite places. *Journal of Environmental Psychology*, **16**, 221–233.

Ley, D. & Olds, K. (1988). Landscape and spectacle: World's fairs and the culture of heroic consumption. *Society and Space*, **6**, 191–212.

Males, J. R. & Kerr, J. H. (1996). Stress, emotion and performance in elite slalom canoeists. *The Sport Psychologist*, **10**, 17–36.

Morris, W. N. & Reilly, N. P. (1987). Toward the self-regulation of mood: Theory and research. *Motivation and Emotion*, **11**, 215–249.

Reisenstein, R. (1983). The Schachter theory of emotion: Two decades later. *Psychological Bulletin*, **94**, 239–264.

Schachter, S. & Singer, J. (1962). Cognitive, social and physiological determinants of emotional state. *Psychological Review*, **69**, 283–290.

Sinclair, R. C., Hoffman, C., Mark, M. M., Martin, L. L. & Pickering, T. L. (1994). Construct assessibility and the misattribution of arousal: Schachter and Singer revisited. *Psychological Science*, **5**, 15–18.

Thayer, R. E. (1989). *The biopsychology of mood and arousal*. New York: Oxford University Press.

# 9
# Sport Participation and Metamotivational Orientation

**Koenraad J. Lindner**

*The University of Hong Kong*

**John H. Kerr**

*University of Tsukuba, Japan*

## INTRODUCTION

Understanding why people enter into, adhere to, and withdraw from sport and physical activity can be important for guiding the promotion of active lifestyles and facilitating decision making by those responsible for managing, organizing, and changing the nature of sport and recreation. Research findings in participation motivation to date suggest that the question of motivation for sport participation and withdrawal is complex. It would appear that, for a fuller understanding, it is necessary to examine specific sport participation motives, as well as identifying the difficulties associated

*Experiencing Sport: Reversal Theory.* Edited by J. H. Kerr.
© 1999 John Wiley & Sons Ltd.

with participation as these relate to particular groupings of the population (Gould, Feltz, & Weiss, 1985; Petlichkoff, 1996).

For example, the importance of factors such as sex and age group differences, geographical location, and individual or parental financial status has been established from research on European samples (e.g., Biddle, 1992; Biddle & Fox, 1988; Colley, Eglinton, & Elliot, 1992; Harahousou & Kabitsis, 1994; Telama & Silvenoinen, 1979; Theodorakis, Doganis, & Bagiatis, 1992) and North American samples (e.g., Gould & Petlichkoff, 1988; Lindner, Butcher, & Johns, 1991, 1994a; Wankel & Kreisel, 1985). In addition, some researchers (e.g., Lindner, Johns, & Butcher, 1991) have argued that the importance of motivational factors may vary between different cultural groups. While some of the motivational factors associated with sport participation for Europeans and North Americans have also been identified for Asian samples (Lindner & Speak, 1995a), some important differences have been found. Fu (1993) reported that the strongest argument for sport participation by Hong Kong and Beijing secondary school children was that it enhances health. Asian sport participants were also found to have different reasons for non-participation, of which *studying, other interests*, and *not being skilful enough* featured importantly (Speak, Lindner, & Li, 1994).

Besides the need for making distinctions between geographical regions, Lindner and his co-workers (e.g., Lindner, Butcher, & Johns, 1994b; Lindner, Johns, & Butcher, 1991; Speak, Lindner, & Li, 1994) have argued that participation, non-participation and withdrawal reasons should be established for different groupings of participants. The utility of establishing prevalence of motives for children and youth in general is questionable, since important factors influencing these motives are not considered in such an approach. Some of these factors are well established and recognized, such as sex and age group differences, but others have just recently presented themselves as potentially important. For sport withdrawal, factors of interest include: sport type, parental social status and economic indicators; level of sport participation at time of withdrawal (particularly elite drop-outs versus lower-level drop-outs); and the number of other sports the drop-out was involved in at the time of withdrawal (Lindner, Butcher, & Johns, 1994b). In recent papers, Lindner and Speak showed that there are significant differences in participation motives among groupings based on frequency of sport and exercise participation (Lindner & Speak, 1995b), and significant differences in participation and non-participation motives when participants were grouped by perceived physical ability and perceived physical fitness (Lindner & Speak, 1995a, 1995c). The same groupings also produced significant differences in opinions on gender and sport-related issues (Lindner & Speak, 1996).

# REVERSAL THEORY

In addition to criticism that participation motivation research has been too general and therefore not meaningful or practical, past research in this area has been blamed for being too descriptive and lacking a theoretical perspective (Weiss & Chaumeton, 1992). It is desirable to locate present research on student motives for recreational sport choice and participation within a relevant theoretical framework. Reversal theory (Apter, 1982) is one such pertinent framework which has already been applied in various ways to the study of participation motivation in sport. A detailed description of this theory is available in the first chapter of this volume and in published books (Apter, 1989; Kerr, 1997). The reversal theory concept of metamotivational dominance has been applied in sport research by examining motivational differences relating to participation in sport and physical activity, and the results of such research have been quite supportive of reversal theory. For example, paratelic dominant sport participants demonstrate a marked preference for sports characterized by impulsive and explosive actions, while telic dominant participants tend to choose endurance sports (Svebak & Kerr, 1989). Similarly, risky sports have been linked with paratelic dominance, whereas safe sports are engaged in preferentially by telic dominant individuals (Chirivella & Martinez, 1994; Kerr, 1991; Kerr & Svebak, 1989; Summers & Stewart, 1993). Links between negativism dominance and sport preferences have also been reported (Braathen & Svebak, 1992; Chirivella & Martinez, 1994).

Up to the present time, metamotivational dominances could be established for only two of the four dyads through established psychometric tests such as the Telic Dominance Scale (Murgatroyd, Rushton, Apter, & Ray, 1978) and the Negativism Dominance Scale (McDermott & Apter, 1988) and this has limited the scope of research in this area. A dominance test for all four dyads, including the interactional dyads, has only very recently been published (Apter, Mallows, & Williams, 1998). In addition, dominance scales measure general metamotivational tendencies of individuals across attitude objects. It is sometimes more useful or desirable to obtain an impression of an individual's motivational position towards a more specific, or even very specific aspect of life. An appropriate label for such a position is *metamotivational orientation*. By using the orientation concept, one can establish the nature of motivation for sport participation in reversal theory terms. In the study reported in this chapter, respondents in a sport participation survey were classified into metamotivational orientation groups on the basis of their ranking of reasons provided for participation. Thus, a person rating 'for leisure and enjoyment' higher than other stated reasons for involvement in sport would be classified as a participant with a paratelic orientation towards sport participation. Similarly, telic-, autic-, mastery-, and sympathy-oriented participants were identified. This allowed comparisons between orientation groups for a variety of sport participation-related variables.

# THE SURVEY METHOD IN METAMOTIVATIONAL RESEARCH

The study of motivational aspects of sport involvement can follow a variety of designs and methods, each with both advantages and drawbacks. The main guides to selecting an approach are the purpose of the study and the nature of its design; in other words, the research question is the key to the choice of method. Thus, if one is interested in mood states and their effect on performance, a different approach would be called for than if one wishes to research potential links between metamotivational dominance and sport type preference. The former study would likely involve a group of participants with common characteristics and could utilize interviews, observation, mood state measuring instruments, or a combination of these. Relevant in-depth details pertaining to the participants would be considered and consequently the study would likely be on a rather small scale. For the latter type of study, using the survey method, large numbers of sport participants could complete one or more existing dominance scale and their sport preference could be established via a questionnaire. Alternatively, participants in specific sport types could be tested and compared for their dominances.

Since the purpose of large-scale survey-type studies is to establish whether a significant relationship exists between variables, the use of a large number of participants in the sample would be advisable, but the disadvantage is that one would not be able to take into account the individual participant's sport involvement in more detail. Both of these approaches, and others such as case studies and time-series analyses, have their place and function in research.

In the study presented here, the objective was to determine if metamotivational orientation toward sport participation is associated with certain elements of participation, such as frequency, preferences and perceived competence, and whether these orientation groups would display differences consistent with reversal theory. An important question was whether the concept of metamotivational orientation is valid: do individuals, assigned to an orientation group based on responses to Likert scale statements, display attributes that are in line with what reversal theory would predict for such a group?

This chapter shows how reversal theory can be applied to sport research by using the metamotivational orientation concept in a survey approach. Specifically, the purpose of the study reported here was to examine differences in sport and exercise participation frequencies, preferences for sport and activity types, and perceived physical ability and fitness in university entrants who were grouped on the basis of their metamotivational orientation to sport participation.

## Method

*Participants*

The participants were 2387 students at the University of Hong Kong, newly admitted in 1995. They were issued a self-administered questionnaire as part of the documentation package sent out annually to incoming students by the university's registry. The return rate was in excess of 90%.

*Instrument*

The questionnaire for this study has been used with consistent results over the past five years for the purpose of programming decision making for student sport and recreation, and for research in sport participation motivation. In addition to a section for demographic information, the current instrument comprised three parts:

1. The frequency of participation in sport or exercise activities during the respondents' school years (excluding physical education classes), and the frequency of their intended participation during their time at university. In addition, motives for past and future participation were queried through Likert-scale statements, for which the respondents indicated the strength of their agreement with stated reasons for participation. Based on these responses, the respondents were subsequently categorized into metamotivational orientation groups (see below).
2. Respondents indicated preferences for 39 different sports and activities offered at the University of Hong Kong, including ball games, combat sports, racquet sports, different forms of dance, swimming, hiking, yoga, etc.
3. The respondents were also asked to rate their own physical ability and physical fitness as compared with people of their own age and sex, and their own ability to swim a distance of 50 metres.

## Procedure for Categorizing Groups by Metamotivational Orientation

In the present study, respondents were classified on the basis of their metamotivational orientation towards sport participation, and were retrospectively grouped according to the motive they rated highest (the 'deciding reason') for their intended participation. Of the original 2387 respondents, 180 stated that they would not participate in sport or physical activity during their university years. A further 837 respondents (380 males, 457 females) did not indicate which of the motives they rated highest and were excluded from the data analysis. The remaining 1370 respondents could be assigned to metamotivational orientation groups on the basis of the rated motives, although 6 respondents did not indicate gender. (Data from these respondents was excluded from the gender analysis.) Those who rated 'health-related fitness' highest were placed in the telic-oriented group, 'leisure and relaxation' in the paratelic-oriented group, 'to be with or make new friends' in the sympathy-oriented group, 'for character-building' or 'for better personal image' in the autic-oriented group, and 'for sport-related skills and fitness' in the mastery-oriented group. There were no statements in the questionnaire that clearly represented conformist, negativistic, or alloic orientations.

## Research Questions

The following research questions were examined:

1. Are there differences among the orientation groups with respect to their activity preferences, sport participation patterns, and self-perceptions of physical capacities such as physical ability, physical fitness, and capacity to swim?
2. Do these differences, if any, support expectations based on reversal theory?

## Data Analysis

Differences in the sizes of the orientation groups and in sport and physical activity preferences were tested through Chi-square procedures. Choices of sport were analysed for the specific sports and by type of sport: *safe–risk, endurance–explosive*, and *team–individual* sports. The safe sport category included 11 sports and activities in which bodily injury is unlikely, such as badminton, archery, table tennis, and yoga, whereas the risk category included 12 sports with potential for injury, such as martial arts, soccer, basketball, and rock-climbing. There were 7 activities or sports each in the endurance (e.g., circuit training, cycling, rowing) and explosive (e.g., track and field athletics, martial arts) categories. The team sport category comprised 9 sports (e.g., volleyball, soccer, and field hockey), while there were

15 activities and sports designated as individual (e.g., fitness training, tennis, swimming, archery). Chi-square tests for differences between meta-motivational orientation groups within each category were performed on the average number of respondents in that category (i.e., the sum of the number of respondents choosing the sports in the category divided by the number of sports in the category). Comparisons between two opposite categories were also made on the basis of percentage contributions of each (e.g., 50–50 would indicate equal numbers selecting safe and risk, or team and individual sports).

The significance of differences among the five orientation groups were tested through one-way and two-way (sex × orientation group) ANOVAs for the following variables: frequency of past and intended future participation, perceived physical ability, and perceived physical fitness. All statistical operations were performed in Abacus's Statview program (Abacus, 1992).

# RESULTS AND DISCUSSION

## Metamotivational Orientations towards Sport Participation

The breakdown in numbers and percentages by gender (males, $N = 630$, females $N = 734$) is shown in Figure 9.1. The vast majority of respondents were classified under the telic- or paratelic-oriented groups, in about equal percentages. This result was somewhat surprising, as one might have expected a broader spread across metamotivational orientation groups. For males, the numbers of students in the telic and paratelic groups were significantly higher than those in the autic and sympathy groups ($\chi^2 = 260.4$, $p < 0.0001$). For females, numbers in the telic and paratelic groups were significantly higher than those in the autic, sympathy, and mastery groups ($\chi^2 = 333.4$, $p < 0.0001$).

The finding of about equal percentages in the telic- and paratelic-oriented groups was perhaps also somewhat surprising as one might have expected a higher proportion of telic-oriented individuals in a sample of university entrants in Hong Kong. Chang and Harrison (1983) found a sample of Singaporean and Macau students to be predominantly telic dominant, much more so than their European counterparts. However, the current study measured orientation towards sport and exercise participation, not relatively non-specific telic or paratelic dominance. To what extent orientation towards sport participation is in concordance with metamotivational dominance is a question that needs to be addressed in future

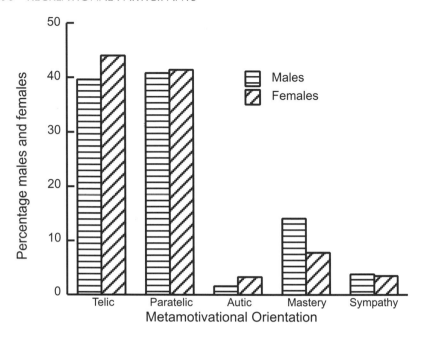

**Figure 9.1** Percentages and frequencies of categorized respondents in the meta-motivational orientation groups

research. Clearly, students in this study participated or intended to participate with two principal motives: to become or stay fit and healthy (a telic orientation), or for leisure and enjoyment (a paratelic orientation). The number of mastery-oriented future participants was relatively greater for males than for females ($\chi^2 = 18.27$, $p < 0.001$). The low numbers in the autic, mastery, and sympathy groups do not permit strong confidence in the generalization of the results reported here for these groups, and caution is required in their interpretation.

## Preferences for Sports and Activities

Basketball, badminton, tennis, swimming, table tennis, cycling, and football (soccer) were the activities most preferred by the males, while all five female orientation groups ranked badminton, tennis, squash, swimming, and cycling in the top eight choices. The least-preferred activities were mostly sports generally unfamiliar in Hong Kong, or perceived by these students to be gender-role inappropriate (e.g., soccer for females; dance for males). The popularity of certain sports with Hong Kong youth is quite pronounced and has dominated the responses to items dealing with choices of intended participation for all metamotivational orientation groups.

For the males, there were significant differences in three sports between the metamotivational orientation groups with respect to the number of respondents selecting these sports: for basketball, the telic group had a significantly lower number than the other groups ($\chi^2$ = 10.01, $p$ = 0.04); for fitness training, the paratelic group displayed significantly less interest ($\chi^2$ = 9.4, $p$ = 0.05); and for tennis, the number of autic-oriented participants was significantly lower than should be expected under a hypothesis of no dif-ference ($\chi^2$ = 12.7, $p$ = 0.013). These results confirm previous research findings (Kerr, 1991; Svebak & Kerr, 1989) which have shown that basket-ball was preferred and performed by paratelic dominant individuals, while weight trainers tended to be telic dominant. Recreational tennis generally involves a degree of interaction between either two or four players and this may be the reason it was not of interest to autic-oriented individuals.

For the females, there were significant differences in nine sports. In basketball ($\chi^2$ = 11.3, $p$ = 0.02), circuit training ($\chi^2$ = 10.7, $p$ = 0.03), survival training ($\chi^2$ = 9.1, $p$ = 0.05), and rugby ($\chi^2$ = 11.9, $p$ = 0.02), the mastery-oriented group had significantly higher numbers of selections, reflecting the usefulness of these sports to females who wish to master sport skills or their own bodies. In their preference for volleyball, both the autic and mastery groups scored significantly higher than other groups ($\chi^2$ = 14.2, $p$ < 0.01). Autic-oriented respondents scored significantly higher than other groups in their preference for windsurfing ($\chi^2$ = 10.4, $p$ = 0.033) and for Chinese martial arts (both individual sports), whereas the sympathy group (prefer-ring activities involving others) scored significantly lower than the other orientation groups ($\chi^2$ = 9.5, $p$ = 0.048) on these sports. Telic-oriented females were significantly high and paratelic-oriented significantly low in their preference for fitness training ($\chi^2$ = 19.3, $p$ < 0.001) and diet and exercise ($\chi^2$ = 14.8, $p$ = 0.005). The telic-oriented group's high interest in serious, goal-directed items, such as fitness and diet and exercise, and the paratelic group's low interest in these items might have been expected and are in line with predictions from reversal theory.

When sports were combined into categories based on risk–safe, endurance–explosive, and team–individual criteria, the differences among the orientation groups were small, but in directions consistent with the theory (see Figure 9.2). Consistent with previous research on telic domi-nance (Kerr, 1991; Kerr & Svebak, 1989), the male telic group preferred safe sports more than did the other male groups. Most of the female groups (with the exception of the sympathy group) preferred safe sports, but differences between these orientation groups on preference for safe or risk sports did not reach significance. The male groups tended to favour explo-sive sports, with the exception of the autic group, but all the female groups

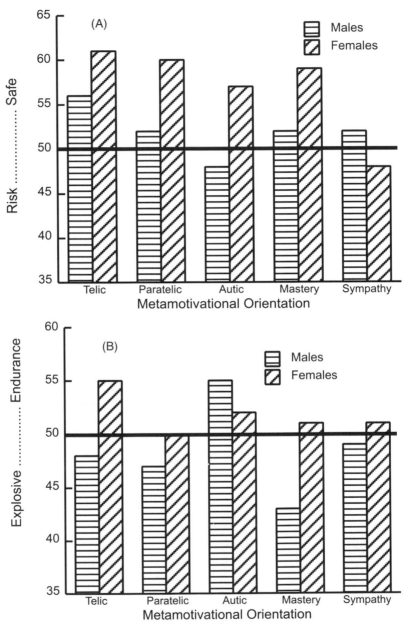

**Figure 9.2** Preferences for sport types of metamotivational orientation groups. (*Note*: The 50-line indicates a 50–50 split in percentage of respondents choosing either alternative. A column extending above the 50-line indicates a preference for (A) safe, (B) endurance or (C) team sports, respectively, while a column ending below the 50-line indicates a preference for (A) risk, (B) explosive, or (C) individual sports.)

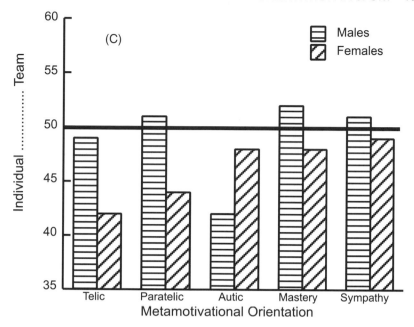

**Figure 9.2**    *(continued)*

indicated a preference for endurance over explosive activities, with the clearest preference shown by the telic group. Differences among male orientation groups were minor (with the exception of the male autic group's preference for individual sports), but the female telic and paratelic groups showed a marked preference for individual sports.

The Chi-square tests performed on average numbers of respondents selecting the risk–safe, explosive–endurance, and individual–team sports categories did not yield significant results, probably due to the overwhelming numbers of choices in the popular sports. However, paratelic-oriented males and females disagreed significantly more strongly with the Likert scale statement 'I prefer or would prefer an individual sport to a team sport', than telic-oriented male and female respondents ($F(5, 2159) = 3.25$, $p = 0.006$).

This study has provided preliminary data on preferences for sport and physical activities in metamotivational orientations as yet unexplored in sport research. While Kerr and Svebak have examined sport preferences in telic- and paratelic-dominant groups, or compared the Telic Dominance Scale scores of participants in telic- and paratelic-type sports (Kerr & Svebak, 1989; Svebak & Kerr, 1989), no previous studies have analysed preference data on groups labelled as autic, mastery, or sympathy in orientation. The autic and mastery groups tended to choose preferentially sports and activities where the outcome of personal performance is important, such as in athletics, martial arts, basketball, and volleyball, whereas sympathy-oriented respondents avoided these direct agonistic and competitive team activities in preference for more sociable sports like tennis. The tendency for telic-oriented male participants to prefer 'safe' sports, and for the paratelic males to lean relatively more towards 'risky' sports, confirms findings by Chirivella and Martinez (1994), Kerr (1991), Kerr and Svebak (1989), Rowland, Franken, and Harrison (1986), and Summers and Stewart (1993), and the finding of the current study – that gender is a factor that may mask orientation preferences for endurance versus explosive sports – is in support of results reported by Svebak and Kerr (1989). However, a marked difference between telic- and paratelic-oriented respondents as regards preference for endurance and explosive sports, which would be expected based on Svebak and Kerr's (1989) results, did not materialize. Preferences for team and individual sports have not yet been reported in the literature, other than results by Braathen and Svebak (1992), which showed that talented teenage team sport participants were less negativistic dominant than participants in endurance and explosive individual sports. The current results are not sufficiently pronounced to warrant firm conclusions.

## Frequency of Sport and Physical Activity Participation

The $F$-test in the two-way ANOVA showed a significant effect of groups for past participation frequency ($F(5, 2185) = 13.2$, $p < 0.001$). For both sexes, respondents in the mastery orientation group had higher participation frequencies than the other groups, with significant differences with the telic and paratelic groups (Figure 9.3).

The results for intended future participation frequency were similar ($F(5, 2182) = 12.85$, $p < 0.001$), with the male mastery group significantly higher than the male telic and paratelic groups, and the female mastery group significantly higher than the female telic, paratelic, and sympathy groups.

Figure 9.3 shows a consistency in overall participation patterns of the metamotivational orientation groups for males and females and for past and future participation: mastery-oriented respondents have the highest participation frequencies. Intended participation was substantially higher than past participation for the female groups only, with the exception of the female sympathy group. Past participation was lowest for the telic groups, possibly because a general telic orientation would encourage focusing on school work rather than on sport, which in Hong Kong society is

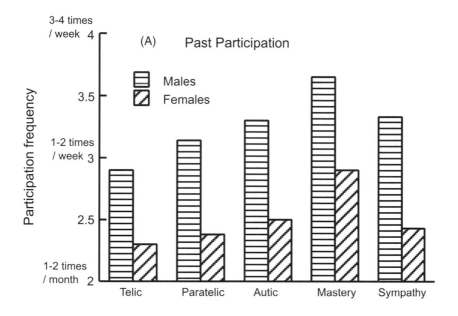

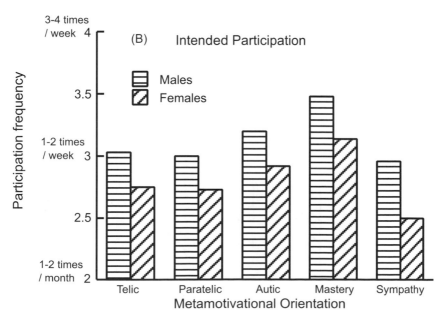

**Figure 9.3**   (A) Past and (B) intended future sport participation by metamotivational orientation groups

viewed as a rather frivolous pastime for children, unlike the North American situation (Roberts, 1984). However, the telic groups increased both in absolute values and relative to the other orientation groups in their intended participation frequency, in line with their telic participation motive of health and fitness.

These are the first reported sport and exercise participation frequency data for metamotivational orientation groups and thus comparison to other studies is not possible. However, these findings will be useful as reference points for future study results.

## Perceived Physical Ability, Fitness, and Swimming Capacity

There was a significant main effect of groups for the perceived ability variable ($F(5, 2184) = 8.97$, $p < 0.001$). The male and female mastery-orientation groups had the highest perceived ability of all groups, significantly higher than the male telic and paratelic groups and the female telic group (Figure 9.4). The male autic group also had a high mean score on perceived ability, but the large variability precluded significance of the differences with other groups. There were no significant differences among

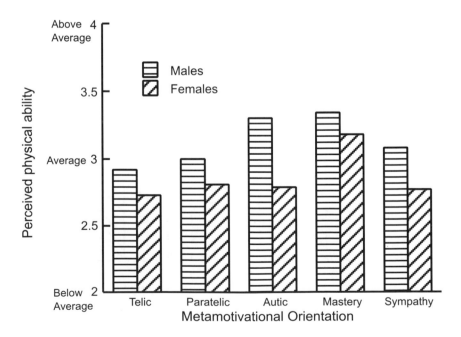

**Figure 9.4**  Perceived physical ability by metamotivational orientation groups

the metamotivational orientation groups for perceived fitness ($F(5, 2185)$ = 1.71, $p > 0.05$).

Perceived ability has been considered to be an important component of sport participation motivation. Theories by Harter (1978) and Nicholls (1984) propose that perceived ability, or perceived competence, results from successful participation experiences which instil a desire in the participant to become more competent. These theories, while different in detail, contend that the perception of one's ability is crucial to sport behaviour and the main mediator of performance and persistence. Roberts (1984) asserts that high perceived ability is an important goal for competitive sport participants for any of three achievement orientations: to demonstrate competence, to achieve mastery, and to attract social approval. Analysis of ability attributions is therefore essential for understanding entry into, functioning in, and withdrawal from sport.

However, it has been argued that all this may well be true and correct where serious, competitive participants are concerned, particularly athletes at higher qualitative levels, but not for a large group of participants who engage in sport principally for other motivational outcomes, such as fun, health and fitness, or the social contacts facilitated by sport involvement (Lindner, 1996). Weiss (1993) writes that the sport psychology literature is consistent in reporting significant relationships between perceived ability and motivation, but that perceived ability and other attributes form only one of three interacting groups of factors that account for children's involvement in organized competitive sport, the other two being socialization influences and available opportunities.

The current results appear to be in support of this view of a selective role of perceived ability: those wanting to achieve competence in sport skills – namely the male and female mastery groups and, to some extent, the male autic group – had higher than average perceived ability scores, whereas the male telic, paratelic, and sympathy groups had relatively lower scores in perceived ability. Female scores on perceived ability were consistent across all groups except the mastery-oriented group and in all cases were lower than male scores. The results of the current study, therefore, cast some doubt on the appropriateness of the competence orientation approach (e.g. Roberts, 1984) to sport participation motivation in populations other than competitive athletes.

There were more swimmers (respondents who indicated they could swim a distance of 50 metres) than non-swimmers in all male orientation groups, but the percentage of swimmers in the male autic (83%) and sympathy (85%) groups was much higher than in the other groups. For the females, there were about equal numbers of swimmers and non-swimmers in most groups, except for the telic group, where the number of non-swimmers exceeded that of swimmers. The autic and sympathy orientation groups also had a higher proportion of swimmers to non-swimmers. Chi-square values did not reach significance within the two sexes, but there were significantly more swimmers in the male than in the female sympathy group ($\chi^2 = 12.71, p = 0.013$).

These results can be rather readily explained in reversal theory terms. Sympathy-oriented individuals, who wish to be with or make new friends through sport participation, may view swimming as an activity with good potential for social contacts with friends and therefore have become reasonably competent and familiar with it. Autic-oriented individuals are also likely to want to acquire the skill for self-preservation, or other egotistical purposes. Differences in proportions of swimmers and non-swimmers among the remaining orientation groups were non-significant. The failure of the mastery group to show higher percentages of swimmers is perhaps surprising, as the reason these participants are involved in sport is most likely to be because they are, or desire to be, good at them. Therefore they might have been expected to also want to have the ability to swim.

# CONCLUSIONS

This chapter has provided an example of application of the survey method in reversal theory research on motivation in sport, and demonstrated the utility of the concept of metamotivational orientation towards sport participation. The results of the study reported in this chapter appear to validate this orientation concept, since differences found among the metamotivational orientation groups were generally in line with what reversal theory would expect in terms of behaviours, attitudes, and perceptions. Another contribution by the present work is the extension of reversal theory sport research to metamotivational dimensions that have not yet been explored empirically, such as the autic, mastery, and sympathy dimensions. The frequencies in the various orientations are what reversal theory theorists might have expected, but have not yet been able to establish: relatively low percentages of individuals involved in recreational sport for autic, mastery, or sympathy motives. However, these results should be interpreted with caution for two reasons:

1. The questionnaire used in this study was not specifically designed to assess metamotivational orientations in the reversal theory framework. Rather, orientations were retrospectively ascribed to those stated deciding reasons that were judged to be telic, autic, etc., in nature. Therefore, there is a possibility that the large proportion of telic- and paratelic-oriented respondents could be a result of the wording of the statements

rather than a true reflection of the distribution of orientations in the population of university entrants. Future research should use reasons statements about students' participation motives that more closely reflect the various orientations, including those that were not represented in the current instrument.

2. Until future study establishes how much concordance there is between rather specific metamotivational orientation and general metamotivational dominance, findings involving the former cannot be generalized to the latter. In other words, the frequencies and the differences found for and between the metamotivational orientation groups cannot be validly applied to metamotivational dominances.

A further question that arises from the current research is how metamotivational orientations, and for that matter dominances, should be analysed in these types of data sets. In the current chapter, overall orientation was used, that is, the statement that received the respondent's highest numerical rating on a 6-point scale was taken as that respondent's metamotivational orientation towards sport participation. However, in reversal theory, metamotivational states are divided into groups of somatic and transactional states, and it might be useful to include this division when deciding on an individual's motivational orientation. A respondent's *somatic* orientation could be assessed as the highest of the telic, paratelic, negativistic, and conformist statements, with or without further criteria. Similarly, *transactional* orientation would be identified from the ratings of the autic, alloic, sympathy, and mastery statements. There may be theoretical arguments in favour of the assessment of four orientations, one for each dyad; for example, is the respondent more telic than paratelic oriented, more autic than alloic oriented, and so on.

Another approach to the measurement of metamotivational orientations stems from the difficulty of formulating participation motivation statements that precisely represent one metamotivational state without overlap with other states. For certain states (e.g., mastery and autic orientations) overlap is extremely difficult to avoid. In subsequent research ongoing at this time, motivation statements have been drawn up which are accurate reflections of state combinations rather than individual states. In this way, for example, an individual may be assigned to an autic–mastery orientation group if the statement favoured indicates a wish to excel for selfish or egoistic reasons. A paratelic–negativistic orientation would be assigned when the statement favoured by a respondent represents rebellious fun-seeking. Future research must determine the most fruitful of these methods of determining metamotivational orientations if a more complete understanding of sport participation motives is to be achieved.

# REFERENCES

Abacus (1992). *Statview: The ultimate data analysis and presentation system.* Berkeley, CA: Abacus Concepts, Inc.

Apter, M. J. (1982). *The experience of motivation.* London: Academic Press.

Apter, M. J. (1989). *Reversal theory: Motivation, emotion and personality.* London: Routledge.

Apter, M. J., Mallows, R. & Williams, S. (1998). The development of the Motivational Style Profile. *Personality and Individual Differences,* **24**, 7–18.

Biddle, S. J. (1992). Sport and exercise motivation: A brief review of antecedent factors and psychological outcomes of participation. *Physical Education Review,* **15**, 98–110.

Biddle, S. J. & Fox, K. R. (1988). The child's perspective in physical education: 11 children's participation motives. *British Journal of Physical Education,* **19**, 79–82.

Braathen, E. T. & Svebak, S. (1992). Motivational differences among talented teenage athletes: The significance of gender, type of sport and level of excellence. *Scandinavian Journal of Medicine and Science in Sports,* **2**, 153–159.

Chang, A. & Harrison, G. (1983, September). *Telic dominance in Singapore and Macau Chinese.* Paper presented at the 1st International Symposium on Reversal Theory, Wales, UK.

Chirivella, E. C. & Martinez, L. M. (1994). The sensation of risk and motivational tendencies in sports: An empirical study. *Personality and Individual Differences,* **16**, 777–786.

Colley, A., Eglinton, E. & Elliot, E. (1992). Sport participation in middle childhood: Association with styles of play and parental participation. *International Journal of Sport Psychology,* **23**, 193–206.

Fu, F. H. (1993). *The development of sport culture in the Hong Kong Chinese.* Hong Kong: Hong Kong Baptist College.

Gould, D., Feltz, D. & Weiss, M. R. (1985). Motives for participating in competitive youth swimming. *International Journal of Sport Psychology,* **6**, 126–140.

Gould, D. & Petlichkoff, L. (1988). Participation motivation and attention in young athletes. In F. L. Smoll, R. A. Magill & M. J. Ash (Eds.), *Children in sport* (3rd edn.) (pp. 161–178). Champaign, IL: Human Kinetics.

Harahousou, Y. S. & Kabitsis, C. N. (1994). Important reasons that motivate Greek women into participation in physical recreation. In F. I. Bell & G. H. Van Gyn (Eds.), *Access to active living. Proceedings of the 10th Commonwealth and International Scientific Congress* (pp. 113–118). Victoria, BC: University of Victoria.

Harter, S. (1978). Effectance motivation reconsidered. *Human Development,* **21**, 34–64.

Kerr, J. H. (1991). Arousal-seeking in risk sport participants. *Personality and Individual Differences*, **12**, 613–616.

Kerr, J. H. (1997). *Motivation and emotion in sport: Reversal theory*. London: Wiley.

Kerr, J. H. & Svebak, S. (1989). Motivational aspects of preference for, and participation in, 'risk' and 'safe' sports. *Personality and Individual Differences*, **10**, 797–800.

Lindner, K. J. (1996). Motivation factors in the promotion of sport participation. *The Hong Kong Journal of Sports Medicine and Sports Science*, **1**, 33–44.

Lindner, K. J., Butcher, J. & Johns, D. P. (1991). *Sport participation and withdrawal by urban children and youths between grades 1 and 10*. Winnipeg: Research Grant report to Sport Canada.

Lindner, K. J., Butcher, J. & Johns, D. P. (1994a). Recall of competitive sports participation by urban Grade 10 students. *Canadian Association for Health, Physical Education and Recreation Journal, Research Supplement*, **1**, 79–95.

Lindner, K. J., Butcher, J. & Johns, D. P. (1994b). Factors affecting withdrawal from youth sport. In K. J. Lindner & M. A. Speak (Eds.), *Sport and exercise participation: Motivation and barriers* (pp. 43–53). Hong Kong: The University of Hong Kong Centre for Physical Education and Sport.

Lindner, K. J., Johns, D. P. & Butcher, J. (1991). Factors in withdrawal from youth sport: A proposed model. *Journal of Sport Behavior*, **14**, 3–18.

Lindner, K. J. & Speak, M. A. (1995a). Self-estimates of ability and fitness level, and reasons for sport (non) participation by university entrants. In R. van Fraechem-Raway & Y. Vanden Auweele (Eds.), *Proceedings of the IXth European Congress on Sport Psychology, Part III* (pp. 1260–1267). Brussels: Université Libre de Bruxelles.

Lindner, K. J. & Speak, M. A. (1995b). Frequency of and reasons for sport participation by students entering university. In F. Fu & M. L. Ng (Eds.), *Sport psychology: Perspectives and practices toward the 21st century* (pp. 295–304). Hong Kong: Hong Kong Baptist University.

Lindner, K. J. & Speak, M. A. (1995c). Reasons for non-participation in sport and activity: Perceived ability, fitness and economic factors. In *Proceedings of the 18th Universiade FISU/CESU Conference* (pp. 295–304). Fukuoka, Japan: Organizing Committee for the Universiade 1995.

Lindner, K. J. & Speak, M. A. (1996). University entrants' opinions on gender and sport issues. In D. J. Macfarlane (Ed.), *Gender issues in sport and exercise* (p. 82). Hong Kong: The University of Hong Kong. (Abstract.)

McDermott, M. R. & Apter, M. J. (1988). The Negativism Dominance Scale (NDS). In M. J. Apter, J. H. Kerr & M. P. Cowles (Eds.), *Progress in reversal theory* (pp. 373–376). Amsterdam: North-Holland/Elsevier.

Murgatroyd, S., Rushton, C., Apter, M. J. & Ray, C. (1978). The development of the Telic Dominance Scale. *Journal of Personality Assessment*, **42**, 519–528.

Nicholls, J. G. (1984). Achievement motivation: Conceptions of ability, subjective experience, task choice and performance. *Psychological Review*, **91**, 328–346.

Petlichkoff, L. M. (1996). The drop-out dilemma in youth sport. In O. Bar-or (Ed.), *The child and adolescent athlete: Encyclopaedia of sports medicine*, Vol. VI, Ch. 28 (pp. 418–430). Oxford: Blackwell Science.

Roberts, G. C. (1984). Toward a new theory of motivation in sport: The role of perceived ability. In J. M. Silva & R. S. Weinberg (Eds.), *Psychological foundations of sport* (pp. 214–218). Champaign, IL: Human Kinetics.

Rowland, G. L., Franken, R. E. & Harrison, K. (1986). Sensation seeking and participation in sporting activities. *Journal of Sport Psychology*, **8**, 212–220.

Speak, M. A., Lindner, K. J. & Li, D. (1994). Participation in sport by students entering The University of Hong Kong: Results of a survey undertaken in September 1993. In K. J. Lindner & M. A. Speak (Eds.), *Sport and exercise participation: Motivation and barriers* (pp. 3–17). Hong Kong: The University of Hong Kong Centre for Physical Education and Sport.

Summers, J. & Stewart, E. (1993). The arousal performance relationship: Examining different conceptions. In S. Serpa, J. Alves, V. Ferriera & A. Paula-Brito (Eds.), *Proceedings of the VIII World Congress of Sport Psychology* (pp. 229–232). Lisbon, Portugal: International Society of Sport Psychology.

Svebak, S. & Kerr, J. H. (1989). The role of impulsivity in preference for sport. *Personality and Individual Differences*, **10**, 51–58.

Telama, R. & Silvenoinen, M. (1979). Structure and development of 11 to 19 years olds' motivation for physical activity. *Scandinavian Journal of Sports Sciences*, **1**, 23–31.

Theodorakis, Y., Doganis, G. & Bagiatis, K. (1992). Attitudes toward physical activity in female fitness programs participants. *International Journal of Sport Psychology*, **23**, 262–273.

Wankel, L. & Kreisel, P. (1985). Factors underlying enjoyment of youth sports: Sport and age-group comparisons. *Journal of Sports Psychology*, **7**, 51–64.

Weiss, M. R. (1993). Psychological effects of intensive sport participation on children and youth: Self-esteem and motivation. In B. R. Cahill & A. J. Pearl (Eds.), *Intensive participation in children's sport* (pp. 39–69). Champaign. IL: Human Kinetics.

Weiss, M. R. & Chaumeton, N. (1992). Motivational orientations in sport. In T. S. Horn (Ed.), *Advances in sport psychology* (pp. 61–99). Champaign, IL: Human Kinetics.

# 10
# Some Final Considerations

**John H. Kerr**

*University of Tsukuba, Japan*

## INTRODUCTION

A recent quote from the late Hans Eysenck provides a timely reminder to all psychologists (including reversal theory sport researchers) of the complexities with which they are dealing:

> Psychologists have to deal with persons, not atoms. It is a person who comes into the laboratory: a person with his or her own ideas, emotions, prejudices, bits of knowledge and information; a person with a specific position on the major dimensions of personality; a person with his or her special IQ and specific abilities. All of this must interact in diverse ways with performance on most, if not all, experimental conditions; it must affect memory, learning, perception, conditioning, emotional reactions, psychophysiology – indeed anything he or she does. The evidence for such large-scale interaction is conclusive (Eysenck & Eysenck, 1985) and makes it imperative for the relevant personality factors to be included in any experimental design. Conversely, such inclusion, governed always by theory, will throw much needed light on the value of the theory in question and will hopefully lead to improvements in that theory, or even substitution by a better theory and the creation of a paradigm.
>
> (Eysenck, 1997, p. 1234)

*Experiencing Sport: Reversal Theory.* Edited by J. H. Kerr.
© 1999 John Wiley & Sons Ltd.

Although it clearly wasn't Eysenck's intention, the quote also neatly encapsulates the very essence of reversal theory and could almost be taken as a kind of 'mission statement' or credo for reversal theory research. Reversal theory certainly recognizes the importance of individual experience and the role that cognition and emotion play in that experience, and reversal theory research is certainly about testing the theory and, where possible, adding to and improving it. In similar fashion, reversal theory sport research is *theory driven*, with the findings not only providing a better understanding of what athletes are experiencing when performing, but also testing and providing support for the concepts and arguments which make up the theory.

Observation of journal and textbook contents over the last 10 years suggests that much of the other work carried out in sport psychology has been data driven, especially in North America. As well as being theory driven rather than data driven, reversal theory sport research has followed what is sometimes known as a *top-down* approach (as indeed has reversal theory research in general; see Apter, 1989, pp. 7–8). This means that, rather than undertaking research studies and then attempting to draw together the results in the formulation of a model or theory, reversal theory itself generates and guides research efforts.

However, as Apter (1989) has pointed out, the structural phenomenology which forms the bedrock of reversal theory means that the theory is also *experience driven* and adopts what he terms an *inside-out* approach. He states:

> The general approach of structural phenomenology is therefore not just 'top-down' but is also what one might call 'inside-out'. It starts from subjective experience and interprets behaviour, or physiological processes, in the light of this experience – rather than starting with external observation and measurement and then (possibly) making inferences about the experience which may lie behind it. Thus in dealing with arousal, instead of starting with an objective measure of cortical or autonomic arousal and then (perhaps) asking how far the subject is being aroused, reversal theory does things the other way round. It starts from the question of whether the subject feels aroused, and then looks to see what the physiological concomitants of this feeling might be, and therefore what might be the best physiological indices.
>
> (Apter, 1989, pp. 7–8)

# QUANTITATIVE AND QUALITATIVE RESEARCH METHODS

Reversal theory sport research also attempts to take advantage of both quantitative and qualitative research methods. This may go against general trends in both psychology and sport psychology. Stevenson and Cooper

(1997), in a recent article in *The Psychologist*, debated the relative values of quantitative and qualitative research. Morgan (1996) had earlier outlined the quantitative position, to which Sherrard (1997) replied on behalf of those favouring the qualitative approach. The debate is a continuing one which resurfaces frequently in psychology writing. Psychology in general has been built up on the positivist approach commonly used in the natural sciences, with the emphasis on the use of the scientific method and quantitative research techniques to collect and analyse data and establish forms of knowledge on the basis of results. By adopting this approach, psychology could gain and maintain respectability in the scientific world. The challenge to this approach came from constructionist views, which argued that knowledge is socially constructed and best understood by the use of qualitative research techniques.

There are some writers who have been highly critical of the scientific method in psychology. They claim that, while the scientific method has worked well as a basis for research in the natural sciences, its use in the study of human behaviour has been less than adequate. Kline (1988), for example, took an extreme view of psychological work based on this method in general (and in experimental, cognitive, social, and animal psychology in particular), claiming that it has failed to produce any real insight into aspects of human behaviour like feelings and emotions.

Likewise, Parker (1989) talked about the crisis in modern social psychology and the disaffection among those involved with traditional approaches in psychology which emphasized laboratory-type experimentation. Parker (1989) argued for a radical approach and a new *realist* social psychology which would challenge the non-existent causal laws sought by positivist social psychologists.

Although he does not refer to these texts (indeed, he deliberately makes no reference to any texts), Salter (1997) adopts a similar standpoint with respect to mainstream British sport psychology which has implications for sport psychology in general. He states:

> I fear that left unrectified British sports psychology is on the point of entering a conceptual and methodological cul-de-sac. I fear that as the position reveals itself the majority of British sports psychologists are adopting a naive realist position with regard to their work. Instead of questioning the unique demands of the sporting context, the profession appears to be content to ride on the coat tails of main-stream empirical psychology. Here, rather than innovate, sports psychologists appear to be content to fulfil their scholarly obligations by referencing the model of the physics laboratory and not the complexity of the world of sport. . . . There is a need to move away from the false certainty of 'hard data' and towards an approach that allows us to capture and work with the difficult to articulate, yet essential, aspects of sporting performance.
>
> (Salter, 1997, pp. 248–249)

Salter's (1997) call for 'a radical psychology of sport' may well be justified, but there is some evidence that changes are already taking place. For example, the Sport and Exercise Psychology section of the British Psychological Society recently published *Quality and quantity: Research methods in sport and exercise psychology* (Robson, Cripps, & Steinberg, 1996). Several of the papers were based on the use of qualitative methods, ranging from repertory grid analysis (Jones & Harris, 1996) to the use of diary methods (Clough, Hockey, & Sewell, 1996). There are also signs of a relatively recent similar change in the publications included in several North American sport psychology journals (e.g., Côté, Salmela, Baria, & Russell, 1995; Jackson, 1992; Van Mele, Vanden Auweele, & Rzewnicki, 1995).

The main thrust of Stevenson and Cooper's (1997) article, mentioned above, was their attempt to explore the middle ground somewhere between the extremes of the advocates for either quantitative or qualitative research only:

> We contend that both positivism and constructivism are problematic. Positivism entails a narrow definition of good science which serves to distance the researcher from the researched. In constructivist research there is no strong methodological position as the relativism implicit in this approach suggests that as all accounts of the world are equally good, all research positions are equally good. The definition of 'knowledge' becomes more fluid.
>
> Rather than adopting a dichotomising description of enquiry, Moon, Dillon and Sprenkle (1991), suggested that inquiry positions lie along a continuum with positivism at one end and constructivism at the other. According to its position on the continuum, any inquiry stance will entail certain suppositions concerning epistemology (how we know) and ontology (what can be known). Implicit in the idea of a continuum is the possibility of adopting some 'middle ground' research position.
>
> (Stevenson & Cooper, 1997, p. 159)

The article goes on to encourage researchers to reflect carefully on the process of their research rather than apply research methods in a routine way. This 'reflexivity' (see Bryman, 1988) should allow investigators to choose research methods appropriate to the phenomenon under investigation.

Reversal theory research has adopted not so much a middle ground approach to understanding human behaviour in sport, but what might be termed a *middle way* or an eclectic multimethod approach. This means that careful reflection on the part of reversal theory researchers has led them to select a wide range of techniques from the quantitative–qualitative reserve (sometimes in combination), which are best suited to unravel the nuances and idiosyncrasies of the individual's thinking in particular contexts (see Figure 10.1). This approach to research, of course, is in keeping with reversal theory's phenomenological underpinnings, where the subjective experience of the individual is considered of crucial importance in understanding his or her motivation and emotion. The advantages and disadvantages of research techniques used in reversal theory research were described and discussed by Apter in Chapter 2.

# REVERSAL THEORY'S ECLECTIC APPROACH TO RESEARCH

A particularly good example of this eclectic approach and the use of quantitative and qualitative methods in combination was provided by Svebak and Murgatroyd (1985). Based on the responses to the Telic Dominance Scale (TDS) (Murgatroyd, Rushton, Apter, & Ray, 1978) by 110 male and female students, they selected two groups, one of extreme telic and the other of extreme paratelic dominant individuals. Having used a survey questionnaire to form these groups, they then went on to use psychophysiological and interview techniques, backed up by a state questionnaire, the Telic State Measure (TSM) (Svebak & Murgatroyd, 1985), to carry out a validation of reversal theory constructs. The results from the psychophysiological experiment indicated biological differences between the two dominance groups (e.g., in muscle tension in striate muscles as indicated by passive forearm flexor EMG-activity). The results from the structured interviews (also rated by five independent judges) showed that telic and paratelic dominant individuals could be identified, and that differences in lifestyle patterns were also apparent. As the authors stated, 'the success of the multimethod approach taken in this study of the validity of theoretical constructs could not have been achieved by the use of any one or pair of methods alone'.

Reversal theory sport research has also taken on board the eclectic approach utilized in more general reversal theory research, as shown by the contributions to this book (see Figure 10.1). In order to tap into the thinking of sport performers in a series of different circumstances and situations in sport, a variety of both quantitative and qualitative research techniques and tools have been used to advantage. In all cases, whether quantitative or qualitative, or involving high-level or recreational performers, attempts were made to ensure ecological validity for the sport activity being investigated.

Surveys, laboratory experiments, field experiments, field studies, and real-life simulations have all been methods used in reversal theory quantitative sport research. The quantitative tools to date have included metamotivational dominance personality measures (e.g., Chirivella & Martinez, 1994; Svebak & Kerr, 1989), metamotivational state measures completed pre/post, or during performance (e.g., Cox & Kerr, 1989a, 1989b; Kerr

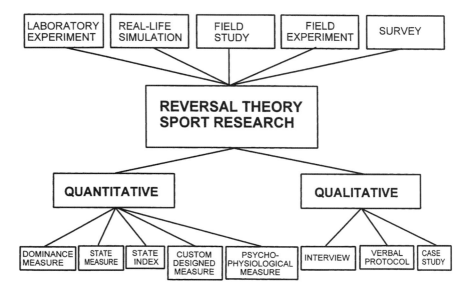

**Figure 10.1**   An overview of reversal theory sport research

& van Schaik, 1995), measures of emotion, stress, and effort (Males & Kerr, 1996; Purcell, 1999), objective indices of metamotivational state (e.g., Kerr & Vlaswinkel, 1993), custom-designed questionnaires (e.g., Apter & Batler, 1997), and psychophysiological measures (e.g., Braathen & Svebak, 1990). Several studies have used these in combination (e.g., Braathen & Svebak, 1994).

Settings for qualitative research have been real sports events, some competitive, some non-competitive. The majority of investigations have been field studies. The techniques used have included semi-structured interviews and the subsequent use of metamotivational coding schedules (e.g., Males, Chapter 5 in this volume; Males, Kerr, & Gerkovich, 1998), verbal protocols (e.g., Purcell, Chapter 4 in this volume), and case studies (e.g., Males, 1995, 1996 – in snooker and slalom canoeing, respectively).

Some studies have used a combination of qualitative techniques and yet others have used a combination of qualitative and quantitative techniques. In Chapter 6 in this volume, Svebak reviews a series of studies in sport which were based on a three-way methodological approach to research involving experimental psychophysiology, survey, and qualitative interviewing (see also Braathen & Svebak, 1990, 1992, 1994). Multimethod studies combining quantitative and qualitative techniques were also used effectively in comprehensive studies of slalom canoeing (Males & Kerr, 1996; Males, Kerr & Gerkovich, 1998; see also Males, Chapter 5 in this volume), and golf (Purcell, 1999).

Parts of this book may have been overly critical of reversal theory measures used in quantitative research to date. In order to redress the balance, as it were, it may be worth mentioning here that since the first measure, the Telic Dominance Scale (Murgatroyd *et al.*, 1978), became available, considerable efforts have been made to develop better and all-inclusive instruments. The recent publication of the Motivational Style Profile (MSP) (Apter, Mallows, & Williams, 1998), after some years spent validating the instrument, means that a dominance measure which covers all four metamotivational pairs is now available.

As far as state measures are concerned, the Telic State Measure has been in use since the early 1980s (and features in several chapters in this book). The best published description of the measure is found in Svebak and Murgatroyd (1985), which is the one usually referred to in the reversal theory literature. Since then, at least two other state instruments have been developed. One, the Somatic State Questionnaire (SSQ) (Cook, Gerkovich, Potocky, & O'Connell, 1993) deals with the telic, paratelic, negativistic, and conformity states, as well as arousal. A second, the Telic/Paratelic State Instrument (T/PSI) (Calhoun, 1995; Calhoun & O'Connell, 1995; see also Cogan & Brown, Chapter 7 in this volume), provides an alternative for measuring whether the telic or paratelic state is operative. These two measures and information about scoring are included as Appendix A and Appendix B, respectively.

A state instrument covering all four metamotivational pairs and several dimensions of arousal is currently being developed by Kerr and Apter. It is specifically designed for use in sport and has been labelled the State of Mind Indicator for Athletes (SOMIFA). It has been revised several times as the process of validation is undertaken and the final version is also included as Appendix C. Until trials and validation are complete, attempts to publish the measure in an academic journal have not yet been made. However, the measure is included in this volume with the idea that those who wish to do so may use the measure in their research, and that their findings might also contribute to the successful development of the SOMIFA.

In summary, reversal theory provides a comprehensive and dynamic theory which has relevance for understanding human behaviour in sport. Reversal theory sport researchers have shown a willingness to make use of a range of research techniques from both the quantitative and qualitative approaches. Indeed, they have shown their versatility in overcoming many of the problems with particular research techniques identified by Apter earlier in this book. This flexible and enthusiastic attitude to research is unlikely to change in the future as old methods are refined and new ones developed.

# FUTURE RESEARCH DIRECTIONS

## General Themes

Several of the contributors to this book have outlined their particular views of how reversal theory sport research can be developed in the future. However, a general theme that could be addressed in future is to show (1) where there is conceptual compatibility between reversal theory and other contemporary approaches in sport psychology and test any overlap empirically, and (2) why reversal theory is better at explaining motivation, emotion, and personality in sport than these other approaches. While this process has already begun, there is considerable scope for further work. Several examples are explored below.

### Sensation seeking

Zuckerman's (1979) notion of sensation seeking has often been used in explanations of motivation in dangerous sports like mountaineering, motorcycle racing, and free-fall parachute jumping. In addition, Zuckerman's Sensation Seeking Scale (SSS) (Zuckerman, 1979) has been used in studies of participants in these sports and the results have indicated that their scores on several subscales of the SSS are higher than those of other sports groups or the general public (e.g., Rowland, Franken, & Harrison, 1986; Zuckerman, 1983). There is a clear overlap here with the concept of paratelic dominance and arousal seeking from reversal theory. Several studies have shown a similar relationship between the performers of dangerous sports and paratelic dominance (e.g., Chirivella & Martinez, 1994; Kerr, 1991) and other studies have also shown statistically significant correlations between SSS subscales and subscales from the TDS (e.g., Trimpop, Kerr, & Kirkcaldy, 1999). However, sensation seeking in Zuckerman's terms is conceptualized as a personality *trait*, a relatively permanent feature of a person's overall personality which is consistent across situations. By comparison, while paratelic dominance is a bias in a person's personality towards spending time in the paratelic state, the concept of dominance is much less fixed or rigid than that of a personality trait like sensation seeking. Although a person may be paratelic dominant and spend the majority of his or her time in the paratelic state, that person will also spend time in the telic state. Therefore, a person with the paratelic state operative may exhibit arousal-seeking behaviour through participation in dangerous sports, but that same person with the telic state operative would be unlikely to engage in arousal-seeking behaviour. In this way, reversal theory's approach to personality and, in this case, arousal seeking is more flexible than Zuckerman's approach.

### State and trait anxiety

Some readers may recognize what has been described in the last paragraph of the previous section as being very similar to state and trait theories of personality. These include Spielberger's idea of state and trait anxiety (e.g., Spielberger, 1966) and Martens' use of this concept in the sports context as multidimensional anxiety theory (e.g., Martens, Burton, Vealey, Bump, & Smith, 1990). While there are some similarities between the state and trait personality approach and the metamotivational dominance and state approach of reversal theory, there is one major difference which gives reversal theory the edge over the other approaches.

Many of the sport psychology texts contain chapters about the effects of anxiety in sport and the majority use the state–trait approach to explain why athletes, faced by a particular set of circumstances, experience performance-debilitating anxiety in competitions. Many of these chapters then go on to describe how athletes can learn to cope with this anxiety. However, a basic tenet of reversal theory is that human behaviour is inherently inconsistent. This means that an athlete may behave in a certain way on one occasion in a particular competitive situation, but in similar circumstances on a different occasion (sometimes for no apparent reason) may behave completely differently. Those readers who are, or who have been, athletes, coaches, or even sport psychologists may well be able to recollect situations and occasions, in sport or perhaps in everyday life, where this has occurred. State and trait theories of anxiety or personality have difficulty explaining inconsistent behaviour in similar circumstances, but, as mentioned above, inconsistency of human behaviour is a fundamental principle of reversal theory.

### Optimal arousal theory, multidimensional anxiety theory, catastrophe theory, and zones of optimal functioning

In addition to multidimensional anxiety theory, the preoccupation with anxiety and performance in sport psychology has led to the use of a number of other theoretical approaches in an attempt to explain the relationship between arousal and performance. The main alternatives include optimal arousal theory (e.g., Hebb, 1955), catastrophe theory (e.g., Hardy, 1990), and zones of optimal functioning (e.g., Hanin, 1993). Apter (1989) has clearly demonstrated the limitations of optimal arousal theory when compared to reversal theory and Kerr (1997) has discussed the advantages of reversal theory over the other three approaches in some detail. There is no need to repeat the arguments here, but as Man, Stuchlíková, and Kindlmann (1995) have shown, when examining state–trait anxiety in top-level soccer players, reversal theory provided a more credible explanation of the results they obtained than other approaches. It should be possible to show the advantages of reversal theory over the other approaches through empirical studies.

*Attribution theory*

Attribution theory (Weiner, 1985) has also received considerable attention in the sport psychology literature. Wilson (Chapter 3 in this volume) has already discussed attribution theory and compared it with reversal theory. Even though attempts have been made to extend and improve on Weiner's (1985) theory in its application to sport (e.g., McAuley & Duncan, 1990; Vallerand, 1987), research results have provided only partial support. Readers should refer to Chapter 3 in this volume, where Wilson underlines his view that attribution theory's major limitations are its inability to describe the full range of emotion and to cover important determinants of emotional experience. According to Wilson, reversal theory does not share these limitations.

*Goal achievement/orientation theory*

Svebak (Chapter 6 in this volume) comments on motivation in sport and the influence of work by, for example, Nicholls (1989) and Duda (1993) on mainstream thinking in sport psychology. He points out that their notions of goal achievement and ego and task involvement or orientation are facets of the telic state in reversal theory. However, Svebak also criticizes this approach, claiming that it is biased and plays down the fact that for some performers and some sports, motivation to perform may be based mainly on the intrinsic fun and enjoyment that particular activities provide. He also questions the psychophysiological relevance of studies of stress responses in athletes which fail to make the distinction between serious, telic orientation and fun, paratelic orientation in sport motivation.

The examples described above serve to illustrate that there is some conceptual compatibility between reversal theory and other contemporary approaches in sport psychology. Clearly, reversal theory does have advantages over other approaches, not the least of which is its comprehensive and systematic, but flexible, framework for explaining human experience of motivation.

Apart from those examples mentioned above, future work might involve examining the large amount of work carried out on goal setting in sport. In

Burton's (1992) review of this work, he discusses differences in goal-setting styles and how they differentially affect goal responses in athletes. How might this relate to different types of dominance or motivational style in reversal theory? How would the effectiveness of goal-setting behaviour relate to behaviour in the telic and paratelic or mastery and sympathy states? These questions and others need answers.

Also, the theory of reasoned action (Ajzen & Fishbein, 1980) has been used to predict exercise behaviour (e.g., Norman & Smith, 1995). Could there be an overlap between this approach and the behaviour of telic dominant exercisers or those who participate in exercise while in the telic state? Should there be a parallel theory of unreasoned or unplanned action to accommodate the concepts of paratelic dominance and paratelic state in which well-planned exercise behaviour is not a feature? Or can reversal theory build on its apparent overlap with the theory of reasoned action and extend and develop it further?

## Specific Directions

If bets were to be taken as to the two specific areas of reversal theory sport research likely to expand in the next 10 years, then the leading contenders would probably be qualitative research on the motivational experience of performers, and Svebak's hypothesized triangular relationship between motivational characteristics, biological composition and sport preference. Svebak, in this volume, described the results of a number of studies which have supported this triangular relationship. Additional possible directions for further examining the three-way relationship are outlined below.

The link that has been established between preference for different types of sport and, for example, a predominance of slow- or fast-twitch muscle fibres, may well mean that there are other biologically-based elements of movement in different sports, such as aspects of neuromotor functioning, which might also support Svebak's hypothesis. Svebak, when talking about biological talent in Chapter 6 in this volume, mentions the importance of central nervous system transmitter-related pathways and the capacity of the brain in the activation and modulation of peripheral biological systems to sports performance.

Explosive sports require sudden, fast, powerful movements, often at short notice (e.g., the sprinter leaving the blocks or the wicketkeeper in cricket moving quickly to make a diving catch). Performing such actions successfully requires the performer to have fast reaction and movement times. Reaction time (the time interval between the presentation of a signal and the initiation of movement) is an aspect of the cognitive operations involved in the planning of voluntary movements in, for example, explosive sports. Fast reaction time would not appear to be a requirement for the successful performance of the repetitive, monotonous movement involved in endurance sports.

Researchers (e.g., Henry & Rogers, 1960; Christina, Fischman, Vercruyssen, & Anson, 1982) have been examining reaction time for a number of years and have differentiated three different types of reaction time. These are *simple*, *choice*, and *discrimination* reaction times. As Rose (1997) has pointed out, simple reaction time is a response to the presentation of a single stimulus (e.g., a sprinter and the sound of the starter's gun), choice reaction time is a response to a number of stimuli involving decision making on the part of the responder (e.g., a quarterback in American football after the snap having to choose between a number of open receivers), and discrimination reaction time involves responding only to one of several signals presented (e.g., the quarterback on the orders of the coach throws only to one receiver even though others may be available).

In addition, the use of surface electromyography (EMG) has led to a more precise measurement of what is termed *fractionated reaction time*, which is divided into *premotor time* and *motor time*. Premotor time is 'the time that elapses between the presentation of a reaction signal and the first change in EMG activity in the muscle that is identified as the prime mover in the action being observed', and motor time 'begins with the first change in electrical activity recorded in the prime-moving muscle and continues until the movement begins' (Rose, 1997, pp. 31–32).

It may be that research could show links between fast or slow premotor reaction time, predominance of fast- or slow-twitch muscle fibres, paratelic or telic metamotivational dominance, and preference for and high-level performance in explosive or endurance sports, respectively. Unlike the percentages of fast- and slow-twitch muscle fibres which remain fixed, reaction time can be improved to some degree through the learning and practice of movements. However, it would seem likely that fast reaction time is a basic biological feature which underlies effective performance in certain explosive sports. Conversely, having slow reaction time may be one of the genetically defined elements which pushes some individuals towards participation in endurance sports.

A second possible research direction might arise from Bailey, Silberstein, and Heskin's (1995) pilot study research which examined patterns of electrical activity in the brain as a function of the telic and paratelic metamotivational states. Electrical activity in the brain was recorded using the Steady State Visually Evoked Potential (SSVEP) technique. Telic and paratelic states were measured by a self-report questionnaire, and a cognitive perceptual task and a funny film were used to induce the telic or paratelic states, respectively, in participants. Increases in the SSVEP in the occipital-parietal regions were found to occur with the inducement of the telic state, and an attenuation of the SSVEP in the occipital-parietal regions with the inducement of the paratelic state. Thus, these findings suggest a decrease in brain activity (in the occipital-parietal regions) in the telic state and an increase of brain activity in the paratelic state. Clearly, this is another example of a biological link to particular metamotivational patterns, and it seems possible that the connection could also be made for sports performers. Although the use of this research technique in active sports would probably be out of the question, it might possibly be used in relatively inactive sports like certain types of shooting and archery, or perhaps chess. It would also be interesting to see if Bailey, Silberstein, and Heskin's (1995) results would also apply to telic and paratelic dominant athletes, or at least, to telic and paratelic dominant athletes with the telic or paratelic state operative.

A third possible research direction involves the recent revolution in genetic research, which currently has led to discoveries being announced almost daily in the media. Genetic research has enormous implications not only for psychology and reversal theory in general, but also for the further establishment of Svebak's triangular relationship in sport.

Owen and McGuffin (1997) predicted that genetics has the potential to change and perhaps even transform psychiatry and pointed out that it has already been shown that there are important genetic influences on severe mental disorders like schizophrenia, manic depression and autism, and milder conditions like mild depression and anxiety (e.g., Plomin, Owen, & McGuffin, 1994; Thapar & McGuffin, 1996). Dimensions of personality like extraversion and neuroticism have also been shown to be influenced by genes. In addition, Plomin, in his 1998 invited address to the British Psychological Society:

> . . . presented a view of the future in which psychologists would collect DNA routinely alongside psychological measures so that genetic influences could be taken into account as individual difference variables. This was not an idealistic vision, but a real practical possibility. Collecting DNA is no longer difficult or expensive. A cotton bud applied to the inside of the mouth and returned by post can already be analysed for thousands of genetic markers.
>
> (Jones, 1998, pp. 61–62)

One discovery which should immediately be of interest to reversal theory sport researchers was the identification of a gene connected to novelty or sensation seeking (Ebstein *et al.*, 1996; Owen & McGuffin, 1997). Returning to Svebak's relationship, the advent of gene research allows the interplay between genes and environment to be explored. Speculation would suggest that there may also be other genetically defined contributions to this relationship.

These are just three possible directions in which reversal theory sport research might attempt to confirm Svebak's thoughts on the relationship between motivational characteristics, biological composition, and sport preference. Undoubtedly there are others.

## TAKING STOCK

This book has included some of the latest reversal theory sport research results and as this final chapter draws to a close it may be useful to take stock of these findings and see how they have taken sport-based work in reversal theory forward.

1. Current knowledge of the emotional experience of elite sports performers in terms of operative metamotivational states has been extended to include all four pairs of states (e.g., Chapter 5).
2. Current knowledge of the emotional experience of athletes has been extended by examining that experience in terms of the full palate of 16 primary emotions from reversal theory (e.g., Chapter 3). Of note was the new-found importance of the transactional emotions.
3. Important links between planning and decision making in sport and athletes' metamotivational experience have been established (e.g., Chapter 4).
4. The hypothesized relationship between metamotivational characteristics, biological composition, and sport preference has been further supported by recent research findings (e.g., Chapter 6).
5. Previous findings on the metamotivation of risk and safe sport participants have been replicated in additional risk and safe sports studies and extended to include the negativism–conformity dimension. In addition, a new link has been made between risk sport participation and prevalence of injuries (e.g., Chapter 7).
6. Previous findings underlining the crucial role that telic- and paratelic-oriented metamotivation plays in recreational sport participation has been confirmed (e.g., Chapters 8 and 9) and current knowledge has been extended to include autic, mastery, and sympathy metamotivational categories (e.g., Chapter 9).
7. The basic tenets of reversal theory have been generally supported, ranging from the expected induction of the paratelic state in sport settings and locations (e.g., Chapter 8) and the confirmation of the importance of such variables as felt arousal (e.g., Chapters 5 and 8) and felt transactional outcome (e.g., Chapter 3) on metamotivation, to the efficacy of reversal theory's 16 primary emotions for describing athletes' competitive experience.

Taken together, these advances in reversal theory sport research are considerable. Traditionally, academics are supposed to be critical of their own work and list a number of possible shortcomings of the theoretical approach they have adopted. Several of the contributors to this book have been quite vigorous in their criticism of previous reversal theory sport research, but the truth is that there were few results from this latest collection which could not be explained by the theory and very few, if any, which seriously challenged any of its basic tenets.

# THE REVERSAL THEORY SPECIAL INTEREST GROUP IN SPORT

As mentioned in the Preface, the majority of the chapters in this book resulted from presentations made at the first reversal theory meeting which focused specifically on sport. Multi-topic international conferences on reversal theory have been organized every two years on a rotating basis between North America, Europe, and Australia. The next one, the ninth, will take place at the University of Windsor in Canada in June/July 1999 and the following one in Hobart, at the University of Tasmania, in 2001. Right from the first international conference held in 1983, there have always been papers concerned with sport. The number has now increased to such an extent that, in October 1996, the *1st International Workshop on Motivation and Emotion in Sport: Reversal Theory* was held in Tsukuba, Japan. By the time this book is published, a second meeting on *The Application of Reversal Theory to Sports Education* will have been held at the University of Hong Kong, and a third is planned for Darwin, Australia, in 2000. It is not that the special interest group in sport has broken away from the main group, but rather that work in reversal theory is growing fast, and where work in specific areas has reached or is about to reach a critical mass, additional meetings focusing on specialist areas will be increasingly necessary. As it happens, among all those doing reversal theory research, the reversal theory special interest group in sport was the first to find itself in this position.

# CONCLUDING COMMENTS

This chapter will close with an account of motivation in sport which illustrates how strongly motivated and determined sport performers can be.

### Made It by a Short Head

To many Japanese, the sport of sumo, with its seventeenth-century Shinto tradition and pageantry, is an exciting spectator sport. Tournaments may have more than 400 bouts in a day. Matches are short and decisive with contestants exhibiting power, deception, and technique to throw or push their opponents out of the dohyo sumo combat ring. Not all the competitors are Japanese, although they are all given Japanese names. Musashimaru, for instance, is one of two Hawaiians currently fighting at the elite level in Japanese sumo. He is 191 cm tall and weighs 188 kg. The other, Akebono, is 203 cm tall and weighs 213 kg. However, the subject of this account is Mainoumi, a Japanese wrestler who is only 171 cm tall and 96 kg in weight, easily the smallest and lightest contestant. In the few years since his arrival in the top divisions he has performed extremely well, given his size. He is rarely impressive in training, but comes into his own during competition, where his speed, agility and ability to use the element of surprise quite often enable him to defeat his much larger opponents.

This story, however, does not end there. The top level of Japanese sumo has a height restriction. After failing twice to be admitted, Mainoumi decided to ensure that the next time he would fulfil the height requirement. He took the unusual and somewhat bizarre step of having a silicon breast implant inserted into the top of his head to give him the extra couple of centimetres he needed. He duly passed the height requirement, was accepted into the top divisions of sumo and later had his implant removed. The lengths to which Mainoumi went to achieve his ambition of competing at the highest level show the inventiveness and creativity of an individual whose motivation in the face of an enormous size disadvantage continues to defy belief.

# NOTE

A reversal theory archive containing almost all reversal theory publications and other material is maintained by Mary Gerkovich in the USA. Those having difficulty finding references, etc., from other sources should contact her at the Midwest Research Institute, 425 Volker Blvd., Kansas City, Missouri 64110. Fax (int) + 1 816 753 7380; e-mail, mgerkovich@mriresearch.org.

# REFERENCES

Ajzen, J. & Fishbein, M. (1980). *Understanding attitudes and predicting social behavior*. Englewood Cliffs, NJ: Prentice Hall.

Apter, M. J. (1989). *Reversal theory: Motivation, emotion and personality*. London: Routledge.

Apter, M. J. & Batler, R. (1997). Gratuitous risk: A study of parachuting. In S. Svebak & M. J. Apter (Eds.), *Stress and health: A reversal theory perspective*. Washington, DC: Taylor & Francis.

Apter, M. J., Mallows, R. & Williams, S. (1998). The development of the Motivational Style Profile. *Personality and Individual Differences*, **24**, 7–18.

Bailey, A., Silberstein, R. & Heskin, K. (1995, July). *A pilot study to investigate brain electrical activity and metamotivational states.* Paper presented at the 7th International Conference on Reversal Theory, Melbourne, Australia.

Braathen, E. T. & Svebak, S. (1990). Task-induced tonic and phasic EMG response patterns and psychological predictors of endurance and explosive sports. *International Journal of Psychophysiology,* **9**, 21–30.

Braathen, E. T. & Svebak, S. (1992). Motivational differences among talented teenage athletes: The significance of gender, type of sport and level of excellence. *Scandinavian Journal of Medicine and Science in Sports,* **2**, 153–159.

Braathen, E. T. & Svebak, S. (1994). EMG response patterns and motivational styles as predictors of performance and discontinuation in explosive and endurance sports among talented teenage athletes. *Personality and Individual Differences,* **17**, 545–556.

Bryman, A. (1988). *Quantity and quality in social research.* London: Unwin Hyman.

Burton, D. (1992). The Jekyll/Hyde nature of goals: Reconceptualizing goal setting in sport. In T. S. Horn (Ed.), *Advances in sport psychology* (pp. 267–297). Champaign, IL: Human Kinetics.

Calhoun, J. E. (1995). *Construct validity of the Telic/Paratelic State Instrument: A measure of reversal theory constructs.* Unpublished doctoral dissertation, University of Kansas School of Nursing.

Calhoun J. E. & O'Connell, K. A. (1995, July). *Construct validity of the Telic/Paratelic State Instrument: A measure of reversal theory constructs.* Paper presented at the 7th International Conference on Reversal Theory, Melbourne, Australia.

Chirivella, E. C. & Martinez, L. M. (1994). The sensation of risk and motivational tendencies in sports: An empirical study. *Personality and Individual Differences,* **16**, 777–786.

Christina, R. W., Fischman, M. G., Vercruyssen, M. J. P. & Anson, J. G. (1982). Simple reaction time as a function of response complexity: Memory drum theory revisited. *Journal of Motor Behavior,* **14**, 301–321.

Clough, P., Hockey, B. & Sewell, D. (1996). The use of a diary methodology to assess the impact of exercise on mental states. In C. Robson, B. Cripps & H. Steinberg (Eds.), *Quality and quantity: Research methods in sport and exercise psychology* (pp. 22–27). Leicester: British Psychological Society, Sport and Exercise Psychology Section.

Cook, M. R., Gerkovich, M. M., Potocky, M. & O'Connell, K. A. (1993). Instruments for the assessment of reversal theory states. *Patient Education and Counselling,* **22**, 99–106.

Côté, J., Salmela, J. H., Baria, A. & Russell, S. (1995). Organizing and interpreting unstructured qualitative data. *The Sport Psychologist,* **7**, 127–137.

Cox, T. & Kerr, J. H. (1989a). Self-reported mood in competitive squash. *Personality and Individual Differences,* **11** (2), 199–203.

Cox, T. & Kerr, J. H. (1989b). Arousal effects during tournament play in squash. *Perceptual and Motor Skills*, **69**, 1275–1280.

Duda, J. L. (1993). Goals: A social cognitive approach into the study of achievement motivation in sport. In R. N. Singer, M. Murphy & L. K. Tennant (Eds.), *Handbook of research on sport psychology* (pp. 421–437). New York: Macmillan.

Ebstein, R. P., Novick, O., Umansky, R., Priel, B., Osher, Y., Blaine, D., Bennett, E. R., Nemanov, L., Katz, M. & Belmaker, R. H. (1996). Dopamine D4 receptor (D4DR) exon III polymorphism associated with the human personality trait of novelty seeking. *Nature Genetics*, **12**, 78–80.

Eysenck, H. J. (1997). Personality and experimental psychology: The unification of psychology and the possibility of a paradigm. *Journal of Personality and Social Psychology*, **73**, 1224–1237.

Eysenck, H. J. & Eysenck, M. W. (1985). *Personality and individual differences: A natural science approach*. New York: Plenum Press.

Hanin, Y. (1993). Optimal performance emotions in top athletes. In S. Serpa, J. Alves, V. Ferriera & A. Paula-Brito (Eds.), *Proceedings of the VIII World Congress of Sport Psychology* (pp. 229–232). Lisbon, Portugal: International Society of Sport Psychology.

Hardy, L. (1990). A catastrophe model of performance in sport. In G. Jones & L. Hardy (Eds.), *Stress and performance in sport* (pp. 81–106). Chichester: Wiley.

Hebb, D. O. (1955). Drives and the C.N.S. (Conceptual Nervous System). *Psychological Review*, **62**, 243–254.

Henry, F. M. & Rogers, D. E. (1960). Increased response latency for complicated movements and a 'memory drum' theory of neuromotor reaction. *Research Quarterly*, **31**, 448–458.

Jackson, S. A. (1992), Athletes in flow: A qualitative investigation of flow states in elite figure skaters. *Journal of Applied Sport Psychology*, **4**, 161–180.

Jones, F. (1998). DNA: Implications. *The Psychologist: Bulletin of the British Psychological Society*, **11**, 61–62.

Jones, F. & Harris, P. (1996). The use of repertory grid technique in exercise psychology. In C. Robson, B. Cripps & H. Steinberg (Eds.), *Quality and quantity: Research methods in sport and exercise psychology* (pp. 3–9). Leicester: British Psychological Society, Sport and Exercise Psychology Section.

Kerr, J. H. (1991). Arousal-seeking in risk sport participants. *Personality and Individual Differences*, **12** (6), 613–616.

Kerr, J. H. (1997). *Motivation and emotion in sport: Reversal theory*. Hove, UK: Psychology Press.

Kerr, J. H. & van Schaik, P. (1995). Effects of game venue and outcome on psychological mood states in rugby. *Personality and Individual Differences*, **19** (3), 407–409.

Kerr, J.H. & Vlaswinkel, E.H. (1993). Self-reported mood and running. *Work and Stress*, **7** (3), 161–177.

Kline, P. (1988). *Psychology exposed*. London: Routledge.

Males, J. R. (1995, July). *Helping athletes perform: Integrating reversal theory and psychosynthesis in applied sport psychology*. Paper presented at the 7th International Conference on Reversal Theory, Melbourne, Australia.

Males, J. R. (1996, October). *'I don't much like myself as a winner'*. Case study presented at the 1st International Workshop on Motivation and Emotion in Sport: Reversal Theory, Tsukuba, Japan.

Males, J. R. & Kerr, J. H. (1996). Stress, emotion and performance in elite slalom canoeists. *The Sport Psychologist*, **10**, 17–36.

Males, J. R., Kerr, J. H. & Gerkovich, M. (1998). Metamotivational states during canoe slalom competition: A qualitative analysis using reversal theory. *Journal of Applied Sport Psychology*, **10**, 185–200.

Man, F., Stuchlíková, I. & Kindlmann, P. (1995). Trait–state anxiety, worry, emotionality and self-confidence in top-level soccer players. *The Sport Psychologist*, **9** (2) 212–224.

Martens, R., Burton, D., Vealey, R. S., Bump, L. A. & Smith, D. E. (1990). Development and validation of the Competitive State Anxiety Inventory–2 (CSAI–2). In R. Martens, R. S. Vealey & D. Burton (Eds.), *Competitive anxiety in sport*. Champaign, IL: Human Kinetics.

McAuley, E. & Duncan, T. E. (1990). Cognitive appraisal and affective reactions following physical achievement outcomes. *Journal of Sport and Exercise Psychology*, **12**, 415–426.

Moon, S. M., Dillon, D. R. & Sprenkle, D. H. (1991). On balance and synergy: Family therapy and qualitative research revisited. *Journal of Marital and Family Therapy*, **2**, 187–192.

Morgan, M. (1996). Quantitative research: a package deal? *The Psychologist: Bulletin of the British Psychological Society*, **9**, 31–32.

Murgatroyd, S., Rushton, C., Apter, M.J. & Ray, C. (1978). The development of the Telic Dominance Scale. *Journal of Personality Assessment*, **42**, 519–528.

Nicholls, J. G. (1989). *The competitive ethos and democratic education*. Cambridge, MA: Harvard University Press.

Norman, P. & Smith, L. (1995). The theory of planned behaviour and exercise: An investigation into the role of prior behaviour, behavioural intentions and attitude variablity. *European Journal of Social Psychology*, **25**, 403–415.

Owen, M. J. & McGuffin, P. (1997). Genetics and psychiatry. *British Journal of Psychiatry*, **171**, 201–202.

Parker, I. (1989). *The crisis in modern social psychology – and how to end it*. London: Routledge.

Plomin, R., Owen, M. J. & McGuffin, P. (1994). The genetic basis of complex brain behaviours. *Science*, **264**, 1733–1739.

Purcell, I. P. (1999). *Expertise, decisions and emotions in the performance of male golfers*. Unpublished doctoral dissertation, Curtin University of Technology, Perth, Australia.

Robson, C., Cripps, B. & Steinberg, H. (1996). *Quality and quantity: Research methods in sport and exercise psychology*. Leicester: British Psychological Society, Sport and Exercise Psychology Section.

Rose, D. J. (1997). *A multilevel approach to the study of motor control and learning*. Boston: Allyn & Bacon.

Rowland, G. L., Franken, R. E. & Harrison, K. (1986). Sensation seeking and participation in sporting activities. *Journal of Sport Psychology*, **8**, 212–220.

Salter, D. (1997). Measure, analyze and stagnate: Towards a radical psychology of sport. In R. J. Butler (Ed.), *Sports psychology in performance* (pp. 248–260). Oxford: Butterworth-Heinemann.

Sherrard, C. (1997). Qualitative research. *The Psychologist: Bulletin of the British Psychological Society*, **10**, 161–162.

Spielberger, C. D. (1966). Theory and research on anxiety. In C. D. Spielberger (Ed.), *Anxiety and behavior* (pp. 3–20). New York: Academic Press.

Stevenson, C. & Cooper, N. (1997). Qualitative and quantitative research. *The Psychologist: Bulletin of the British Psychological Society*, **10**, 159–160.

Svebak, S. & Kerr, J. H. (1989). The role of impulsivity in preference for sports. *Personality and Individual Differences*, **10** (1), 51–58.

Svebak, S. & Murgatroyd, S. (1985). Metamotivational dominance: A multimethod validation of reversal theory. *Journal of Personality and Social Psychology*, **48**, 519–528.

Thapar, A. & McGuffin, P. (1996). Genetic influences on life events in childhood. *Psychological Medicine*, **26**, 813–820.

Trimpop, R. M., Kerr, J. H. & Kirkcaldy, B. (1999). Comparing personality constructs of risk-taking behavior. *Personality and Individual Differences*, **26**, 237–254.

Vallerand, R. J. (1987). Antecedents of self-related affects in sport: Preliminary evidence on the intuitive reflective appraisal model. *Journal of Sport Psychology*, **9**, 161–182.

Van Mele, V., Vanden Auweele, Y. & Rzewnicki, R. (1995). An integrative procedure for the diagnosis of an elite athlete: A case study. *The Sport Psychologist*, **9**, 130–147.

Weiner, B. (1985). An attributional theory of achievement motivation and emotion. *Psychological Review*, **92**, 548–573.

Zuckerman, M. (1979). *Sensation seeking: Beyond the optimal level of arousal*. Hillsdale, NJ: Erlbaum.

Zuckerman, M. (1983). Sensation seeking and sports. *Personality and Individual Differences*, **4**, 285–293.

# APPENDICES

# APPENDIX A: SOMATIC STATE QUESTIONNAIRE

The Somatic State Questionnaire (SSQ) (Cook, Gerkovich, Potocky, & O'Connell, 1993) is concerned with the so-called somatic states in reversal theory. These are the telic–paratelic and negativistic–conformist metamotivational states. In addition, the SSQ measures arousal preference. Arousal is thought to be the most important and influential variable for individual experience when the somatic states are operative. The SSQ consists of 12 items forming three subscales. The *playfulness* subscale has 4 items (items 5, 6, 7, 11) relating to the telic and paratelic states, the *negativistic* subscale has 4 items (items 1, 3, 9, 12) relating to the negativism and conformity states, and the *arousal preference* subscale also has 4 items (items 2, 4, 8, 10) relating to arousal seeking–arousal avoiding behaviour. Each item has a 6-point rating scale (1 to 6) with pairs of statements at each end (e.g., *feeling cautious–feeling adventurous*). Scoring is straightforward, with the sum of the four items within each subscale providing a total score for that subscale. The rating scales for items 1, 4, 5, 6, 7, 9, 11 are scored in the normal direction (i.e., from 1 to 6), and for items 2, 3, 8, 10, 12 in the reverse direction (i.e., from 6 to 1). Respondents should be made familiar with the measure prior to its use and should be given clear instructions as to how they should respond to the items (e.g., reporting how they feel at the time of completion).

To select the general format of the SSQ and make an initial evaluation of the items, Cook *et al.* (1993) carried out several pilot studies involving more than 250 participants. They experimented with unipolar and bipolar

*Experiencing Sport: Reversal Theory.* Edited by J. H. Kerr.
© 1999 John Wiley & Sons Ltd.

rating scales and adjective checklists. Bipolar rating scales produced the most consistent results and this format was adopted. The pool of items was scrutinized by a panel of reversal theory experts for content validity and then tested and refined using collected data. Internal reliability tests using Cronbach's alpha procedure (see Cronbach, 1951) indicated scores of 0.86 for the playfulness subscale, 0.75 for the negativistic subscale, and 0.78 for the arousal preference subscale. Therefore, the three subscales were considered to have good internal reliability and preliminary studies have shown that they are valid. Full details can be found in Cook, *et al.* (1993). Two useful examples of how the questionnaire has been used in research are Cook *et al.* (1995) and Cook, Gerkovich, and O'Connell (1997).

**Table A.1**  Somatic State Questionnaire (SSQ) (Cook, Gerkovich, Potocky, & O'Connell, 1993)

| Code: | Age: | Male/Female: |
|---|---|---|

Below are pairs of items that are opposites. Please circle the number for each pair that indicates how you feel **RIGHT NOW**. For example, if the pair were:

Hot  1 2 3 4 5 6  Cold

and you were feeling too hot you would circle the '**1**'; if you were too cold, you would circle the '**6**'; and if you were just a little hot you would circle the '**3**'.

| | | |
|---|---|---|
| 1. | Not feeling angry  1 2 3 4 5 6  Feeling angry | |
| 2. | Seeking excitement  1 2 3 4 5 6  Not seeking excitement | |
| 3. | Feeling rebellious  1 2 3 4 5 6  Not feeling rebellious | |
| 4. | Feeling cautious  1 2 3 4 5 6  Feeling adventurous | |
| 5. | Feeling serious-minded  1 2 3 4 5 6  Feeling playful | |
| 6. | Trying to accomplish something  1 2 3 4 5 6  Just having fun | |
| 7. | Want activity to have  1 2 3 4 5 6  Don't want activity to have important consequences     important consequences | |
| 8. | Feeling adventurous  1 2 3 4 5 6  Not feeling adventurous | |
| 9. | Feeling compliant  1 2 3 4 5 6  Feeling defiant | |
| 10. | Feel like taking chances  1 2 3 4 5 6  Don't feel like taking chances | |
| 11. | Want to do something  1 2 3 4 5 6  Don't want to do something important     important | |
| 12. | Wanting to break rules  1 2 3 4 5 6  Wanting to go along with rules | |

# REFERENCES

Cook, M. R., Gerkovich, M. M., Hoffman, S. J., McClernon, F. J., Cohen, H. D., Oakleaf, K. L. & O'Connell, K. A. (1995). Smoking and EEG power spectra: Effects of differences in arousal seeking. *International Journal of Psychophysiology*, **19**, 247–256.

Cook, M. R., Gerkovich, M. M. & O'Connell, K. A. (1997). Differential EEG effects of smoking in the telic and paratelic states. In S. Svebak & M. J. Apter (Eds.), *Stress and health: A reversal theory perspective* (pp. 103–116). Washington, DC: Taylor & Francis.

Cook, M. R., Gerkovich, M. M., Potocky, M. & O'Connell, K. (1993). Instruments for the assessment of reversal theory states. *Patient Education and Counseling*, **22**, 99–106.

Cronbach, L. T. (1951). Coefficient alpha and the internal structure of tests. *Psychometrica*, **16**, 197–334.

# APPENDIX B: TELIC/ PARATELIC STATE INSTRUMENT

The Telic/Paratelic State Instrument (T/PSI) (Calhoun, 1995; Calhoun & O'Connell, 1995) was designed to improve on previous state measures for the telic–paratelic pair of metamotivational states. The authors sought to do this by developing a state measure which would be sensitive to state at all levels of arousal and provide clear cut-points to be used for classifying individuals as telic or paratelic.

The 12-item scale has two subscales. The *serious-minded/playful* (SM/P) subscale has 7 items and the *arousal-avoidant/arousal-seeking* (AA/AS) subscale has 5 items. Testees respond to each item on a 6-point scale and scores are added to provide a score for each subscale. The total of the two subscale scores provides a total T/PSI score. Scores above a cut-point indicate that the individual is in the paratelic state and below that the individual is in the telic state. Instructions for scoring the T/PSI are included below. Respondents should be made familiar with the measure prior to its use and should be given clear instructions as to how they should respond to the items (e.g., reporting how they feel at the time of completion).

Both the serious-minded/playful subscale and the arousal-avoidant/ arousal-seeking subscale had excellent internal reliability scores (Cronbach's alpha SM/P = 0.932; AA/AS = 0.827) (see Cronbach, 1951).

The construct validity of the T/PSI was evaluated by putting together a group of carefully constructed scenarios that represented telic and paratelic

---

*Experiencing Sport: Reversal Theory.* Edited by J. H. Kerr.

states at low, medium, and high levels of felt arousal. These scenarios were assessed by a number of reversal theory experts and classified, for example, as 'telic low arousal' or 'paratelic high arousal'. A group of volunteer respondents ($N = 572$), all over the age of 18, were then asked to remember when they were in these specific situations and asked to complete the T/PSI according to how they felt during these remembered incidents. Analysis of this data revealed that, over all three felt arousal levels, the T/PSI correctly identified 88% of the participants who responded to telic scenarios as telic, and 87% responding to paratelic scenarios as paratelic (Calhoun, 1995).

A good example of the use of this scale can be found in Chapter 7 of this volume.

## SCORING INSTRUCTIONS FOR THE T/PSI

1. The following items comprise the serious-minded/playful (SM/P) sub-scale: 1, 3, 4, 6, 8, 10, 11.
2. The following items comprise the arousal-avoidant/arousal-seeking (AA/AS) subscale: 2, 5, 7, 9, 12.
3. Recode items: 1, 4, 5, 8, 10, 12, so that a response of 1 equals a 6, a response of 2 equals a 5, a response of 3 equals a 4, a response of 4 equals a 3, a response of 5 equals a 2, and a response of 6 equals a 1.
4. Low values (1, 2, or 3) reflect the telic state. Higher values (4, 5, or 6) reflect the paratelic state.
5. Summed scores that are higher reflect the paratelic state; summed scores that are lower reflect the telic state. Sum over the items for each subscale: SM/P: 1, 3, 4, 6, 8, 10, 11; AA/AS: 2, 5, 7, 9, 12. Sum over the two subscales for a total T/PSI score.
6. Range of possible scores: SM/P: 7–42; AA/AS: 5–30; T/PSI: 12–72.
7. Suggested cut scores:
   SM/P:      telic: <23; paratelic: >22
   AA/AS:     telic: <18; paratelic: >17
   T/PSI:     telic: <41; paratelic: >40

**Table B.1**   The Telic/Paratelic State Measure (T/PSI) (Calhoun, 1995; Calhoun & O'Connell, 1995)

Below are 12 pairs of words that are opposites. Please circle the number that is located **BETWEEN** each pair of words that best indicates how you were feeling in the **LAST FEW MINUTES**, just before you started filling out this questionnaire. For example, if the pair were:

Happy 1 2 3 4 5 6 Sad

and you were definitely feeling happy, you would circle the **'1'**. If you were definitely feeling sad, you would circle the **'6'**. If you were feeling just a little bit sad, you would circle the **'4'**.

| | | | |
|---|---|---|---|
| 1. | Feeling playful | 1 2 3 4 5 6 | Feeling serious-minded |
| 2. | Wanting peace and quiet | 1 2 3 4 5 6 | Wanting adventure |
| 3. | Trying to accomplish something | 1 2 3 4 5 6 | Just having fun |
| 4. | Doing activity just for the fun of it | 1 2 3 4 5 6 | Doing activity because it may affect my future |
| 5. | Wanting to feel excitement | 1 2 3 4 5 6 | Wanting to feel calm |
| 6. | Wanting to be serious | 1 2 3 4 5 6 | Wanting to be playful |
| 7. | Concerned about the future effects of my current activity | 1 2 3 4 5 6 | Not concerned about the future effects of my current activity |
| 8. | Wanting to just have fun | 1 2 3 4 5 6 | Wanting to accomplish something |
| 9. | Wanting to feel less aroused | 1 2 3 4 5 6 | Wanting to feel more aroused |
| 10. | Living for the moment | 1 2 3 4 5 6 | Focusing on the future |
| 11. | Feeling serious | 1 2 3 4 5 6 | Feeling playful |
| 12. | Feeling adventurous | 1 2 3 4 5 6 | Not feeling adventurous |

© 1996, Judith Elaine Calhoun.

# REFERENCES

Calhoun, J. E. (1995). *Construct validity of the Telic/Paratelic State Instrument: A measure of reversal theory constructs*. Unpublished doctoral dissertation, University of Kansas School of Nursing.

Calhoun J. E. & O'Connell, K. A. (1995, July). *Construct validity of the Telic/Paratelic State Instrument: A measure of reversal theory constructs.* Paper presented at the 7th International Conference on Reversal Theory, Melbourne, Australia.

Cronbach, L. T. (1951). Coefficient alpha and the internal structure of tests. *Psychometrica*, **16**, 197–334.

# APPENDIX C: STATE OF MIND INDICATOR FOR ATHLETES

## THE DEVELOPMENT OF THE SOMIFA

Kerr and Apter's aim in developing a prototype version of the State of Mind Indicator for Athletes (SOMIFA) was to construct an easily administered, short state-type scale for identifying operative metamotivational states (covering all four pairs of states) in sport situations. By asking athletes to choose one from each of four pairs of statements (each statement representing one metamotivational state) about their state of mind during performance, they could pinpoint which states were operative and, by use of an additional question, which state was salient at the time. Arousal items were also included as the authors thought that the level of felt arousal experienced by athletes would be an important factor in successful sport performance.

The concept of *felt arousal* in reversal theory is how 'worked up' a person feels himself or herself to be in a given situation. Felt arousal is phenomenologically different from two other concepts of arousal often found in psychology writing: (1) how awake or sleepy a person feels and (2) how energetic or tired a person feels. As Apter (1989, p. 9) pointed out, a person can feel wide awake but not be worked up about anything in particular, or a person can feel sleepy but be feeling worked up or emotional.

*Experiencing Sport: Reversal Theory.* Edited by J. H. Kerr.
© 1999 John Wiley & Sons Ltd.

In addition, one can feel energetic but be completely composed and not worked up at all, or feel tired and at the same time worked up and upset about something. Items dealing with these three 'arousal' dimensions were included in the prototype version of the SOMIFA. In addition, a dimension assessing the performers' perceptions of how well they thought they had performed was included. Checks for syntax and clarity were made by a language expert.

Following this, the SOMIFA was administered to a number of different groups of athletes at various sport sites. In each case, prior to administration, coaches were asked for permission to use the SOMIFA and were asked to check the items involved for suitability and ease of understanding. Also prior to SOMIFA administration, athletes were made familiar with the measure. All athletes who subsequently completed the SOMIFA did so on a voluntary basis.

Initial trials with the SOMIFA involved participants in four sports: field hockey, rugby, judo, and basketball. The particular sports and situations were selected to test the utility and validity of the scale in a variety of circumstances, for example, team and individual sports, elite level competition and recreational sport, practice sessions and competitive games, and across consecutive games (win/lose). A brief summary follows:

1. The members of a top-level field hockey team from Western Australia completed the SOMIFA after each one of five consecutive games. Of these five games, four were wins and one was a defeat. There were a number of interesting contrasts (e.g., the win and the defeat were against the same team – the win was in the grand final and the defeat in an earlier match; some games were close-fought, but in others the winning margin was large).
2. Two rugby teams, the 1st XV (high level) and 2nd XV from a Japanese university, completed a Japanese version of the SOMIFA* on two occasions, the first after training and the second after a competitive game. Both teams won their games after close matches. (University rugby in Japan is of a high standard with university players frequently selected to play for their national team.)
3. Five elite Japanese judo players taking part in the 1995 Kodokan Cup tournament (the top Judo tournament in Japan and a qualifying tournament for the Atlanta Olympics) completed a Japanese version of the

---

* A Japanese version of the SOMIFA was translated from the English version independently by two bilingual sports people and translated back from Japanese to English independently by two others. Disagreements in translation were discussed and the correct meaning of terms agreed by consensus among the translators. This procedure ensured that the translation of the SOMIFA into Japanese was as accurate as possible.

SOMIFA after each match as they progressed through to the final stages of the tournament.

4. A women's recreational basketball team (both on-court and bench players) completed a Japanese version of the SOMIFA after each one of four consecutive matches: three games were won and one was lost by a narrow score.

Since the SOMIFA has no multiple-item subscales, statistical procedures for measures with subscales, such as item analysis, item-to-subscale correlations, and factor analysis were inappropriate. In addition, since it is a state-type measure, consistent responses across situations would not be expected and therefore test–retest reliability calculations were also considered inappropriate.

The results of the initial trials were presented to a group of reversal theory sports experts at the *1st International Workshop on Motivation and Emotion in Sport: Reversal Theory* in October 1996. Following discussion and feedback, Kerr and Apter revised and fine-tuned the instrument by changing the wording of two questions and expanding Part II to include preferred arousal items which would allow arousal discrepancy scores to be calculated for each of the arousal items. The SOMIFA is currently being administered to other groups of athletes and its validity is being checked against other reversal theory state scales.

# USING THE SOMIFA

The State of Mind Indicator for Athletes (SOMIFA) is usually completed post-performance, with the initial instructions requesting the athlete to answer the questions about his or her state of mind during the preceding performance. However, the instructions could also be adapted to allow the measure to be used prior to an athletic event, or during performance in sports, like golf, that might allow for this. Apart from initial biographical information, the measure has two parts.

## Part I

In Part I of the SOMIFA, a series of eight statements (each one representative of one metamotivational state) are paired together in four separate

**Table C.1**   State of Mind Indicator for Athletes (SOMIFA) (Kerr & Apter)

Name:                                                                 Age:
Date:                                                                  Sport:
Occasion/Event:                                              Outcome:

**INSTRUCTIONS:**
*Please answer the following questions about the sporting event or the specific part of the event indicated.*

I   Choose one from each of the following pairs of statements which most closely describes your feelings during this performance. (Check the appropriate box in each case.) Please try to judge in terms of **THE TIME YOU WERE ACTUALLY PERFORMING (NOT** how you felt immediately before or after, how you should have felt, how you feel now, or how you usually would have felt).

**I WANTED TO:**

1.a. ☐  achieve something important to me (e.g., status, money, improved skill).
1.b. ☐  simply enjoy the fun of participating in the event.

2.a. ☐  keep to the instructions and expectations of coaches and others.
2.b. ☐  do my own thing whatever the consequences.

3.a. ☐  be tough with and dominating over my opponent(s) during performance.
3.b. ☐  be friendly and sympathetic with my opponent(s) during performance.

4.a. ☐  perform well for myself.
4.b. ☐  perform well for others (e.g. my coach, team, supporters, etc.).

5.   Of all the items which you chose above, which is the **ONE** that you were most aware of during performance.    ☐
     (Please write the number and letter in this box.)

**II   Please circle the appropriate point on the scales below.**

1. How **DID YOU FEEL** in relation to each of the following dimensions? (Please circle the appropriate point.)

calm | | | | |'worked up'

sleepy | | | | | wide awake

fatigued | | | | | energetic

2. How **WOULD YOU HAVE LIKED TO HAVE FELT** in relation to each of the following dimensions?

calm | | | | | 'worked up'

sleepy | | | | | wide awake

fatigued | | | | | energetic

3. How well do you consider you performed by your own standards? (Average means **YOUR** average, etc.)

well below average | below average | average | above average | well above average questions. Forced choice responses to each pair of statements indicate which metamotivational states were operative during performance. An indication of which of these states was salient during performance is provided by question 5, which asks athletes to indicate the state that they were most aware of during performance.

## Part II

Part II of the SOMIFA contains items which are included to differentiate between reversal theory's different concepts of arousal and has items concerning each one. It employs 5-point rating scales. In question 1, individuals are asked to respond in terms of *how did you feel* to each of the arousal items. In question 2, the same three items are repeated and, this time, individuals are asked to respond in terms of *how you would have liked to have felt* in relation to each of the three arousal dimensions. This then also allows discrepancies between experienced and preferred levels of each dimension to be calculated by subtracting the scores for question 1 from the scores for question 2. Previous sport research using the Telic State Measure (Svebak & Murgatroyd, 1985) has shown that discrepancies between levels of felt and preferred arousal are important in distinguishing between successful and unsuccessful athletes (e.g., Cox & Kerr, 1989; Males & Kerr, 1996). Finally, in question 3, respondents are asked to provide a subjective rating of their own performance.

## REFERENCES

Apter, M. J. (1989). *Reversal theory: Motivation, emotion and personality.* London: Routledge.

Cox, T. & Kerr, J. H. (1989). Arousal effects during tournament play in squash. *Perceptual and Motor Skills*, **69**, 1275–1280.

Males, J. R. & Kerr, J. H. (1996). Stress, emotion and performance in elite slalom canoeists. *The Sport Psychologist*, **10**, 17–36.

Svebak, S. & Murgatroyd, S. (1985). Metamotivational dominance: A multimethod validation of reversal theory constructs. *Journal of Personality and Social Psychology*, **48** (1), 107–116.

# AUTHOR INDEX

# SUBJECT INDEX

# *Related titles of interest...*

## Adherence Issues in Sport and Exercise
Edited by STEPHEN BULL
*0471 988480    220pp    due June 1999    Paperback*


## Training in Sport
**Applying Sport Science**
Edited by BRUCE ELLIOTT
*0471 978701    440pp    January 1999    Hardback*

## Understanding Psychological Preparation for Sport
**Theory and Practice of Elite Performers**
LEW HARDY, GRAHAM JONES and DANIEL GOULD
*0471 957879    320pp    1996    Paperback*

## Sports Psychology
**Theory, Applications and Issues**
T. MORRIS and J. SUMMERS
*0471 335495    672pp    1995
Paperback*